I0729563

ねこと国芳

金子 信久

Cats in Ukiyo-e: Japanese Woodblock Prints of UTAGAWA Kuniyoshi

KANEKO Nobuhisa

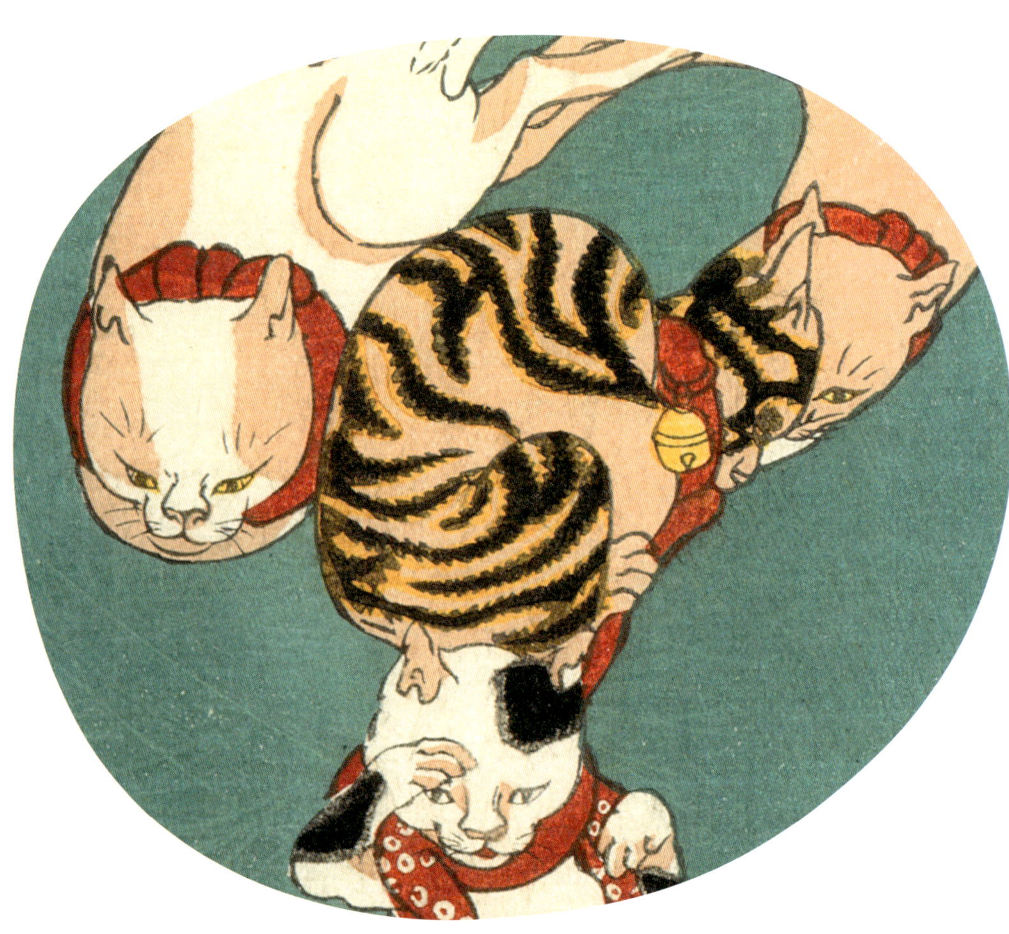

はじめに

　江戸時代の日本の画家で、今日、京都の伊藤若冲と並ぶ人気を誇るのが、江戸の浮世絵師、歌川国芳 (1797-1861) である。勢い、色彩の力、意表をつくアイディア。とりわけ奇想天外な構図の中を縦横無尽に活躍する武者たちの絵は、国芳を「造形家」として評価しようとする人々を中心に賞賛されてきた。しかし考えてみれば、迫力いっぱいの国芳の武者絵は、みな空想の産物。当たり前だが、国芳の家に鎧兜を身につけた武者たちがいたわけではない。

　では、国芳の家にいたものはといえば、猫である。弟子の言によれば、周りには常に何匹もいて、懐にも入れていたらしい。猫に戒名を与えた話も伝わる。日々、超絶的な武者絵を作り出す国芳を、猫たちが「うなうな」と見守っていたわけだ。国芳が描いた猫は、いわば「家族の肖像」である。行き届いた観察眼と愛。家族だからこそなせる描写の数々が、版画となり、売られ、大衆を喜ばせたのである。

　この本は、そんな国芳の猫を味わい尽くそうというもの。国芳や浮世絵は好きだが猫は今ひとつ……という方もいらっしゃるだろうが、ぜひ本書を通して、「猫好き」の心のうちを知っていただけたらと思う。何よりそれが、国芳その人の心でもあるのだから。

　そして、猫好きを自認する方には、本物の猫や猫の写真を見るように楽しんでいただきたい。一人の猫好きの勝手な解説を読みつつ、ご自身で独自のポイントを見つけるのも良いかもしれない。たとえば、この本の中で最も「いやっちい猫」を探すというのは、いかがだろうか。もちろん「いやっちい」というのは、「たまらなく魅力的」という意味。国芳の猫たちを、思う存分かわいがっていただきたい。

Introduction

The Edo period painter boasting popularity rivaling that of Kyoto's Ito Jakuchu is the Edo (Tokyo) ukiyo-e artist, Utagawa Kuniyoshi. In an oeuvre characterized by dynamism, the intense use of color, and out-of-the-box ideas, Kuniyoshi's arresting images of samurai warriors rendered using the strangest of composition have tended to be singled out, chiefly by those who seek to rate the artist as a "designer." But consider this: Kuniyoshi's powerful pictures of samurai were all products of his own imagination. Obviously Kuniyoshi did not happen to have warriors in full armor hanging around his house.

What Kuniyoshi did have were cats. Disciples testify to the artist always being surrounded by cats, even carrying them down the front of his clothing. Word also has it he gave his cats posthumous Buddhist names, like humans. These cats were in truth keeping a critical eye on Kuniyoshi as day-in, day-out he produced those extraordinary warrior paintings. The cats Kuniyoshi painted were family portraits, so to speak, product of careful observation, and great affection. All these depictions made possible precisely because their subjects were part of the family were turned into woodblock prints, sold, and gave joy to the public.

This book aims to offer a feast of Kuniyoshi's cats in all their myriad manifestations. No doubt there will be some keen on Kuniyoshi and ukiyo-e, but less enamored of cats: I urge you to peruse these pages anyway, and gain a little insight into the cat-lover's heart, for no other reason than that this heart was also Kuniyoshi's own.

As for those fully aware of their own love of cats: enjoy the pictures here as if you were looking at real cats, or photos of cats. Read the unashamedly biased comments of one cat-lover, but seek out your own personal highlights. One suggestion would be to find the most adorable feline in the book. Kuniyoshi's cats are certainly worthy of your adoration.

Columns

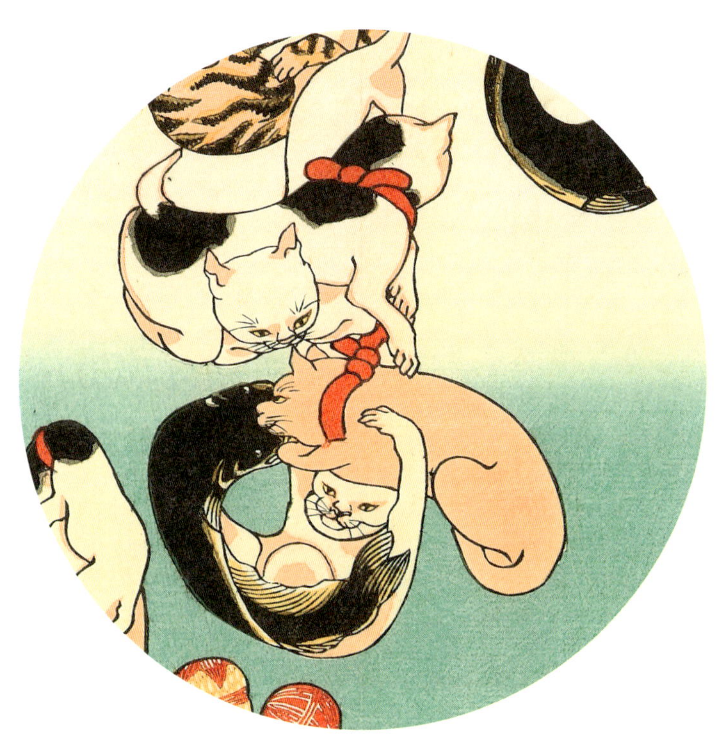

歌川国芳　UTAGAWA Kuniyoshi
寛政 9 年－文久元年　(1797－1861)

本書に出てくる年号　　　Japanese era names appearing in this book

文政	1818－1830	Bunsei	1818－1830
天保	1830－1844	Tenpo	1830－1844
弘化	1844－1848	Koka	1844－1848
嘉永	1848－1854	Kaei	1848－1854

I.

ねこ、
ややこしくも
愛おしい家族

Cats:

complex but cherished

family members

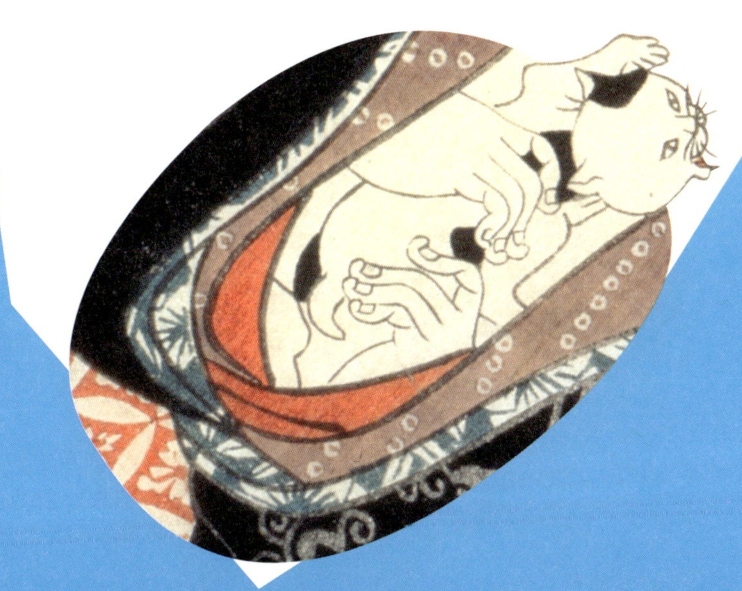

01 風流六花撰 百合 ふうりゅうろっかせん ゆり

　首輪をした猫を抱き上げる女性の足元で、もう1匹が鳴いている。自分もかわいがって欲しいと訴えているのかと思いきや、首輪の猫を追って来たら女性が助けたので、怒っているようだ。ジャンプしそうな体の動きに、こわばった尾。猫の世界の緊迫感が伝わってくる。一方、追いかけられた猫は、もう安全なのに、必死に前足を伸ばして襟につかまり、後ろ足の置き場をバタバタと模索している。

　平安時代の歌人の六歌仙になぞらえ、美しい花と女性を描いたシリーズの一つで、百合の花の描写も見どころである。

Fashionable Selection of Six Flowers *(Furyu rokkasen):* Lilies

A woman scoops a collared cat up into her arms, while at her feet, another meows. Initially one imagines the second creature to be demanding the same affection, but in fact it appears to have been chasing the collared cat, and is angry to have it snatched away to safety by the woman. The body hunched as if about to jump, the stiff, bristling tail tell of tension in the feline domain. Meanwhile, though now safe, the cat being pursued desperately extends its front paws and clings to the woman's collar, its back legs frantically scrabbling for a foothold.

Modeled on the Heian poets known as the Rokkasen, or Six Poetic Geniuses, *Furyu rokkasen* depicts beauty of the floral and feminine varieties, Kuniyoshi's rendering of the lilies a further highlight.

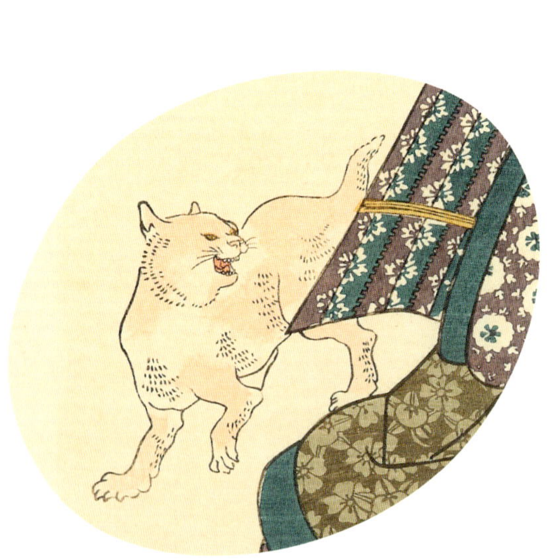

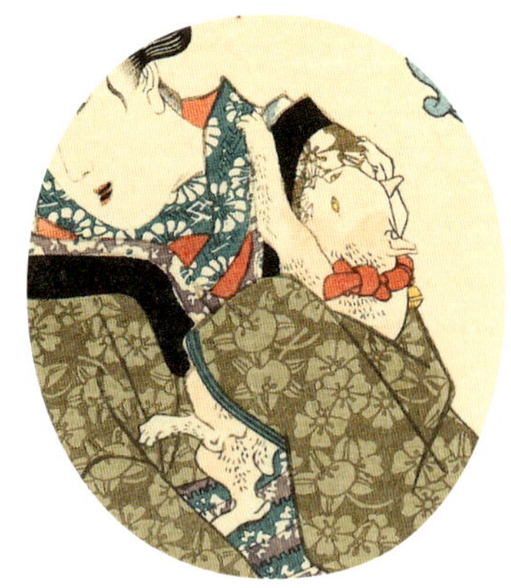

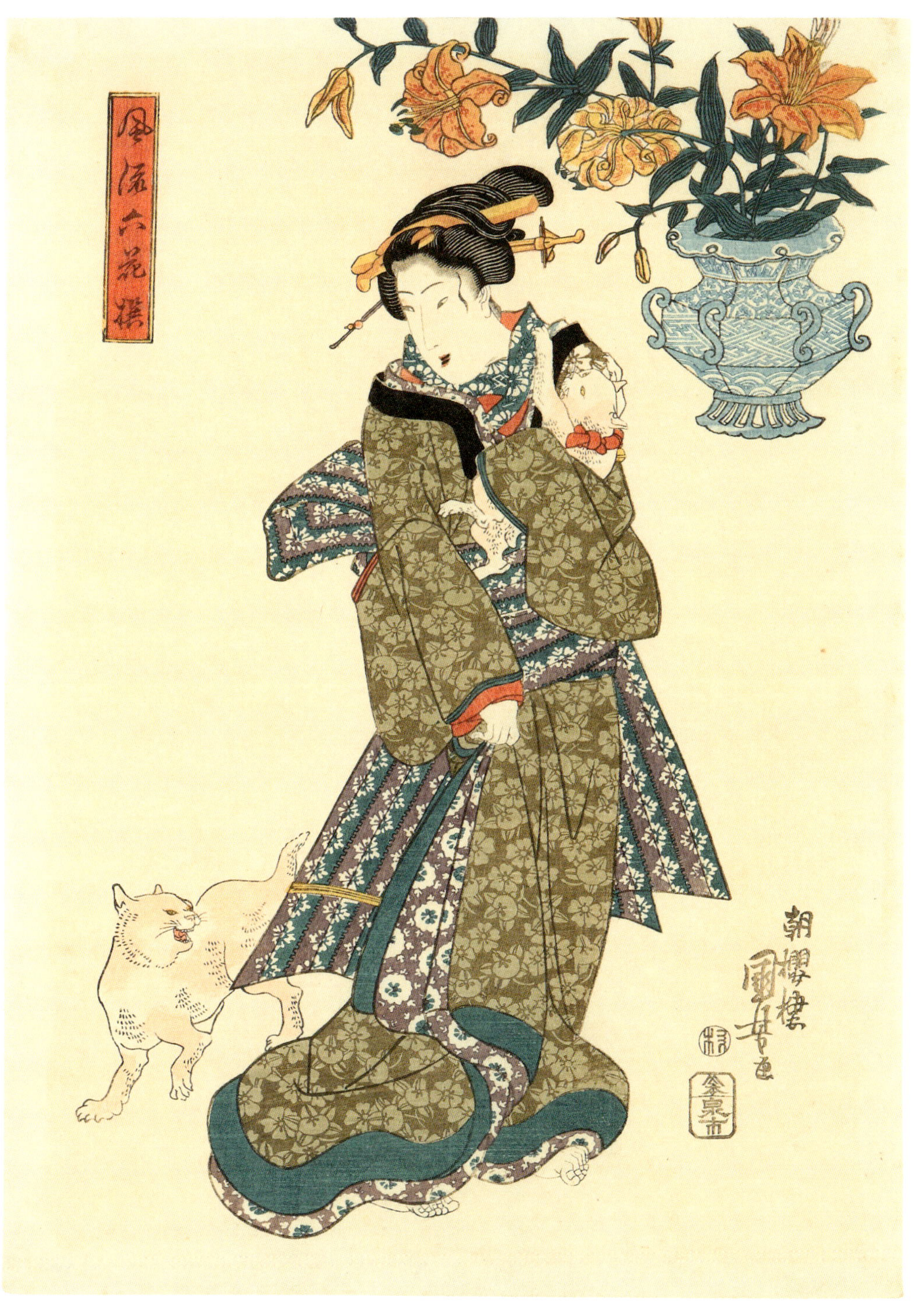

風流六花撰
朝櫻樓
國芳画

02 時世粧菊揃 こどもがあるかときく いまようきくそろい こどもがあるかときく

子猫の1匹は母猫にへばりついている。もう1匹は女性の懐に抱かれて、あごの辺りをかじっているようにも、ペロッとなめているようにも見える。くにゃくにゃと動いてじっとしていない、やんちゃぶり全開の様子である。

ところが画中の歌は、「もらはるゝ先を案じる親心 これも子故にまよふ雉子猫」。

子猫たちはよそにもらわれていく運命にあって、女性もその行く末を心配しているのだろう。幸せそうな母猫、けなげな2匹の子猫を見ていると、こちらまで切なくなる。

タイトルの周りに菊の花があしらわれている。副題がすべて「きく」という言葉で終わるシリーズである。

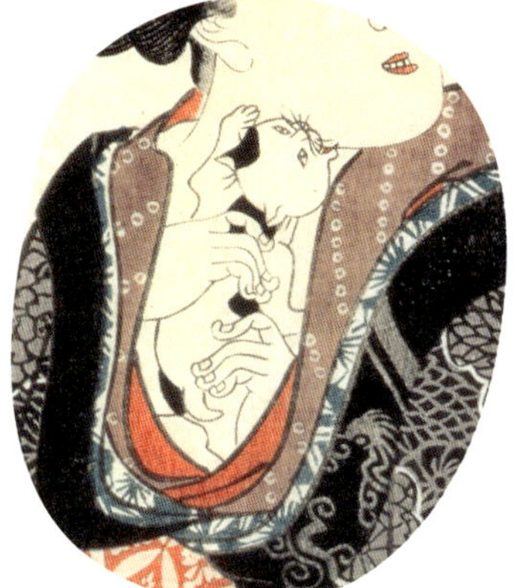

Modern Chrysanthemum Varieties: News of potential little ones
(Kodomo ga aru ka to kiku)

One of the kittens is clinging to the mother cat. Another is clutched to the woman's bosom and appears to be biting her jaw, or perhaps licking it. The overall picture is one of mischievous wriggling creatures, constantly on the move.

The accompanying verse however speaks of "a parent's heart troubled about the place that will take her young, the tabby cat too lost at her children's fate." The kittens are destined to be given away, and the woman is probably also worried about their new homes. Witnessing the contented-looking mother cat and two innocent kittens, even the viewer starts to feel sorry for them.

Chrysanthemums garland the title of the print, one of a series in which the subtitles all end in the word kiku punning on the word chrysanthemum.

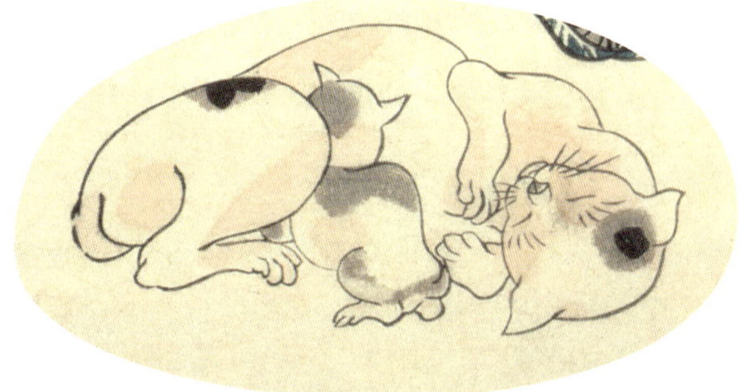

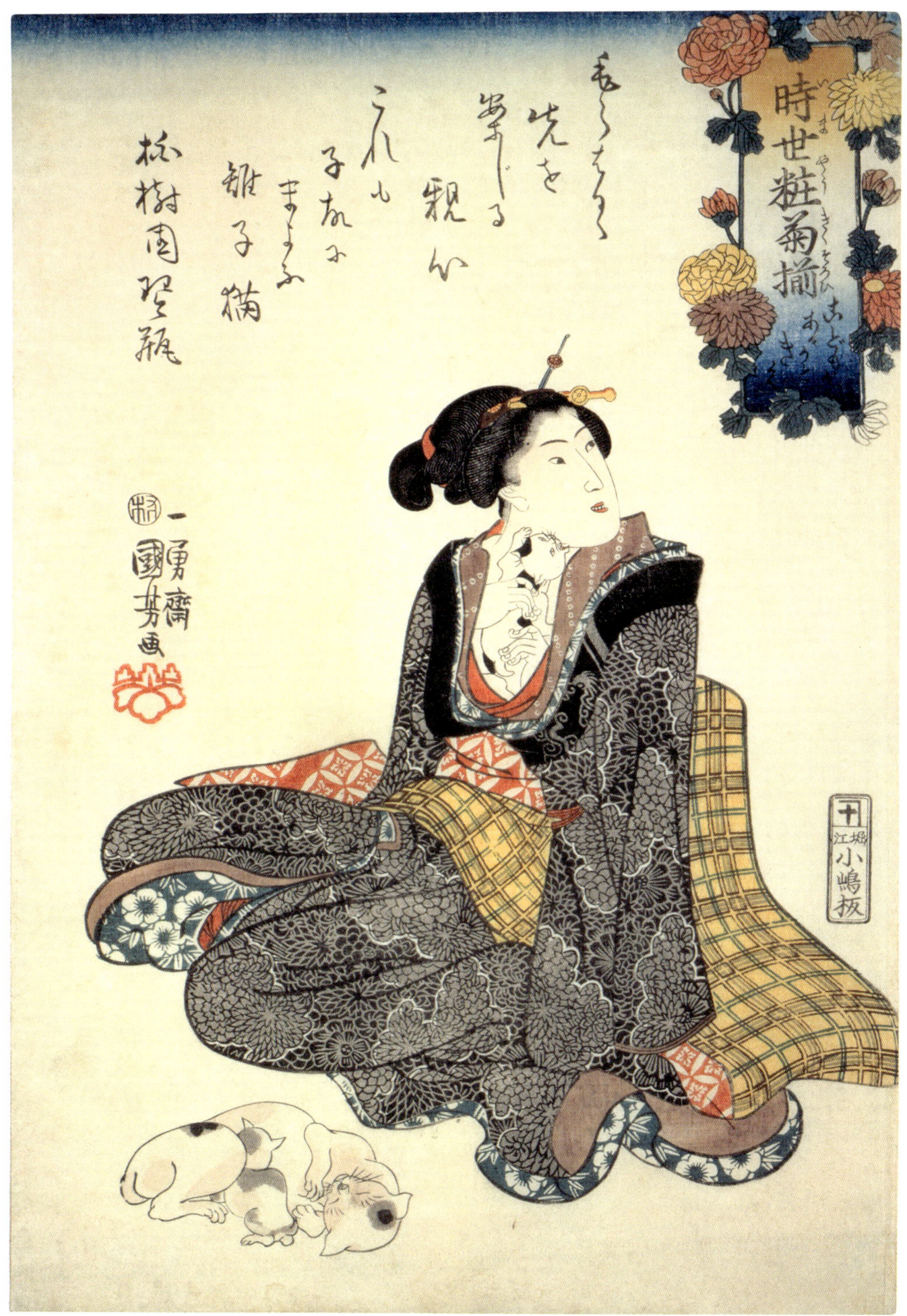

時世粧菊揃
一勇齋國芳画

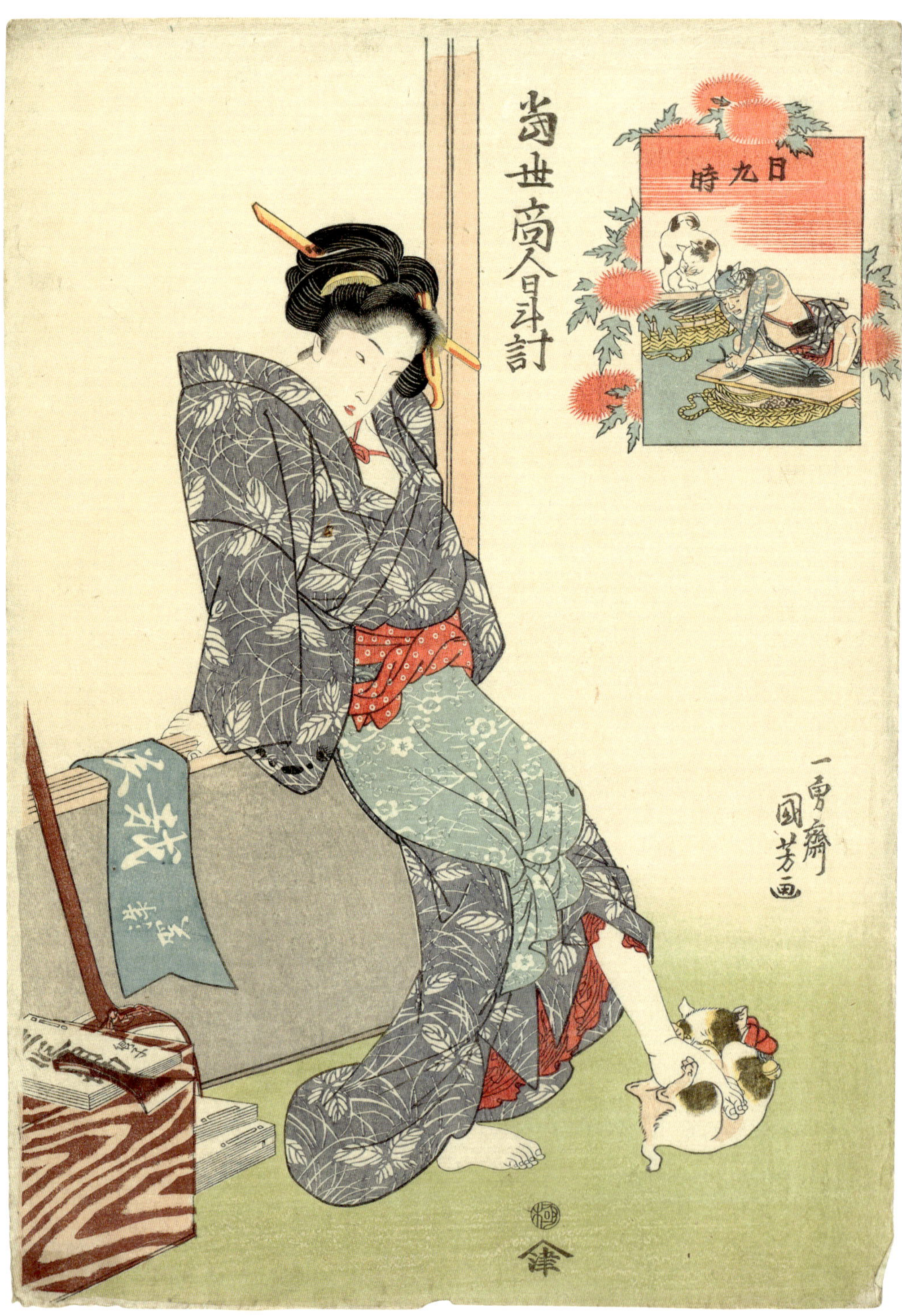
當世商人日斗計
日九時
一勇齋
國芳画

03 当世商人日斗計 日九時 とうせいあきんどひどけい ひここのつどき

　次々と新商品を発売するのが浮世絵の世界だから、人気のある美人画でも、あれこれ趣向を凝らす。この図は、商人の一日の暮らしを題材にしたシリーズの一つ。

　女性の足先にじゃれる、いや、足で遊ばれている猫。嬉しくて遊び始めたのだろうが、弱点のお腹を攻められ、もがいている。顔にも足の様子にも必死さが見える。猫の切迫した状況に対して、女性は何か考えているのか、「心ここに在らず」といった風情。鈴付きの首輪をしてもらいかわいがられている猫だが、時々こんなことに陥るのでは、愛玩動物としての暮らしも楽ではなさそうだ。

Sundial of Modern Tradesmen: Noon

The world of ukiyo-e was one of new products constantly arriving on the market, so even in the popular *bijinga* portraits of beautiful women, artists experimented with ways of ringing the changes. This print is one of a series on a day in the lives of different merchants and tradesmen.

And here is the star: The cat playing at the woman's feet, or rather being teased by her feet. No doubt puss was initially eager to play, but wriggles uncomfortably now the woman has gone for her underbelly, her weak spot. Face and feet both speak of desperation. The woman meanwhile appears oblivious to her pet's distress, lost in thought; in any case, her heart is not really in the game. Sporting a bell on its collar, this is obviously a well-loved cat, but if things descend to this level from time to time, it would seem life as a plaything is no picnic.

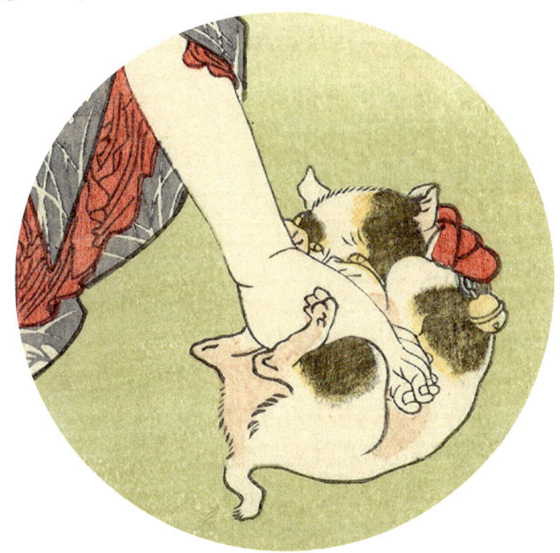

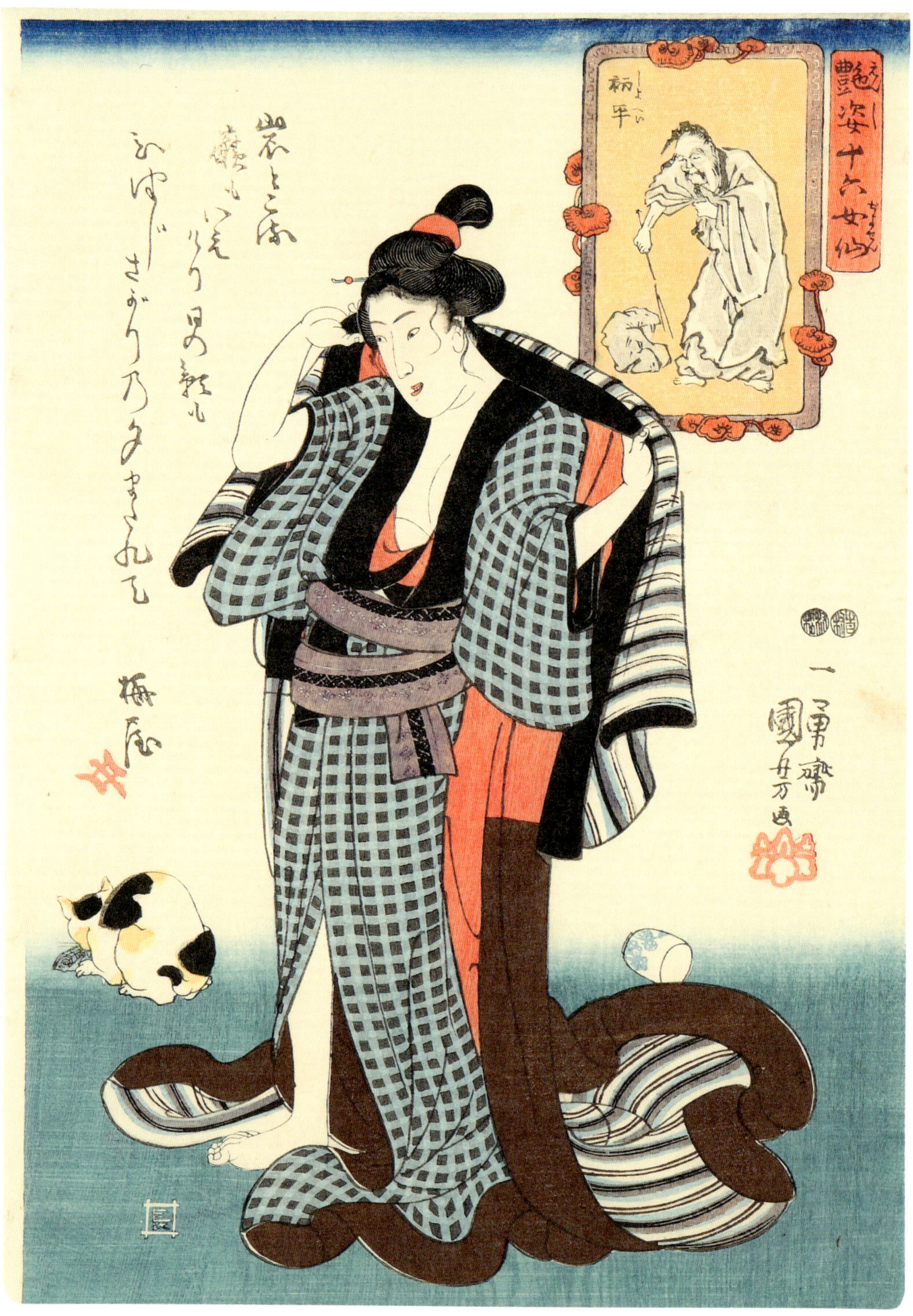

04 艶姿十六女仙 初平 えんしじゅうろくじょせん しょへい

　画中の歌によると、女性は胸やお腹が痛くなる病にあるらしい。具合が良くなり、起きてきたところである。猫はそんな状況に構わず、背を向けて、ひたすら魚を食べている。小山のように盛り上がった背中が、無我夢中の境地を物語る。

　右上の「コマ絵」、つまり小さな枠の中の絵は、中国の仙人、黄初平。白い石を数万頭の羊に変えたというエピソードの持ち主である。それとは縁もゆかりもない江戸時代の女性の姿を重ね合わせるという、浮世絵にはよくある趣向だが、黄初平の意のままになる羊と、わが道をゆく猫が対照的である。

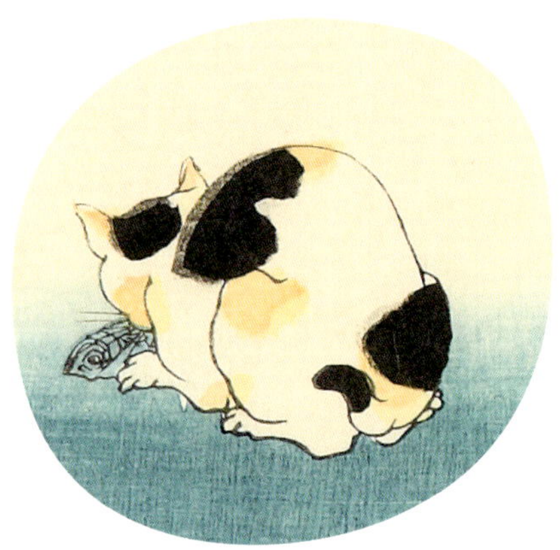

Beautiful Figures of Women Linked to the Sixteen Taoist Immortals: Tai Sin

According to the verse, the woman has been suffering from an illness that induces chest and stomach pains. Now better, she has arisen from her sickbed. Not even faintly interested in its mistress's return to health, the cat is turned away tucking into a fish, its hunched back indicating its total absorption in dinner.

The "single panel cartoon" at top right, ie the picture in the inset, depicts the Chinese Immortal Wong Tai Sin, renowned for transforming white stones into thousands of sheep. Conflating him with the entirely unrelated figure of an Edo-period beauty is a common enough scenario in ukiyo-e, but the cat determinedly doing its own thing offers a stark contrast to the sheep produced at will by the great holy man.

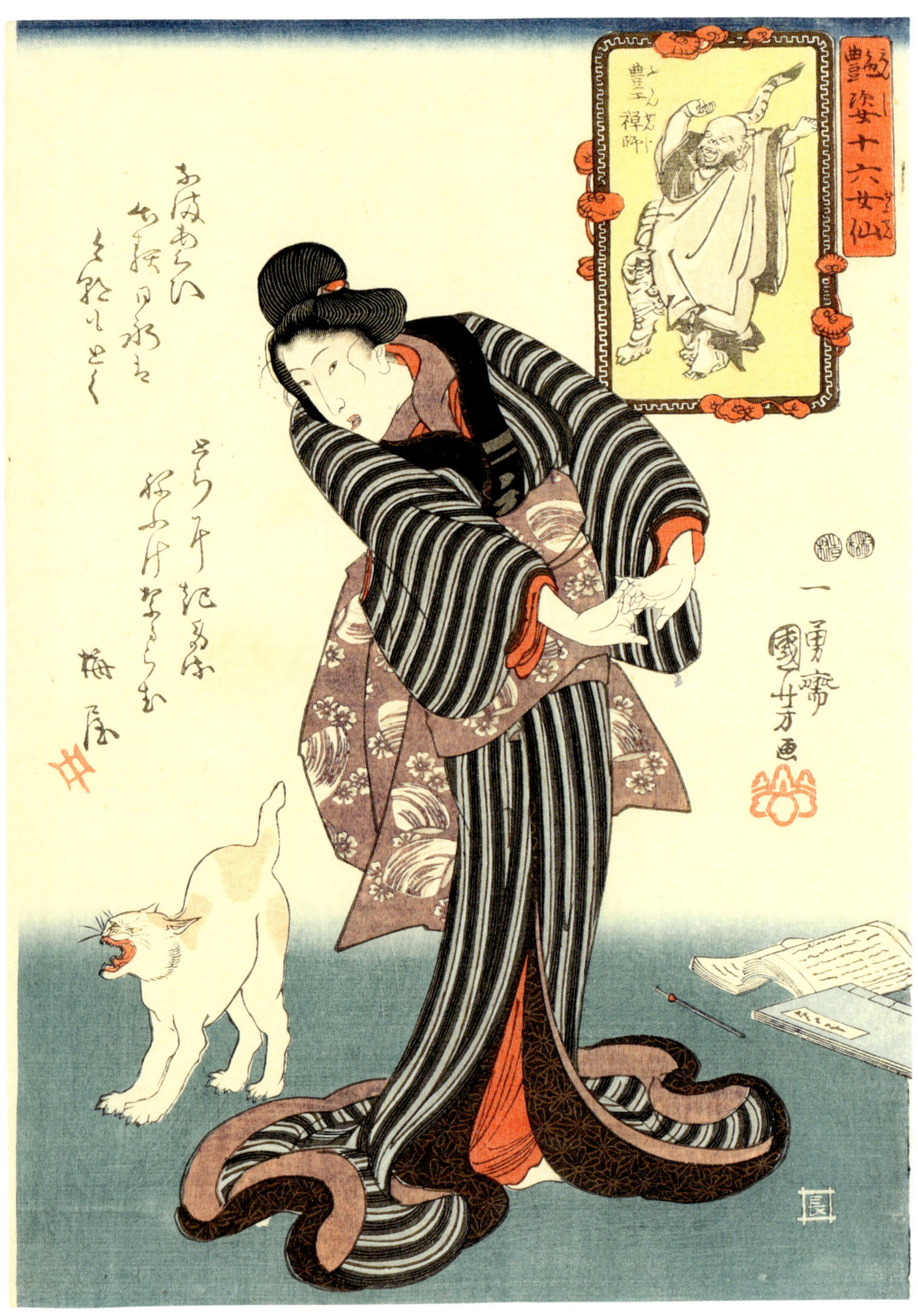
艶姿十六女仙

よゝんなゝ
豊王ゝ禅酔

あはあらに
ちゝ楼ゝ水を
そゝれゝとく

そら千紀ゝゝ
ゝゝ片ゝゝゝゝ

梅屋

一勇齋
國芳画

05 艶姿十六女仙 豊干禅師

えんしじゅうろくじょせん　ぶかんぜんじ

　04と同じシリーズで、サブタイトルは「豊干禅師」。虎を手なずけた中国の僧である。豊干が虎と一緒に眠る絵は、江戸時代の人たちによく知られていた。右上のコマ絵は、その豊干が目覚めたところ。主役の女性は、けだるそうに手をのばしている。画中の歌は「なまあくひ出る日永は今朝もとて　とらに起たるねふけなるらむ」。早朝「寅の刻」に起きたので、眠気に襲われ生あくび、というわけである。

　豊干とともに起きた虎さながら、茶ぶちの猫も思い切りあくびする。足の先からしっぽの先、さらにヒゲの先まで、全身に力が入る。そんな時の顔のひどさも、さすがに国芳は見逃さない。しかし猫という動物は、次の瞬間、何ごともなかったかのように、平静に戻るのである。

Beautiful Figures of Women Linked to the Sixteen Taoist Immortals: Bukan, a Zen Buddhist

A print from the same series as fig. 04, the subtitle refers to the tiger-taming Chinese monk. Pictures of Bukan sleeping with the tiger would have been widely recognized in the Edo period. The frame at top right shows Bukan on waking. The woman is flexing her hands drowsily, the verse indicating that she has arisen early at the "hour of the tiger," hence the sleepy yawning.

Just like the tiger waking up with Bukan, the cat with the brown patches is also yawning dramatically, putting every last effort into the act from its toes to the tip of its tail, and even the ends of its whiskers. Nor does Kuniyoshi overlook the cat's less than flattering countenance at such a moment. In the next instant though, a cat will return nonchalantly to calm normality.

06 妙でんす十六利勘 降那損者 みょうでんすじゅうろくりかん ふるなそんじゃ

　お釈迦さまの弟子、十六羅漢にひっかけて 16 の「利勘」、つまり「得なこと」を連ね
たシリーズだが、中身は「損」なことばかり。「富楼那尊者」をもじったこの図では、「ふ
る」ことがいかに損か、とうとうと語られる。旅で雨が降れば川止めをくらい、尾を
振って来る飼い犬には手を食われ、大手を振って歩けば人に憎まれ、頭を振れば頭痛
がすると、本当に馬鹿馬鹿しいが面白い。

　猫は、長火鉢の縁から着物の中へ入ろうとしている。文中にも、雪が降れば犬は喜
ぶが、猫は嫌がるとある。少しでも暖かい場所を察知し、そそくさと移動するしたた
かさ。しかし、いかんせんしっぽの短い猫はお尻が見えてしまい、後ろ姿は無防備で
ある。

Sixteen Wonderful Considerations of Profit (*Myodensu juroku rikan*): Furuna Sonja

This series features a lineup of sixteen "profits" (*rikan*) ie "beneficial things" in a play on *juroku rakan*, the sixteen arhats that were disciples of the Buddha, but with contents consisting entirely of "losses." This illustration, a pun on Furuna Sonja (the Venerable Punna) tells eloquently of losses associated with the many meanings of the verb *furu*. Rain *falling* on one's travels may cancel a ferry; one may have a hand chewed by a pet dog that comes *wagging* its tail; swaggering triumphantly (ie *swinging* one's arms) many attract people's ire, and when we *shake* our head we get a headache: all in all rather silly, but interesting.

The cat is trying to sneak into the woman's kimono from the edge of the brazier. The text also notes that dogs love snow, but cats loathe it. Detecting a slightly cosier hideaway, the cat stealthily tries to sneak in there. But regretfully the short-tailed cat's backside sticks out, leaving it defenseless from behind.

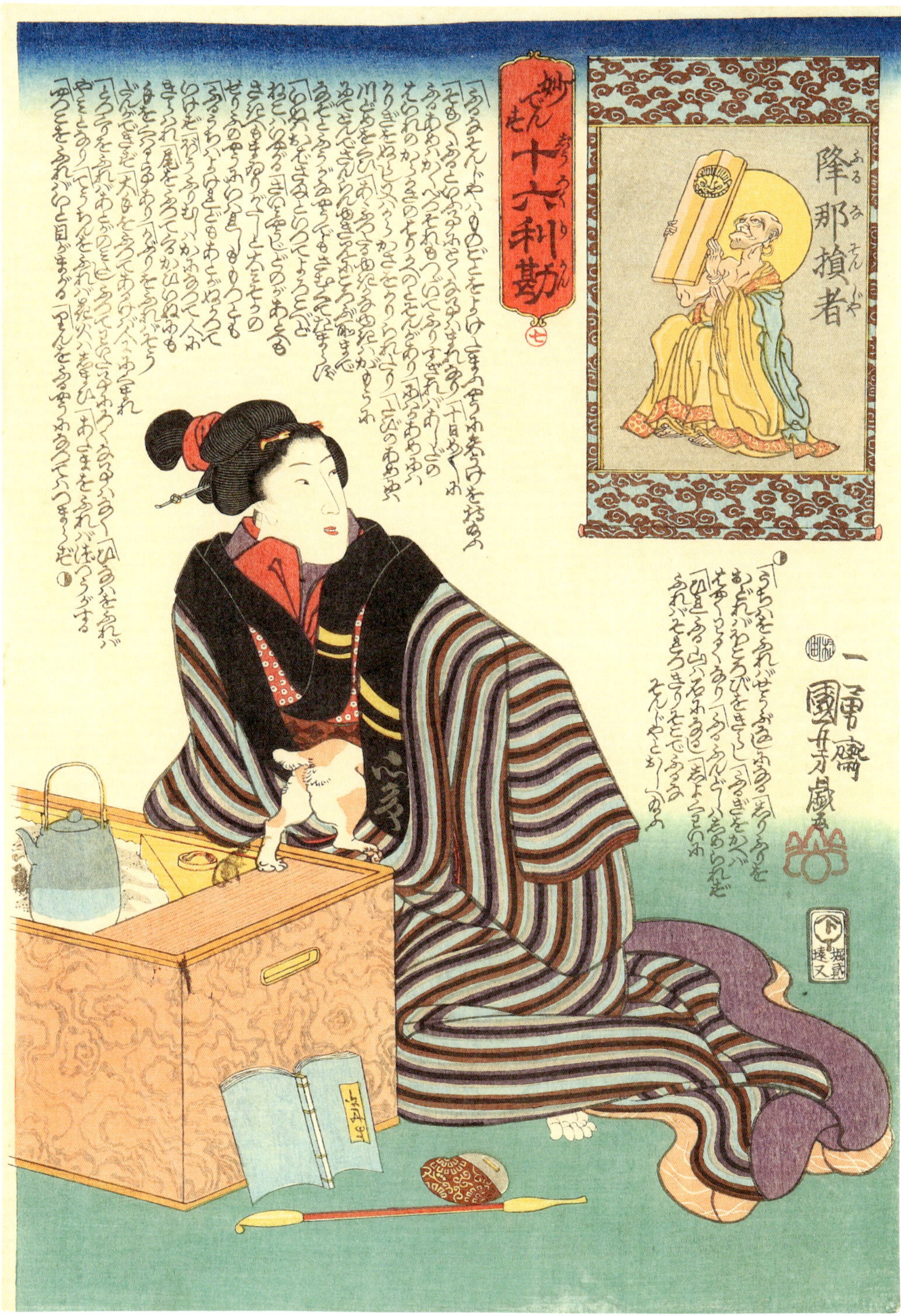

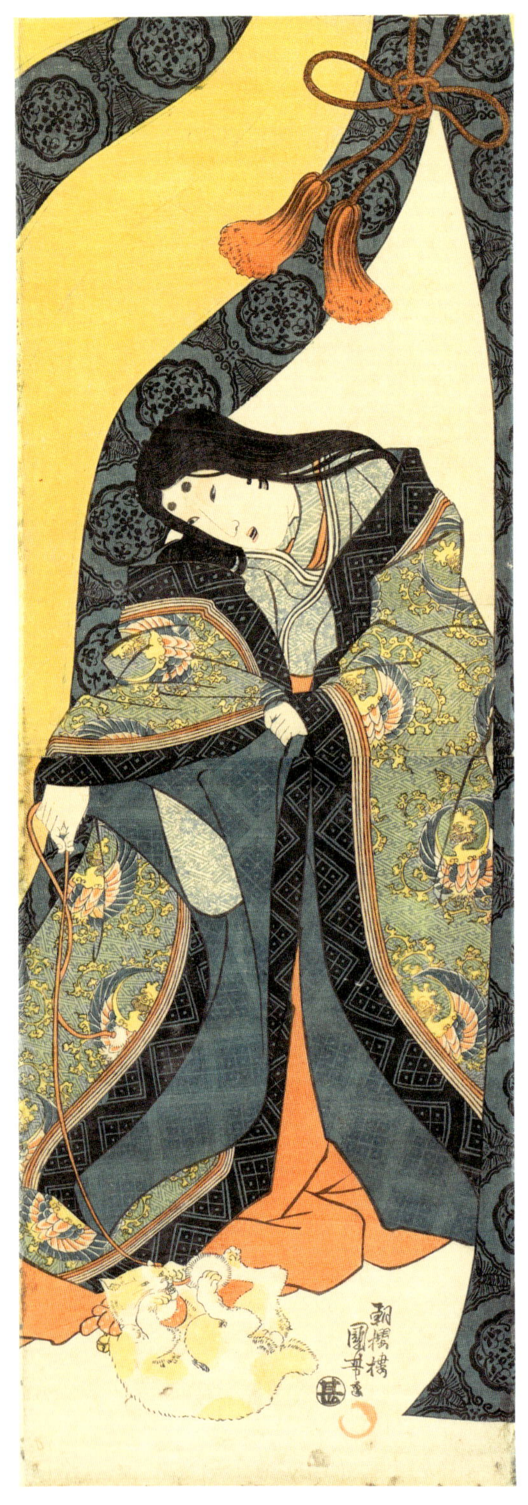

07 女三宮　<ruby>おんなさんのみや</ruby>

　画中にタイトルはないが、紫式部が書いた『源氏物語』の登場人物、女三宮である。飼い猫が、つながれていた綱で御簾（みす）を引き上げてしまい、庭にいた柏木は彼女の姿を垣間見る。二人の不義のきっかけとなったこのエピソードは、江戸時代にも広く知られていた。国芳に限らず、女三宮と猫を描いた浮世絵は多いが、実は、本章で数々ご覧いただいている「猫と女性」という絵のパターンも、そこから派生したといわれている。

　国芳の絵にしてはどことなく立体感に乏しく、まるで千代紙を貼り付けたかのような画面。着物や御簾を、古典的な模様によって典雅に表し、いにしえの貴族の世界を演出しようとしたからである。

　そして猫。房飾りのついた紐にじゃれているが、歯や目を見てほしい。必死の形相である。

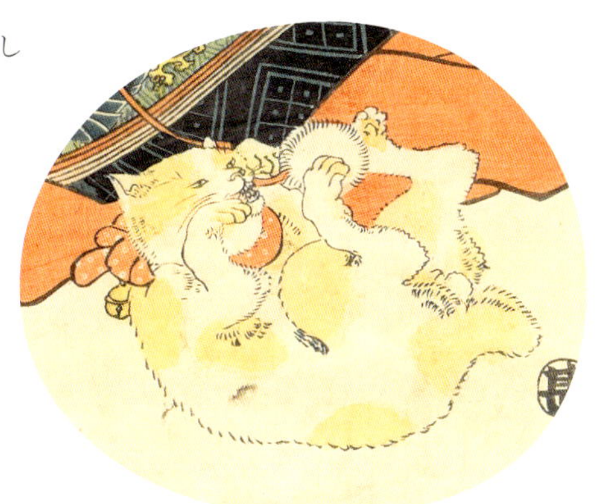

Onna Sannomiya

Though no title is indicated, this is Onna Sannomiya, a character from Murasaki Shikibu's *The Tale of Genji*. Sannomiya's pet cat inadvertently lifts a blind with the attached cord, allowing Kashiwagi in the garden to catch a glimpse of her. This episode, which led to the pair's illicit affair, was also widely known in the Edo period. Kuniyoshi is only one of many ukiyo-e artists to depict Onna Sannomiya and her cat, and the "cat + woman" format of which there are several in this chapter is also said to have emerged from here.

The print somehow lacks the usual three-dimensionality of Kuniyoshi's pictures, appearing more like a piece of chiyogami paper glued on to backing. This is because he has endeavored to use classical designs to give the kimono and blind a certain elegance and thus an old-style, aristocratic feel.

Then there's the cat of course. It attacks the tassled cord playfully, but its teeth and eyes indicate that it means business.

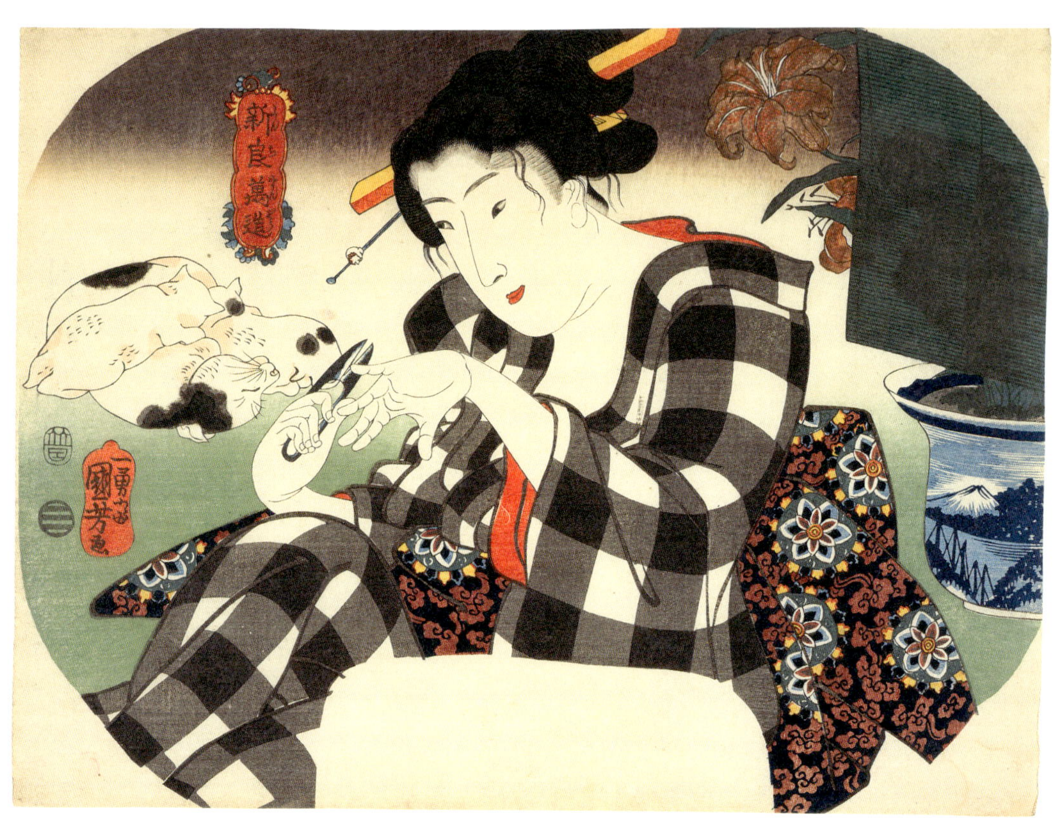

08 新良万造 しんらまんぞう

　団扇に貼る絵を描くのも、浮世絵師の仕事の一つ。扇風機のない時代、こだわりの「マイ団扇」を求める楽しみを想像してほしい。消耗品なので、現代まできれいな状態で残ることは少なく、本書に収録した図はどれも珍しいものばかりである。
「森羅万象」をもじった題だが、意味はわからない。爪を切る女性と百合の花、そして猫。母猫は眠っているようだが、子猫はお乳を飲んでいるようにも、寝ているようにも見える。左の子猫の母親に乗っかる姿が、ほのかなおかしさを醸し出す。女性の着物に猫の白と黒、色づかいも美しい。

Shinra manzo

Painting illustrations to stick on fans was another job of the ukiyo-e artist. Imagine the fun to be had seeking out a personal favorite fan in the days before the electric variety. Being consumables, few fans in decent condition remain today, and every one in this volume is a rare example.

The title is a play on the phrase *shinra manzo* meaning "the whole of creation," but the significance here is unclear. The fan depicts a woman trimming her nails, lilies, and cats. The mother cat appears to be asleep, and the kittens either suckling, or sleeping themselves. The kitten at left on top of the mother looks slightly odd. Kuniyoshi's use of color is also exquisite: the woman's kimono rendered in the same black and white as the cats.

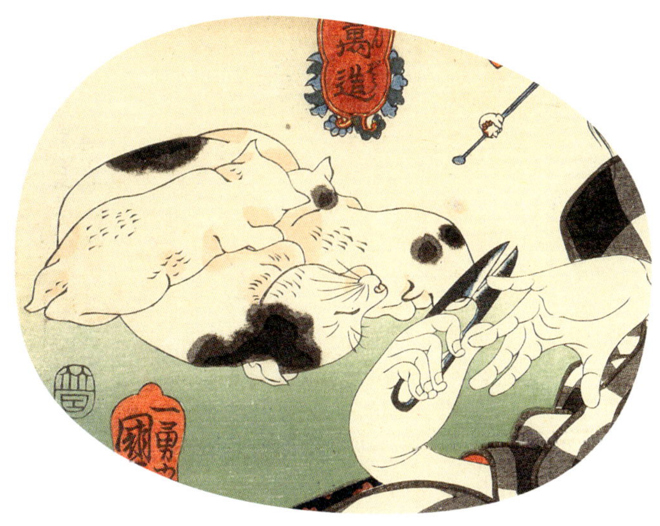

09 五行之内 針の金性 ごぎょうのうち はりのかねしょう

　五行、つまり、すべてのものは木、火、金、土、水から成るという五行思想に引っ掛けたシリーズ。裁縫をする女性が使う針が「金」というわけだが、要するに、単調になりがちな美人画を、何かにかこつけて面白く見せようとする努力なのである。

　薄茶色の大きなぶち模様の猫が、背中を向けて寝ている。がっしりとした、割に大きい猫のように見受けられる。体の微妙な起伏や曲がり具合の描写も十分である。もう一つの注目ポイントは、頭の下からのぞく足先だろう。

The Five Elements: Needle, Metal

Part of a series based on the five elements, that is, the idea that all things are composed of the elements of wood, fire, metal, earth and water. The needle used by the woman sewing is thus "metal." In short, this is Kuniyoshi's effort to use some pretext to make *bijinga*, a genre tending toward the simplistic, appear a little more interesting.

A cat with large light brown patches on its coat sleeps with its back to us. It appears a big, solid beast. Kuniyoshi has also rendered more than adequately the subtle bumps and hollows and curves of the animal's body. Another notable feature is the tip of the paw peeking out from beneath the head.

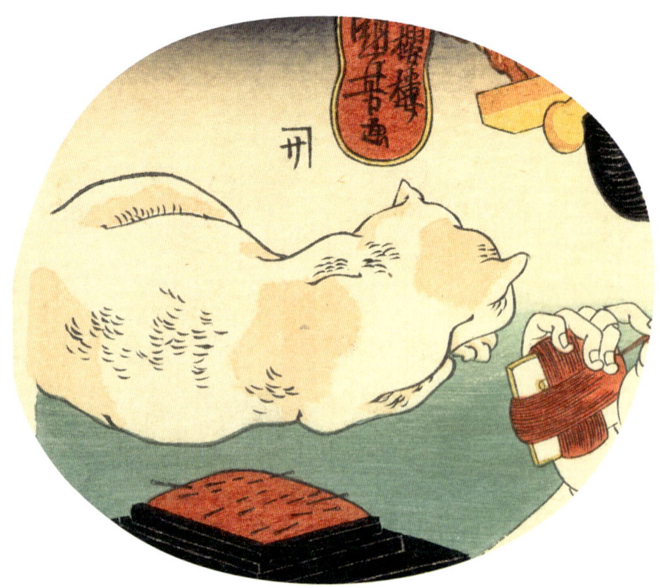

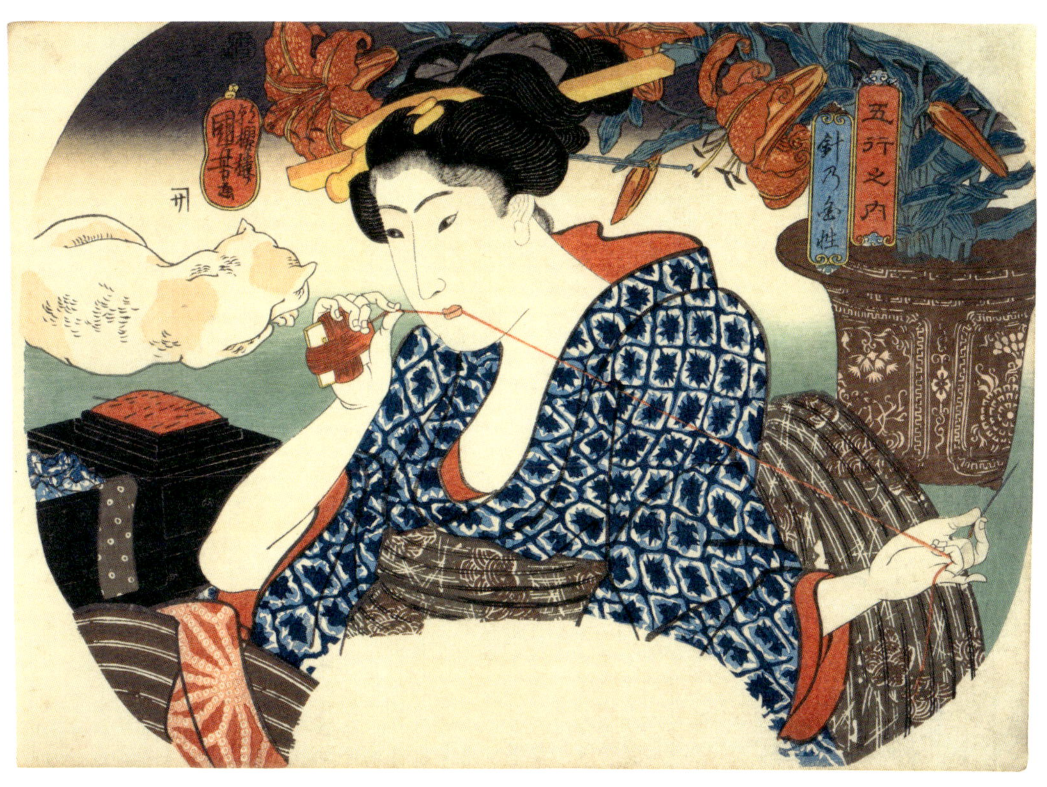

五行之内
針乃金性
一勇斎國芳画

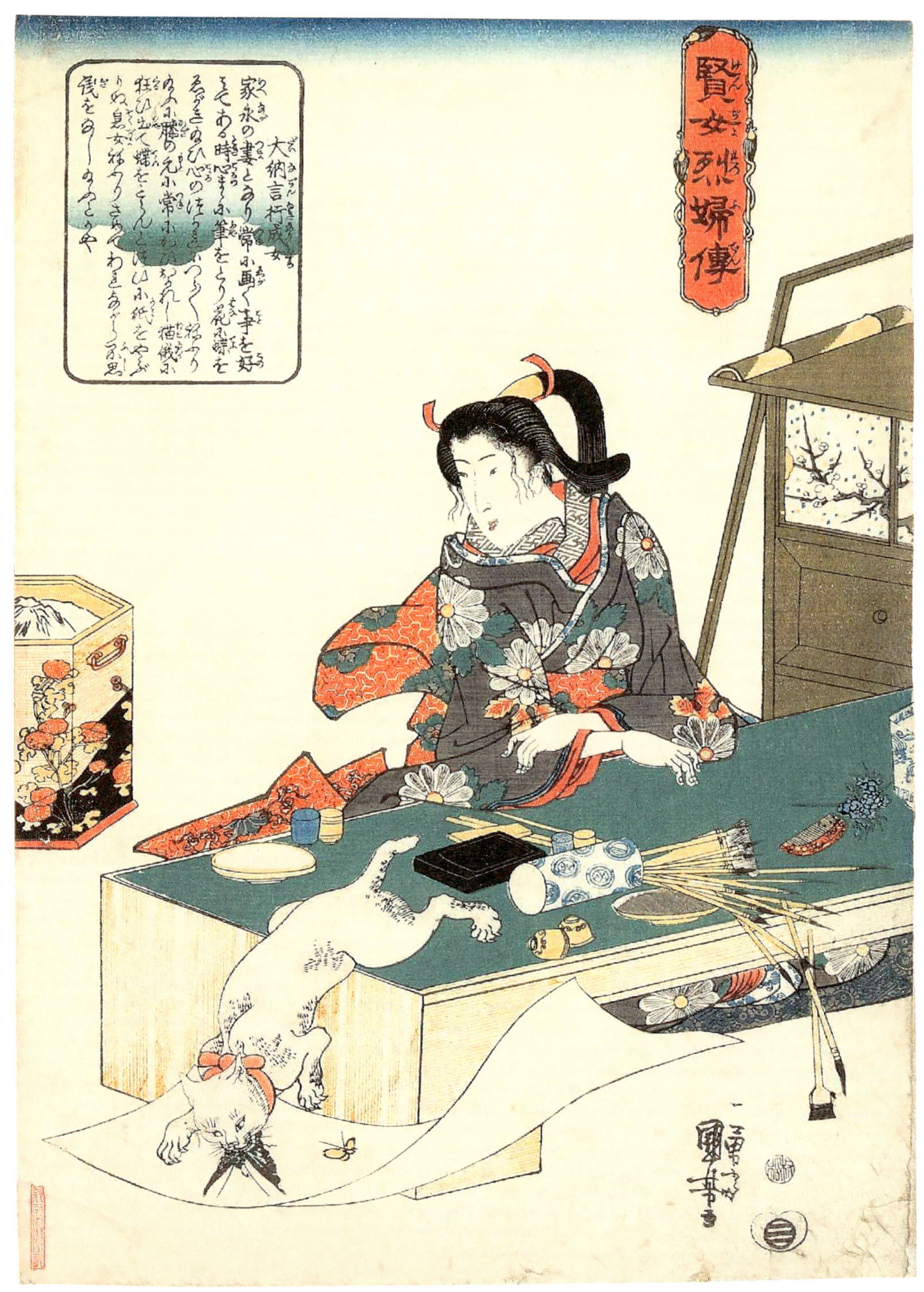

東京都立中央図書館東京誌料文庫所蔵

10 賢女烈婦伝 大納言行成女 けんじょれっぷでん　だいなごんゆきなりむすめ

　歴史上の女性を描いたシリーズの一作。藤原行成といえば平安時代の書の名手だが、その娘が主人公。こんな説明がある。行成の娘は絵を描くのが好きで、ある時、花と蝶を描いていたが、うたた寝してしまった。すると、いつも膝の上にいる猫が、描かれた蝶を捕えようと飛びつき、紙を破いてしまった。

　愛猫は、かわいらしい首輪とは裏腹に、絵を描く道具をなぎ倒し、爪を鋭く立ててワイルドな面をみせている。現代人には意外だが、江戸時代には、猫は蝶を食べるものだという通念があったらしい。たとえば本書の6章に登場する「おこま」もその1匹。うっかり食べてしまったことが、大事件につながるのである。

Biographies of Wise Women and Virtuous Wives: The Daughter of Dainagon Yukinari

One of a series depicting historical female figures. Fujiwara no Yukinari was a famous Heian-period calligrapher, and it is his daughter who features here. One explanation runs thus: Yukinari's daughter liked painting pictures, and on one occasion while painting flowers and butterflies, she nodded off to sleep. The cat that was a permanent fixture dozing on her knee then pounced on the butterfly in the picture in an attempt to catch it, and tore the paper.

Belying its cute collar, the girl's much-loved pet has cut a swath through her painting tools, unsheathing claws and displaying its feral side. Though unfamiliar to modern viewers, in the Edo period it was widely thought that cats ate butterflies. The cat named Okoma that appears in Chapter 6 is another such feline. Thus a casual snack ends up causing mayhem.

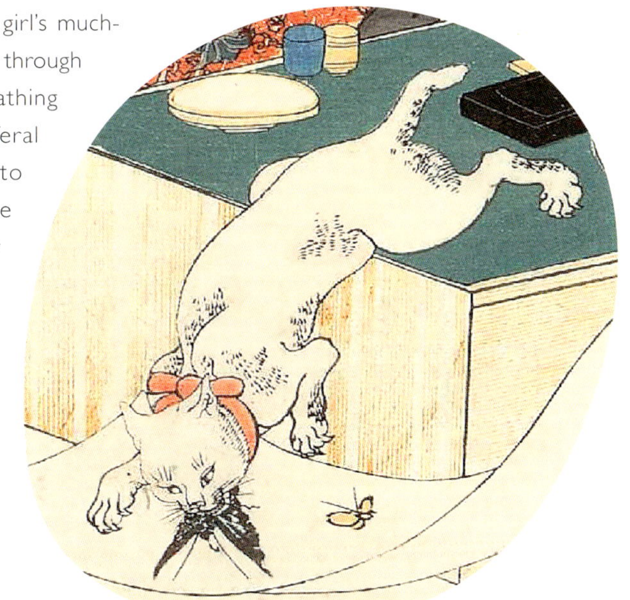

11 嘘真言心之裏表　<ruby>うそとまこと こころのうらおもて</ruby>

　一見むずかしそうなタイトルだが、ある一つのことをめぐる嘘と真、つまり建前と本音の違いがテーマである。ある日、立派な海老と鯛の届け物。「お使いの方、ご苦労さま。お気づかいをいただいて、どうかご隠居さまにもくれぐれもよろしく」というのが建前、つまり嘘。本音は「なんだい今頃になって礼とは。どうせ誰かに言われてようやく贈ってきたんだろ。どこにもやる所がないから、うちで食べるけど」。

　そして猫。嗅ぎ付けて、すぐにやって来たのだろう。かっと口を開けて、体を少し引いて、いきなり戦闘態勢である。しかし、女性は下女のまつに、「それそれ猫が。気をつけなよ」と注意を促す。残念ながらご馳走にはありつけなかったか。

Falsehood and Truth: Both Sides of the Heart

At first glance the title of this print suggests difficult subject matter, but essentially the theme is that of the lies and truth surrounding any particular thing, ie the *tatemae* and *honne*. One day, a splendid gift of crayfish and sea bream is delivered to the door. "Thank you for delivering this," the woman says to the servant. "Please express my gratitude to your master for his thoughtfulness" is the *tatemae*, in other words the falsehood. The *honne*, ie what is really running through her mind, goes more like this: "Bit late to be thanking us now, really. You've only sent that because someone told you to. We will eat it though, because we've got no one to give it away to."

Then the cat. Having sniffed out the tempting treats, it is hot on the trail. Mouth ajar, body drawn back slightly, it has suddenly assumed a fighting position. But the woman cautions her maid Matsu, "Look look, there's a cat. Watch out." Unfortunately it's unlikely puss will score this particular feast.

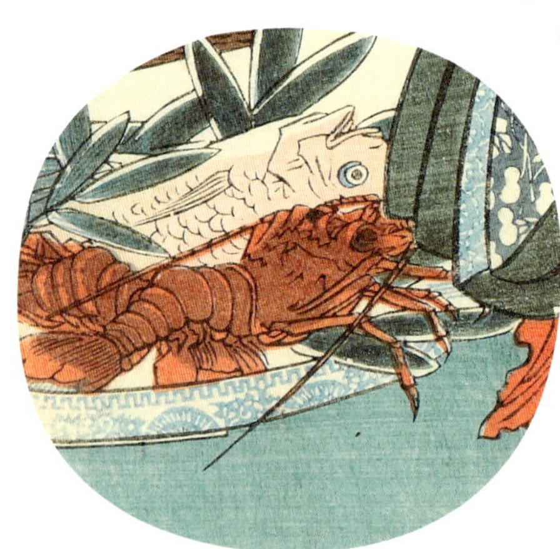

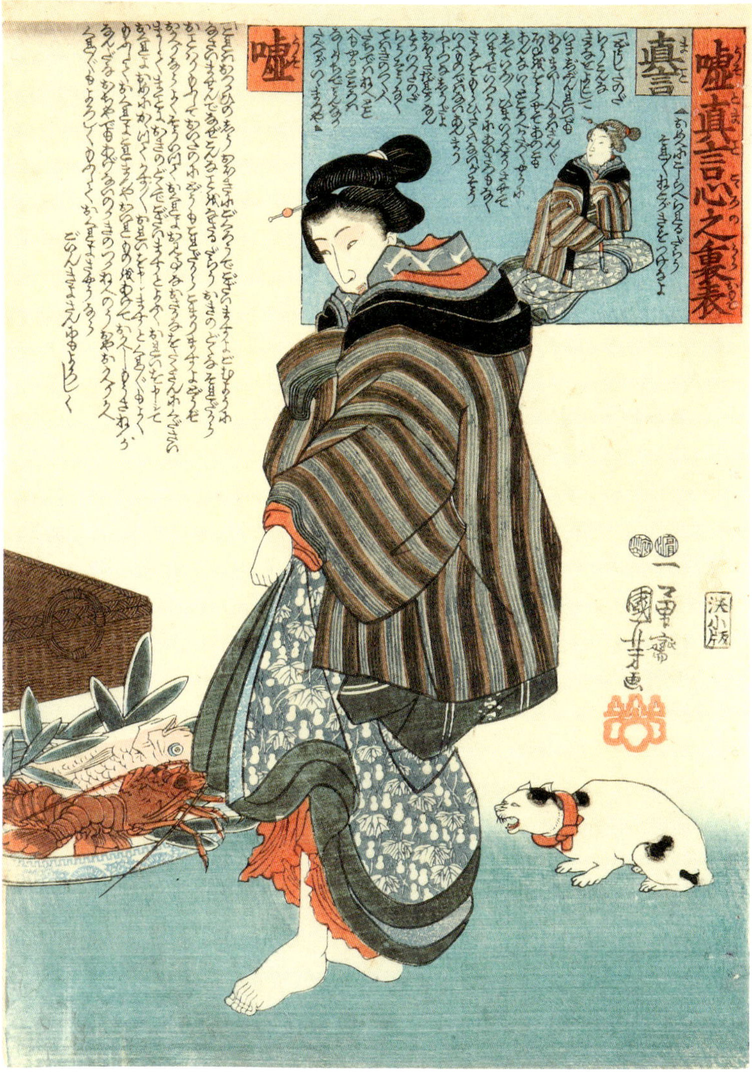

嘘
真言
嘘真言心之裏表
一勇齋　國芳画

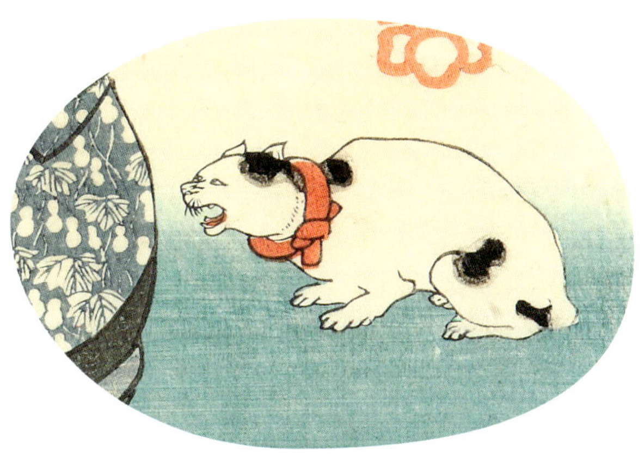

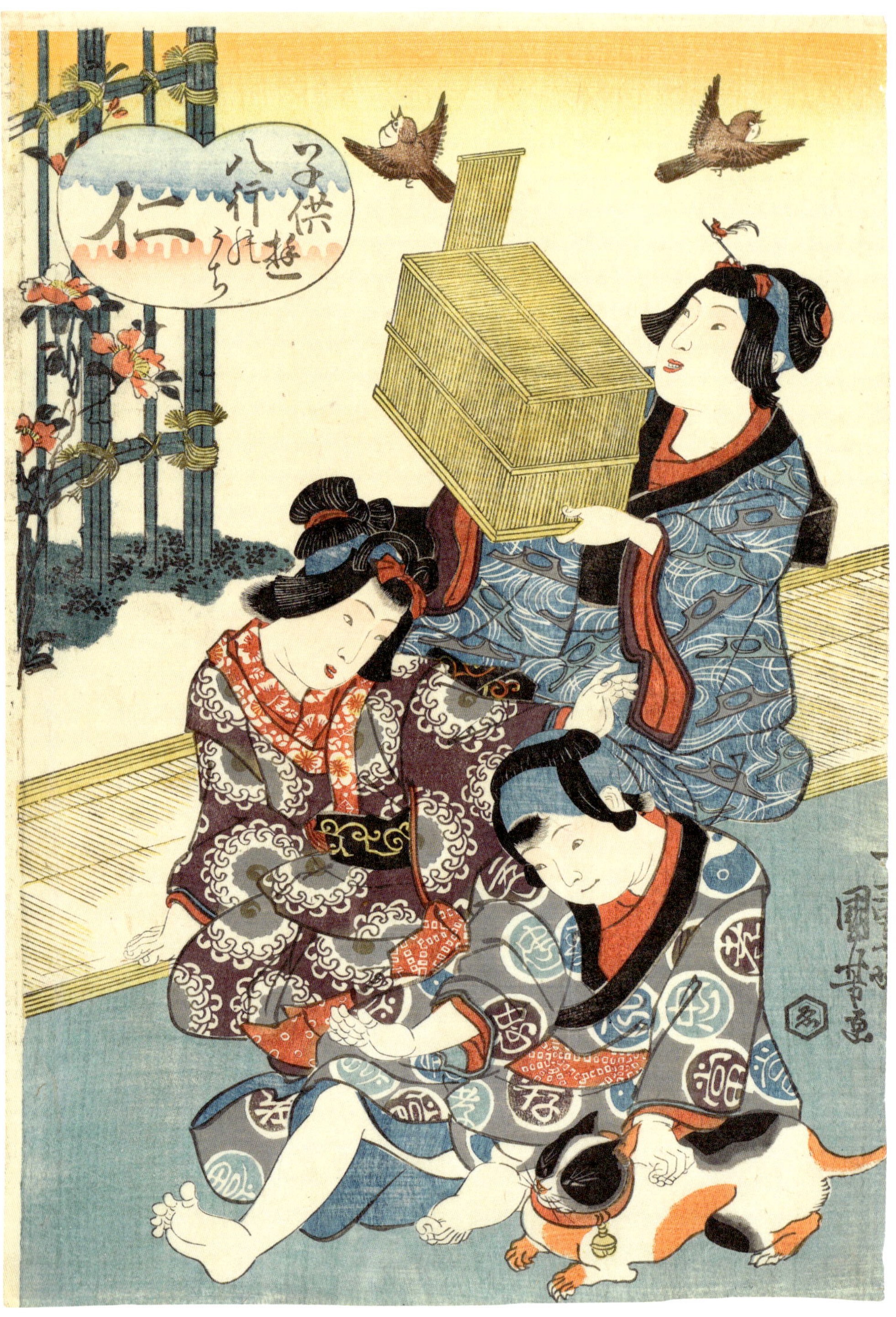

子供八行躾
仁
しつけ

12 子供遊八行のうち 仁 こどもあそびはっこうのうち じん

　よくいる三毛猫なのに、何だろうこの猫は、と首をかしげるような相当変わった趣である。

　かわいそうなことに、男の子に悪さをされているらしい。子供のしぐさが優しげで、あまりそう見えないが、女の子がいさめている。鳥を籠から放つ子もいるが、放生という、動物を自然に帰す仏教の儀式からきている。「仁、義、礼、智、忠、信、孝、悌」という儒教の八つの道徳を表したシリーズの一つで、これは「仁」。つまり、思いやりや慈しみがテーマである。猫は憮然としながらも、じっと耐えている。

The Eight Virtues in Children at Play: Benevolence

Calico cats are common enough, but it's hard to know what to make of this rather odd example.

The poor creature appears to be the object of some meanness on the part of the small boy. Though her childish gestures are gentle, making it less than obvious, one girl is remonstrating with him. Another is releasing birds from a cage, an image inspired by the Buddhist ritual of returning animals to nature. Part of a series of prints depicting the eight Confucian virtues of benevolence, righteousness, courtesy, wisdom, fidelity, loyalty, filial piety, and service to elders, this is benevolence. In other words, the themes here are those of thoughtfulness and affection. Though its dignity has been affronted, the cat stoically endures its lot.

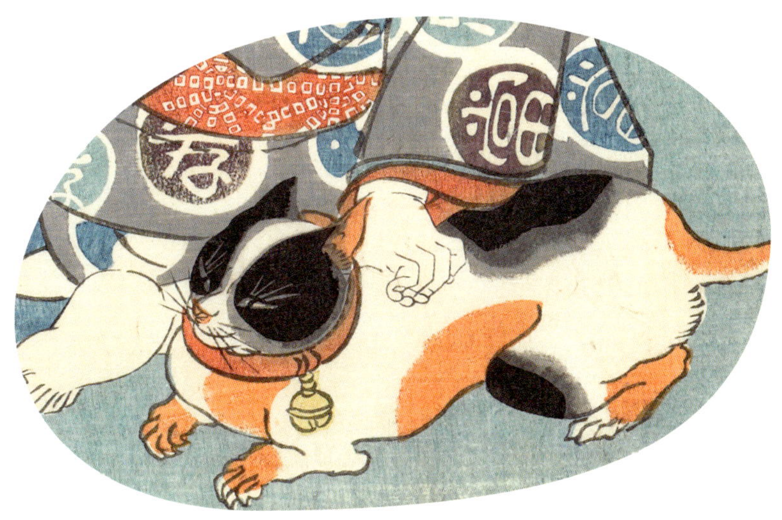

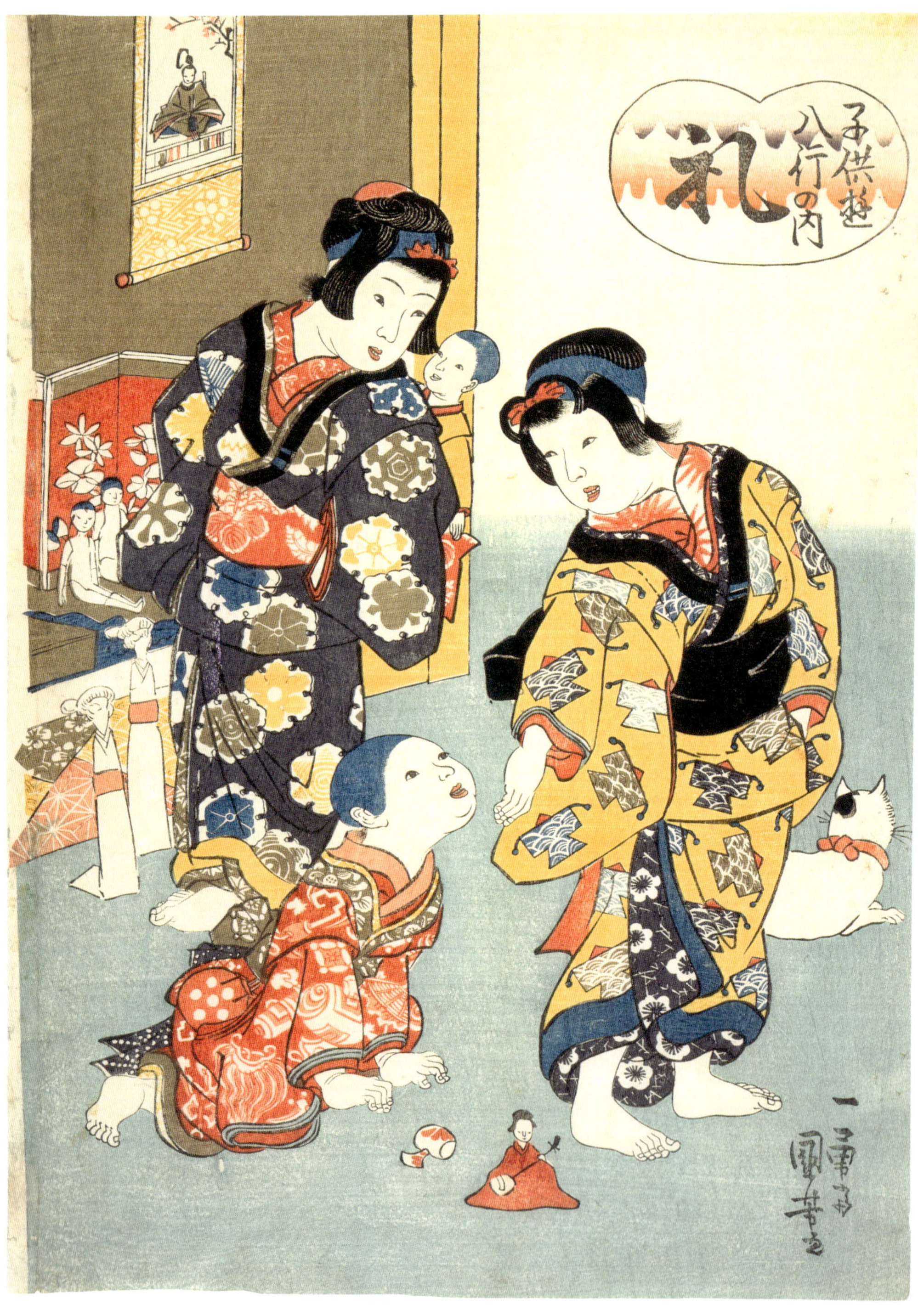
子供遊 八行の内
礼
一勇斎
國芳画

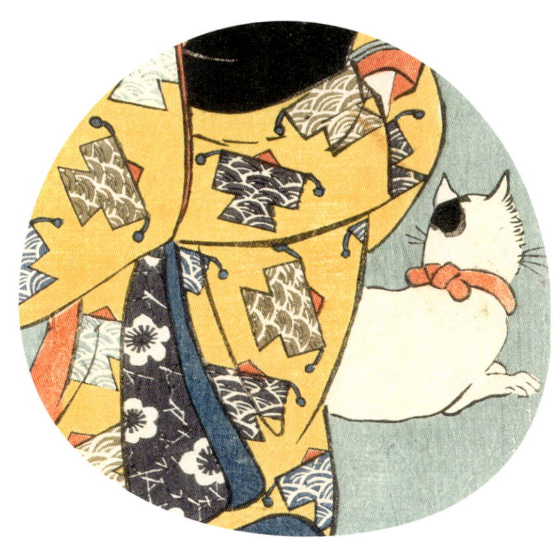

13 子供遊八行の内 礼 こどもあそびはっこうのうち れい

　前のページと同じシリーズの一つで、こちらは「礼」。社会の秩序を保つために必要な人間関係の心得が説かれている。だから年長の子が小さな子の面倒をみたり、遊びのなかでも人形を背負い、母親のまねをしているのである。

　そして、猫の後ろ姿。後ろ姿というのは、かえって強力な存在感を醸し出す。まるで、人間の世界など「わたしは無関係よ」と主張しているかのようである。体をくねらせ座り込む姿を見ると、「つらくないのか？」と心配したくなるが、猫は実に不思議な体を持った動物である。

The Eight Virtues in Children at Play: Courtesy

One of the same series as the print on the previous page, this time the theme is courtesy. The picture preaches the importance of cultivating the interpersonal relationships required to maintain social order. Thus the older children are looking after the young one, and one girl is playing with a doll on her back, copying her mother.

Now note the cat facing away. This back view conversely has a powerful impact, as if the creature is deliberately asserting its detachment from the petty world of *Homo sapiens*. Seeing the twisted form of the seated animal one wonders how it can really be comfortable, but cats' bodies defy logic.

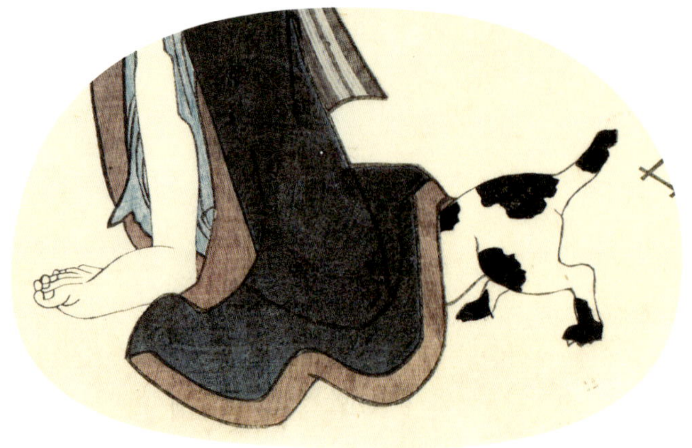

14 於竹大日如来の由来　おたけだいにちにょらいのゆらい

　江戸の豪家に仕えるお竹さんは、仏を敬い、慈悲の心にみちた女性。台所の流しにくくりつけた布の袋にたまった雑菜を食べ、自分の食事は貧しい人に与えたほどで、ついには大日如来として往生し、人々の尊崇を集めた。嘉永2年 (1849)、その「お竹大日如来」の遺品が江戸で公開されて評判となり、数々のお竹さんの絵が作られ、売り出された。

　お竹さんがくわえているのは房楊枝という今の歯ブラシのようなものだが、どういう場面なのか文中に説明はない。そして黒ぶちの猫。てくてくと着物の中へ入っていく。お竹さんを慕ってのことだろうが、だからといって、愛情表現がストレートすぎて思わず苦笑させられる。

Origin of Otake Dainichi Nyorai

Servant of a wealthy Edo family, Otake was a woman who revered the Buddha and was possessed of great compassion, to the extent that she would live off scraps accumulated in a cloth bag tied to the kitchen sink, giving her own food to the poor. Eventually reincarnated as a Dainichi Nyorai (Vairocana), she became an object of religious devotion. In 1849 relics of Otake Dainichi Nyorai were placed on public display in Edo, attracting considerable interest, and numerous pictures of her were produced and sold.

In Otake's mouth is a tufted toothpick, equivalent to the toothbrushes of today, but the text does not explain what is happening in the scene. Also we see a cat with black patches, sneaking into her kimono. No doubt a sign of its attachment to Otake, but even so, as an expression of feline affection it seems far too direct, prompting a wry grin in the cat lover.

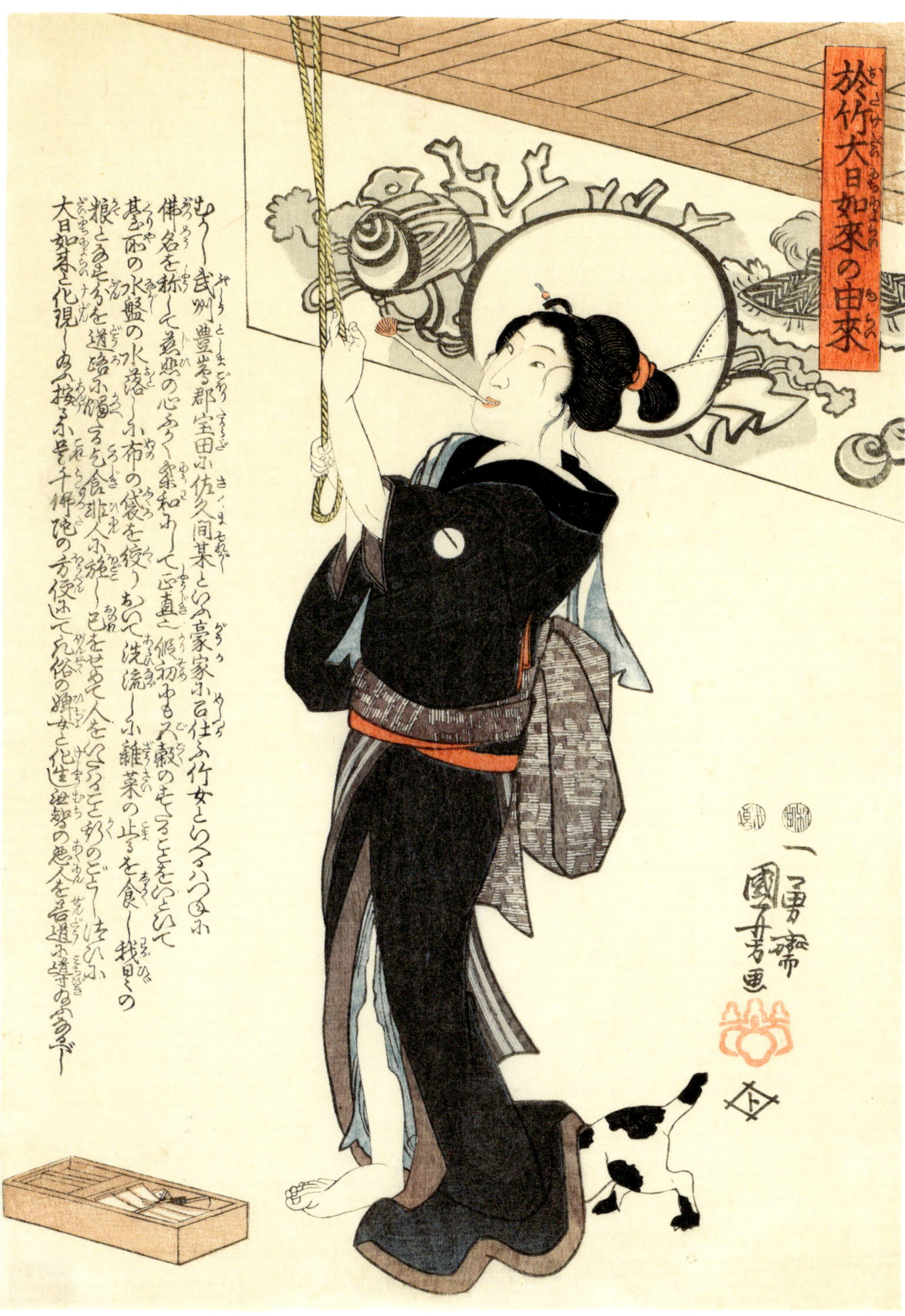

於竹大日如來の由來
もゝ武州豊嶌郡宝田の佐久間某といふ豪家の召仕ふ竹女とてらくハつよく佛名を称へて慈悲の心ふかく柔和にして正直に候初ゟもゝ穀のそこることをおしみて臺所の水盤の水落し小布の袋を絞りおいて洗流し小雜菜の止るを食し我身くの粮とあるをろを道路の小偏るら倉班人小旅し已をせめて人をいくろじ乳のごとし法ひ小大日如來と化視しのゝ按る小ろ千佛陀の方便迷て凡俗の婢女と化生逆悪の悪人を吾道ふ導のふあるゞ
一勇齋國芳画

15 八代目市川団十郎死絵

はちだいめいちかわだんじゅうろう しにえ

　歌舞伎役者の 8 代目市川団十郎は、絶世の美しさで大変な人気者だった。ところが、32 歳の若さで突如、巡業先の大坂で自ら命を絶つ。衝撃はあまりに大きく、在りし日の姿を偲んだり、冥福を祈るための絵がたくさん作られた。地獄の鬼に腕をつかまれる団十郎。同じく冥界にいる奪衣婆や白い衣の亡者までが、あの世へ連れていかないでと懇願する。もちろん大勢のファンは必死ですがり、帯を引っ張る下女もいる。

　そして、一番後ろで加勢しているのが犬と猫。猫は前足を広く開き、着物の裾をかんで、踏ん張っている。役に立っているかどうかはともかく、よくがんばっている。

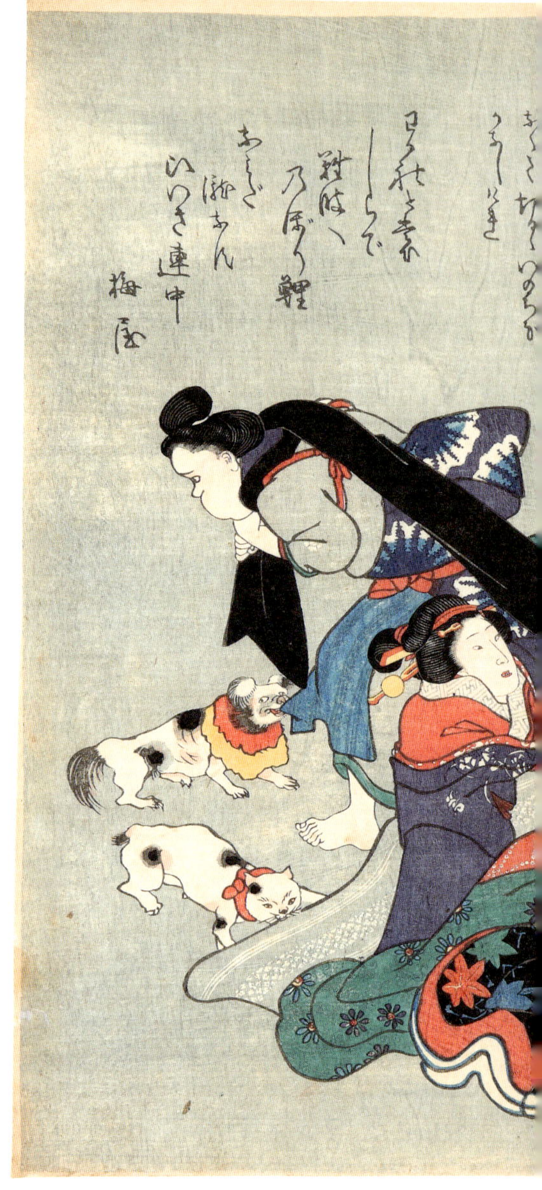

Memorial Portrait of Actor Ichikawa Danjuro VIII

Kabuki actor Ichikawa Danjuro VIII's unrivalled good looks made him an extremely popular figure until at the age of 32 he suddenly took his own life in Osaka while on tour. A huge shock, his suicide prompted the production of numerous pictures recalling how he looked during his career, and as a way to pray for his repose. In this print a demon from hell is grasping Danjuro's arm. Even the hags of hell, and one of

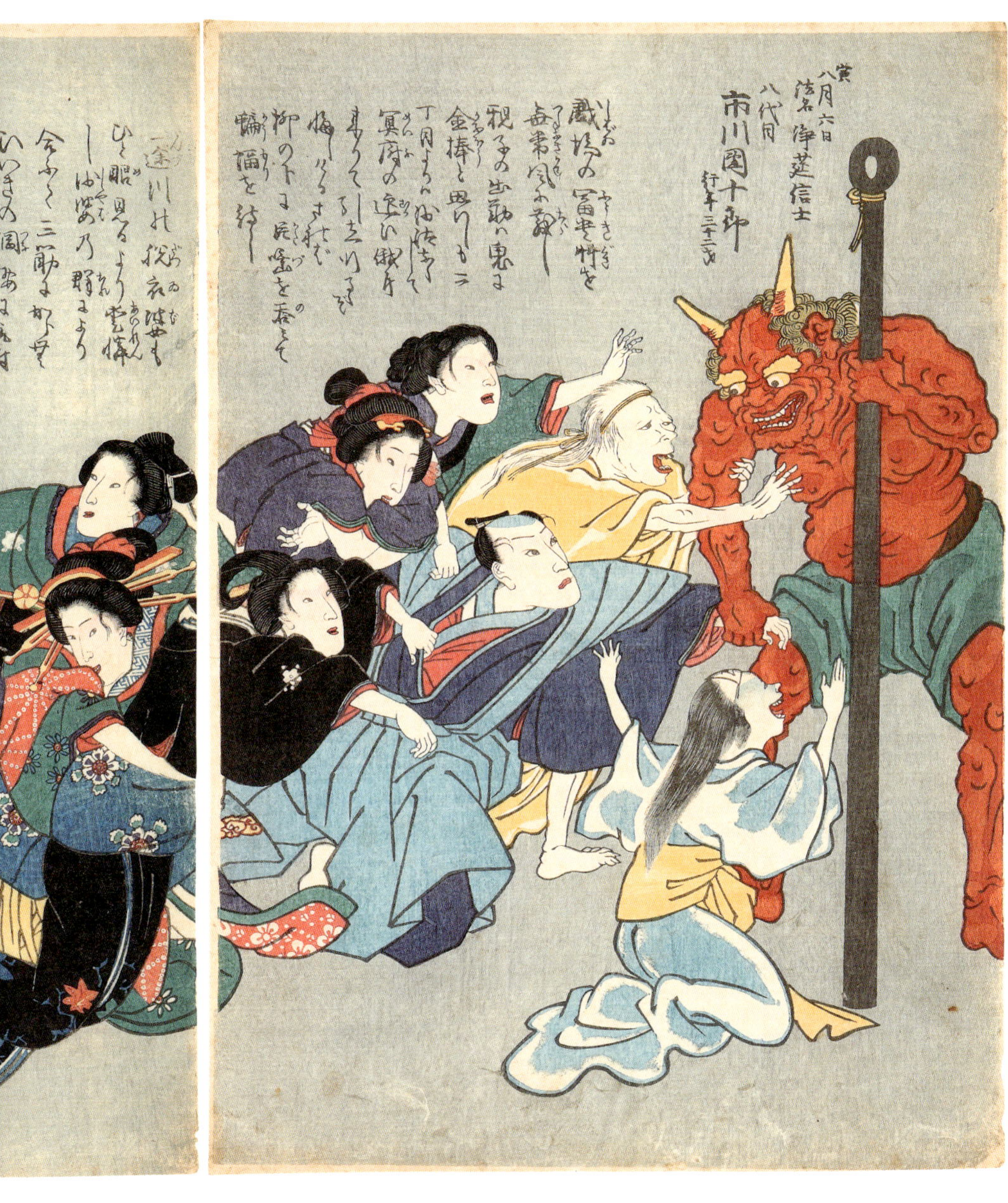

the dead, garbed in white robes, fellow inhabitants of the underworld, are pleading with the demon not to take Danjuro to the other side. Naturally his legions of fans are also desperately clinging to him, a maid even pulling on his sash.

Assisting at the rear are a cat and dog. The cat has its front legs wide apart, the hem of the kimono in its mouth, and is bracing itself with feet firmly planted. Whether it's doing any good or not is a moot point, but in any case, it's trying hard.

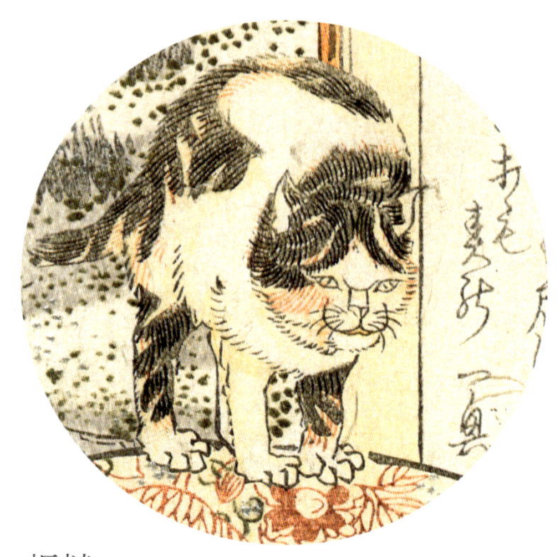

16 風俗女水滸伝 百八番之内 炬燵
ふうぞくおんなすいこでん ひゃくはちばんのうち こたつ

　女性を中国の長編小説『水滸伝』の登場人物になぞらえたシリーズの一つ。画中の歌から察すると、猫を、物語に出てくる虎に見立てているらしい。なるほど、だから前足をぴんと突っ張って、江戸時代の虎の絵によくあるポーズをとっているのである。表情も尋常ではない。

　現代人からみたら限りなく突飛なこんな趣向も、浮世絵には珍しくない。しかし、猫がこんな態度で突如現れたら、びっくり仰天である。実は少しエロティックなところも盛り込まれた絵なのだが、女性は猫に驚いてひっくり返っているようにしか見えない。

Elegant Women's *Water Margin* –
One Hundred and Eight Sheets: In the Kotatsu

One of a series that takes female figures and places them in Chinese novel the *Water Margin*. From the verse in the inset it may be surmised the cat is standing in for the tiger that appears in the story, hence the stiff, straining front legs, a pose common in Edo period images of tigers. There is nothing ordinary either about the expression on its countenance.

Such a scenario, though very odd to modern eyes, is not unusual in ukiyo-e. Still, the sudden appearance of a cat looking like this would indeed by surprising. While there is also a hint of the erotic here, the only conclusion one can draw is that the sudden appearance of this feline intruder has caused the woman to fall over in surprise.

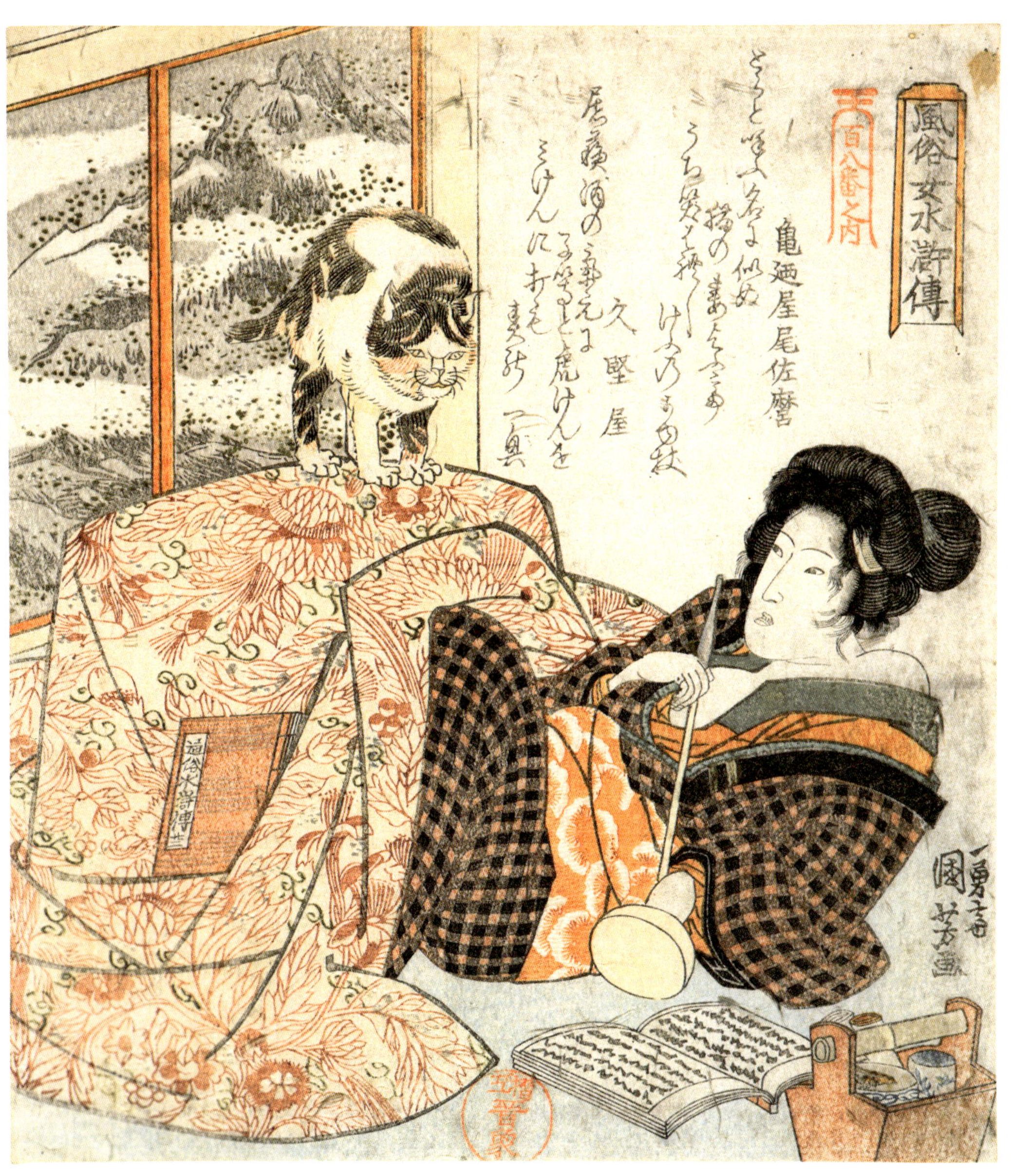

風俗女水滸傳
二百八番之内
亀延屋尾佐麿
久堅屋

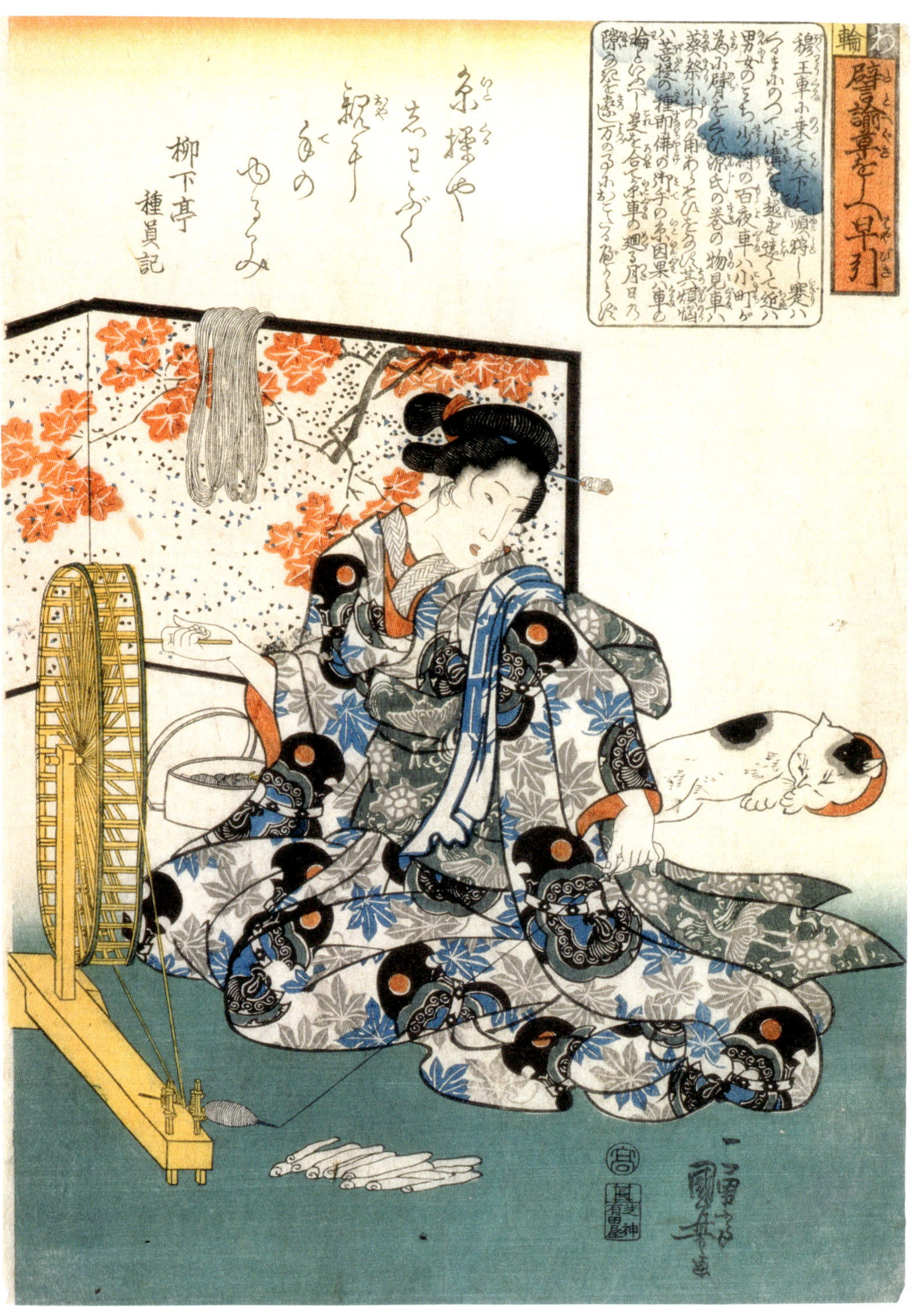
輪

とくゆきことをはやびき
譬諭草を一早引

糸棷や
志ほぐく
親と手に
自の
ゆるみ

柳下亭
種員記

17 譬諭草をしへ早引 輪 　たとえぐさおしえはやびき わ

　大切なことを何かにたとえて教えようというシリーズである。この図は「輪」。文中、有名な古典のエピソードなどを挙げながら、すべては車の輪のようにつながっているから、万事、怠りのないように、との教訓が示されている。また、「糸操や　しわぶく親に手のゆるみ」の句は、糸車を回していたら年老いた親が咳をして、ふと手がゆるんでしまったという内容。そういう時でも、回す手を止めてはいけないのである。

　さて、前足を枕に眠る猫の姿は、相当かわいい。口のあたりが隠れているところ、むっくりした足のいかにも柔らかそうなところも見どころだが、見落としてはいけないのが後ろ足。揃ってしまっているのが、猫好きの心をくすぐる。

Instructive Index of All Sorts of Proverbs: Wheel (*Wa*)

Part of a series aiming to teach important moral lessons by example. This illustration is *wa* (the wheel). The text, citing famous episodes in the classics, teaches that we should apply ourself diligently to whatever we do, because everything is connected like a wheel. The line "The hand of the spinner slackens with the coughing of a parent" means that while the woman is spinning the wheel her elderly parent coughs, causing her to lose the rhythm momentarily; the lesson being that even under such circumstances, the turning hand must always keep moving.

Turning to the cat sleeping with its front paws on the pillow, we find a rather delightful little animal. Highlights include its coyly concealed mouth and its lovely plump, padded paws, but don't miss the back legs. The way they are neatly aligned will elicit a sigh from any cat lover.

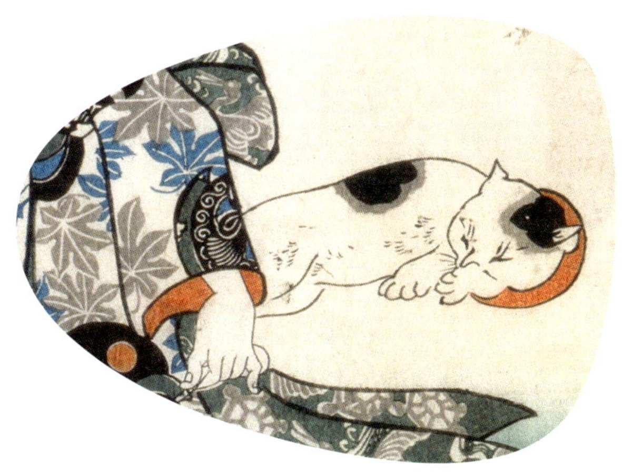

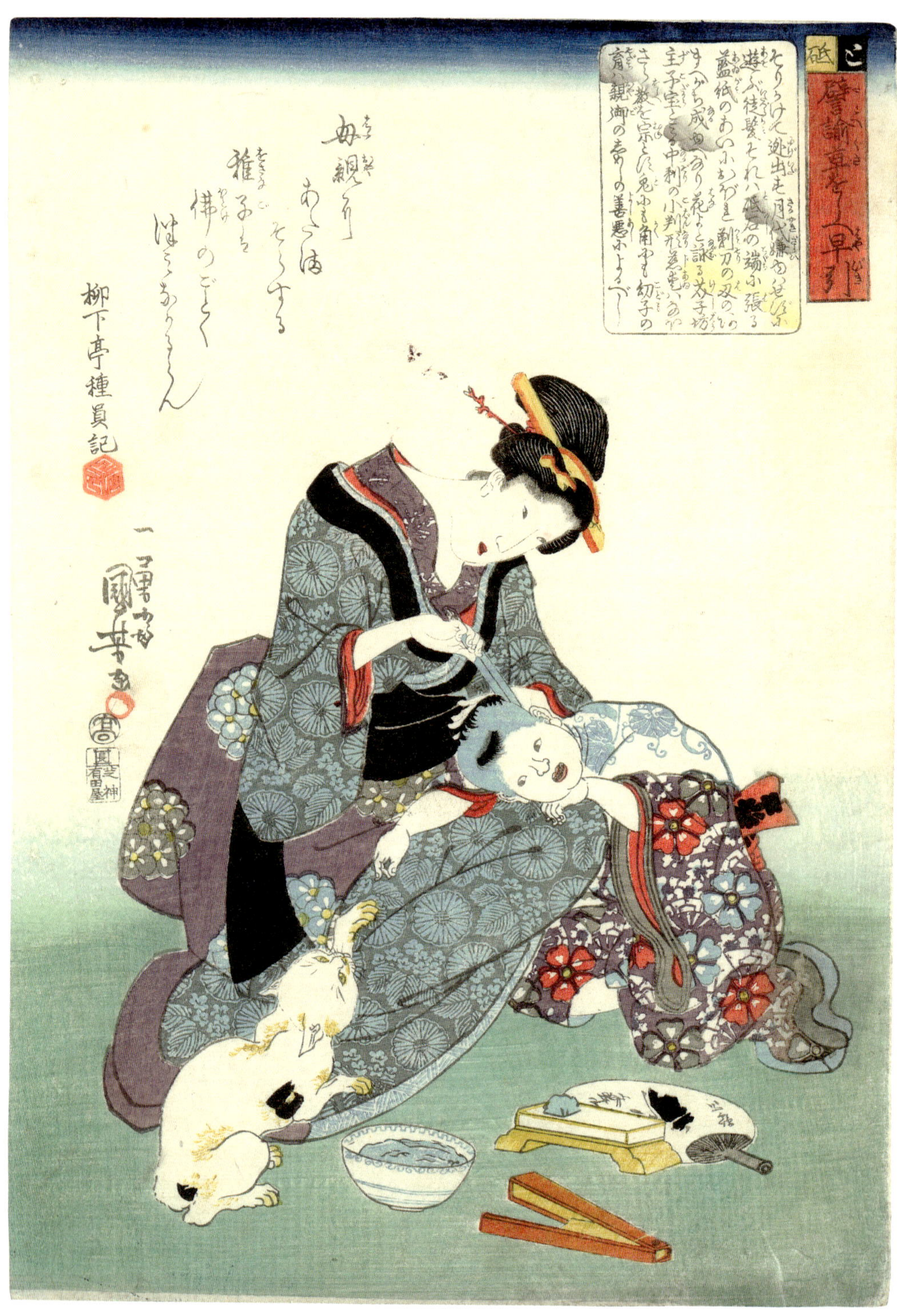

18 譬諭草をしへ早引 砥 _{たとえぐさおしえはやびきと}

　前の図と同様、何かを例に出して大切なことを教えるシリーズの一つ。この図は「いろはにほへと…」の「と」。それを刃物を研ぐ砥石の「砥」に引っ掛けて、子供の頭を剃る親を題材にしている。

　画中の歌は「母親にあたまそらする稚子は　仏のごとくつみなかるらん」。子供に罪はないが、じっとしているのはつらいこと。でも、そこで甘やかさないのが肝要だ、という趣旨である。

　この子はなんとか辛抱しているが、たまたまやって来た猫に手を出した。猫の方は何かもらえるとでも思ったのか、後ろ足で立ち、にゃっと前足を伸ばした。そんな一瞬を捉えている。いたずらっぽい子供の目もなかなかである。

Instructive Index of All Sorts of Proverbs: Whetstone (*To*)

Another of a series teaching important lessons by example, this time featuring the *to* of *i-ro-ha-ni-ho-he-to* – the first line of a poem used to signify the traditional order of the Japanese kana alphabet – associating it with the *to* (whetstone) used to sharpen blades, and by extension a mother shaving a child's head.

The verse may be translated as "The young boy having his head shaved by Mother is as innocent as the Buddha." Meaning a child may do no wrong, but finds it hard to stay still, the gist being not to therefore indulge him too much.

Enduring his ordeal, the lad extends his hand to a passing cat. Thinking some treat is in the offing, the cat stands up on hind legs, stretching out its front paws. The boys' impish expression is another notable feature.

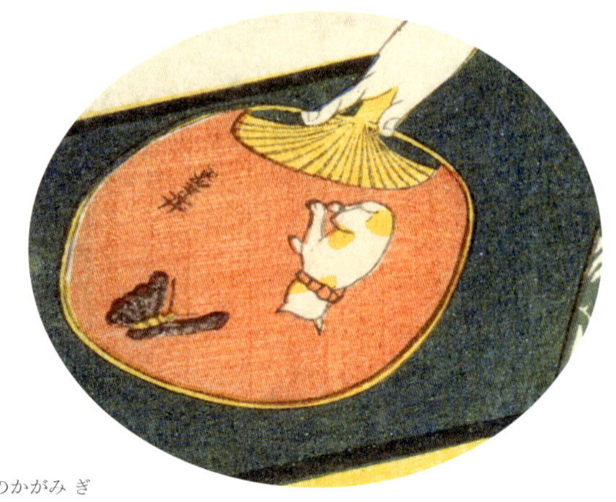

19 貞操千代の鑑 義 ていそうちよのかがみ ぎ

　地道な暮らしから社会の建て直しを図ろうとした幕府の政治改革、天保の改革。役者の似顔絵や遊女の絵が禁止され、浮世絵師や版元らは、食べていくために、まじめな教訓画を装った浮世絵をたくさん作り出した。

　この図も儒教の徳の一つ「義」がテーマだが、内容は、音が同じ「宜」に置き換えている。宜しきに叶う、つまり何ごとも程よくすれば、人から好かれ、夫婦仲も良好に保てると説いている。

　猫は団扇の中にいる。団扇にある画家のサインは「芳」という字に似ているが、国芳の弟子の芳藤がそこだけ描いたのかもしれない。それはともかく、蝶と猫。小さい描写だが、左の前足をちょっと上げた姿からは愛らしさが滲み出ている。もはや、この絵の主役としか思えない。

Mirror of Eternal Feminine Virtues: *Righteousness (Gi)*

The Tempo reforms were instituted by the Tokugawa shogunate to facilitate social reconstruction through austerity. Caricatures of actors and pictures of prostitutes were banned, and to make a living ukiyo-e artists and printers instead produced a stream of ukiyo-e in the guise of pictures illustrating serious moral lessons.

The theme for this print is the Confucian virtue of *gi* (righteousness), but actually substitutes this *gi* for a homonym meaning fitting or proper, preaching that doing what is right, that is doing all things in moderation, will ensure one is liked by others, and maintain marital harmony too.

The cat here is on the fan. The artist's signature resembles the character 芳, indicating that Kuniyoshi's apprentice Yoshifuji may have painted just this section. In any case, we have a butterfly and a cat. A small rendering, still the cat with its left paw delicately raised cuts a delightful figure that makes it in reality the main character.

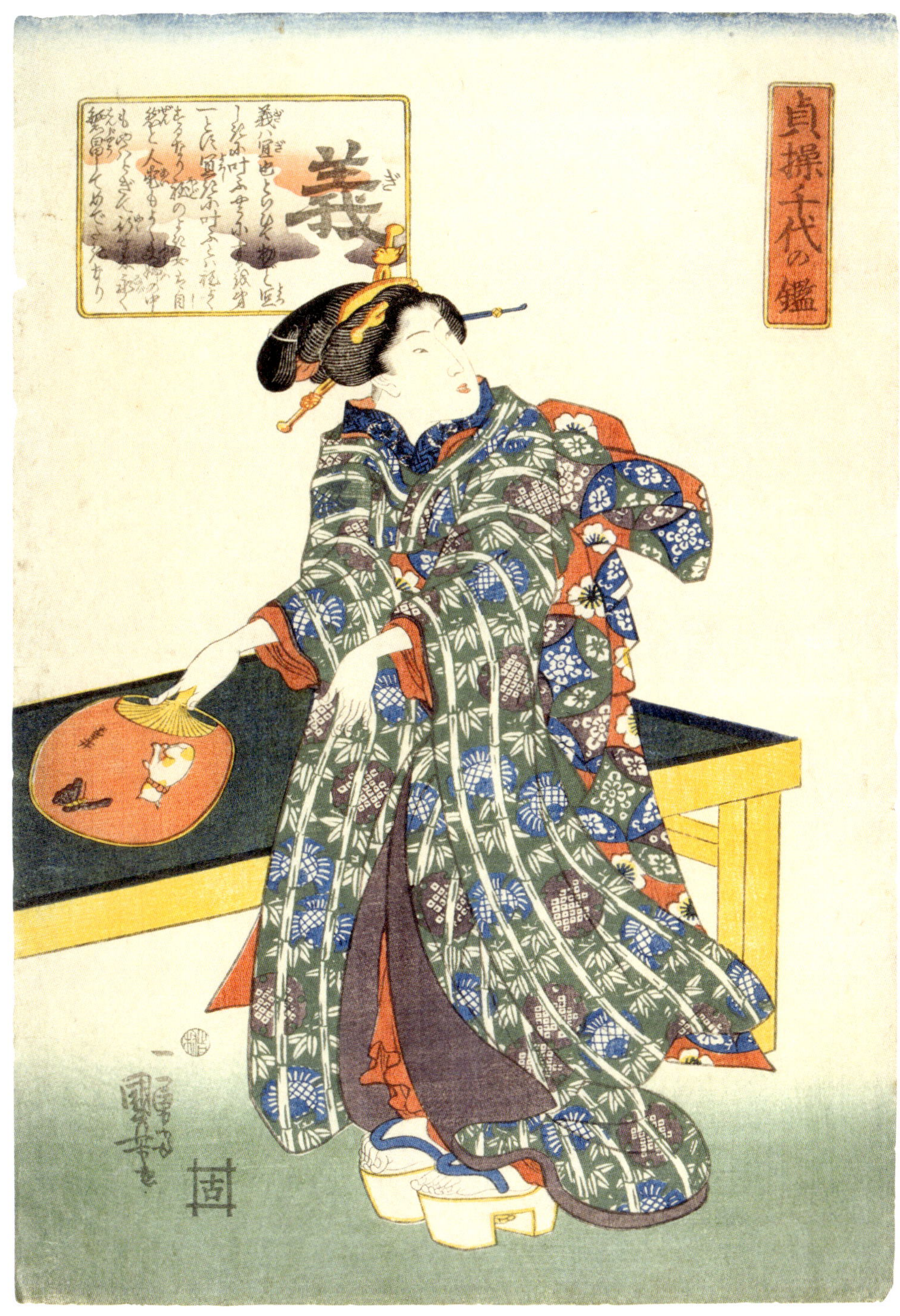
貞操千代の鑑
義
義ハ宜也とらひそく物して

20 源氏雲浮世画合 柏木　<ruby>げんじぐもうきよえあわせ かしわぎ</ruby>

　江戸時代当時の芝居を、似通った『源氏物語』の中のエピソードにかこつけて、一枚の絵にしたシリーズ。画面の女性は、「艶容女舞衣」という演目に登場する三かつ。三かつは不義の末に、娘、おつうを生んだが、それを、光源氏の正妻である女三宮が、柏木との間に薫をもうけた話に重ね合わせているのである。上の歌は『源氏物語』で柏木が詠んだもの。

　ではもう一人、いやもう1匹の登場人物は誰か。実は、柏木が女三宮を見初めたのは、女三宮の飼い猫が、走って御簾をめくり上げた時だった。いわば猫は、二人を複雑な運命へと導いた張本人だが、もちろん悪気など全くない。そんな風情が無心に食べる後ろ姿からも発散されている。互いに背中合わせの三者。罪のないわが子と愛猫ゆえに、三かつの心は複雑だろう。おつうが「三味線」の稽古をしているのが、少々ほろ苦い。

Genji Clouds Matched with Ukiyo-e Pictures: Kashiwagi

From a series linking Edo period plays to similar episodes in *The Tale of Genji*. The woman is Sankatsu from *Hadesugata onna maiginu*. Sankatsu gave birth to a daughter Otsu, product of an adulterous affair, and this is overlaid on the story of Hikaru Genji's lawful wife Onna Sannomiya bearing Kashiwagi's son Kaoru. The verse at the top is recited by Kashiwagi in *The Tale of Genji*.

So who is the other, not necessarily human, character? Kashiwagi actually first spied San-no-Miya when her scampering cat flicked up a bamboo blind. Thus it is the cat that guided the pair to their complex destiny, but naturally without any malicious intent. This is also obvious from the cat's rear view as it eats, oblivious. The trio have their backs to each other; Sankatsu's heart no doubt conflicted as she looks at her blameless child and beloved pet. Showing Otsu practicing the shamisen, in the mode of her courtesan mother, is bittersweet.

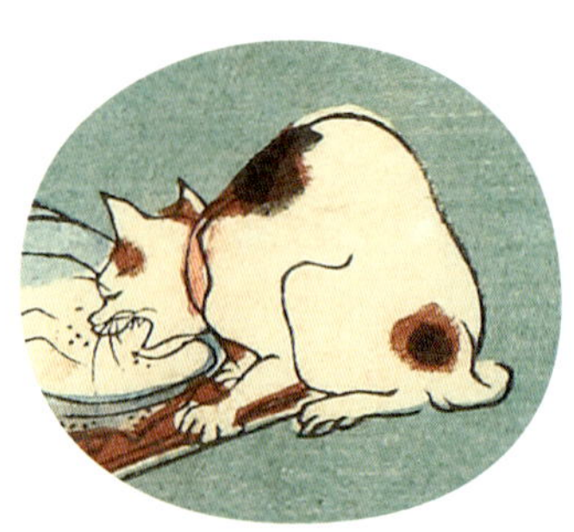

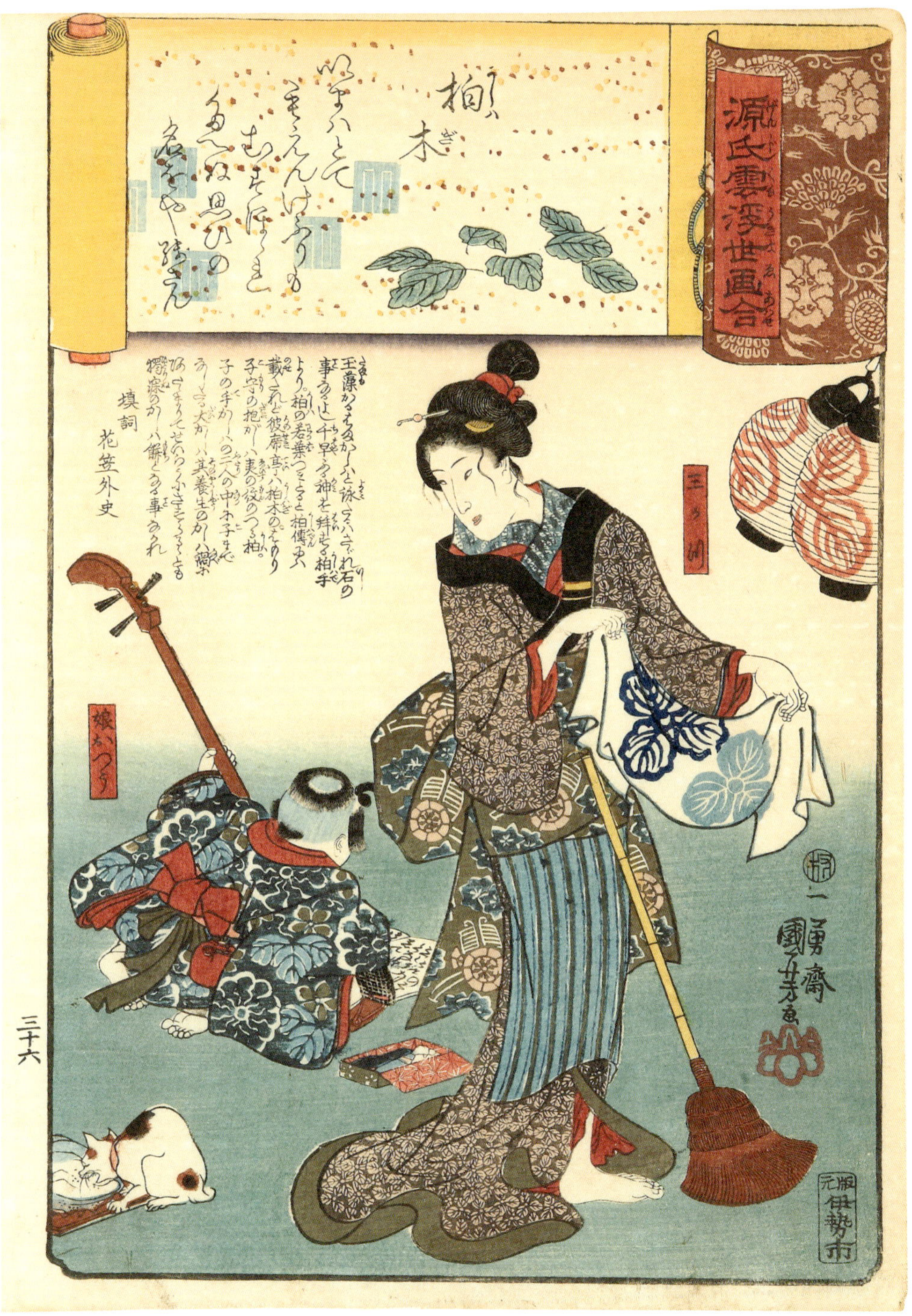
柏木
源氏雲浮世画合
填詞
花笠外史
三十六
一勇齋
國芳画

21 源氏雲浮世画合 若菜 下　げんじぐもうきよえあわせ わかなげ

　前のページと同じ、『源氏物語』とそれに似た江戸時代の芝居を重ね合わせたシリーズ。『源氏物語』の「若菜」の巻には、「桜」咲く庭で柏木たちが蹴鞠をする場面があり、一方「菅原伝授手習鑑」の三段目には、「桜丸」の妻、八重が義理の父の祝いの膳のために「若菜」を摘む場面がある。そこで両者を結びつけたのである。

　猫は上のコマ絵の中。単なる脇役ではなさそうな存在感である。猫は、その蹴鞠のとき、女三宮と柏木の道ならぬ恋のきっかけを作った。三毛猫は遺伝学上ほぼメスだが、国芳はそれを意識して、猫を女三宮、鞠を柏木になぞらえたのでは、という見方もされている。

　猫は鞠に乗っかっているわけではなく、じゃれようとしている。次の瞬間どうなるかわからない、あやうい様子である。

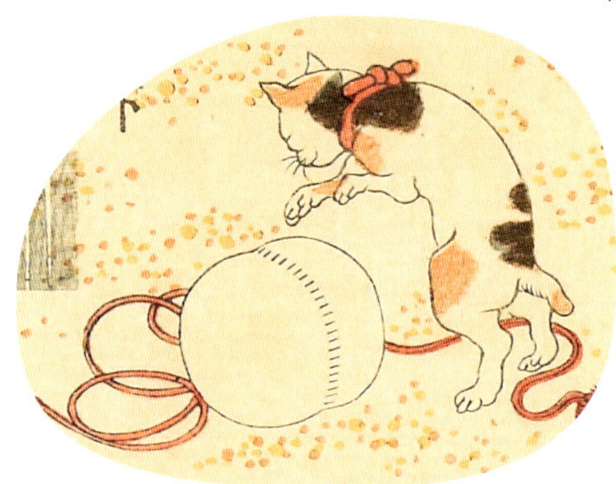

Genji Clouds Matched with Ukiyo-e Pictures: Wakana

Like the previous page, one of a series intermeshing *The Tale of Genji* and a similar Edo period play. The "Wakana" chapter of *Genji* contains a scene in which Kashiwagi and others are kicking a ball around in a garden of flowering cherry trees (*sakura*). Meanwhile, in the third part of the play *Sugawara Denju Tenarai Kagami* there is a scene in which Yae, wife of "Sakuramaru" plucks *wakana* (herbs) for a celebratory meal for her father-in-law. Thus the connection between the two.

The cat is in the inset at top, and exudes a presence that suggests it to be more than a supporting player. During the football game, the cat created the chance for the illicit love of Onna Sannomiya and Kashiwagi to blossom. Genetically calico cats are almost always female, and it has been suggested that Kuniyoshi consciously likened the cat to Onna Sannomiya, and the ball to Kashiwagi.

The cat has not pounced on the ball but is toying with it. The appearance is one of a risky scenario in which what happens next is anyone's guess.

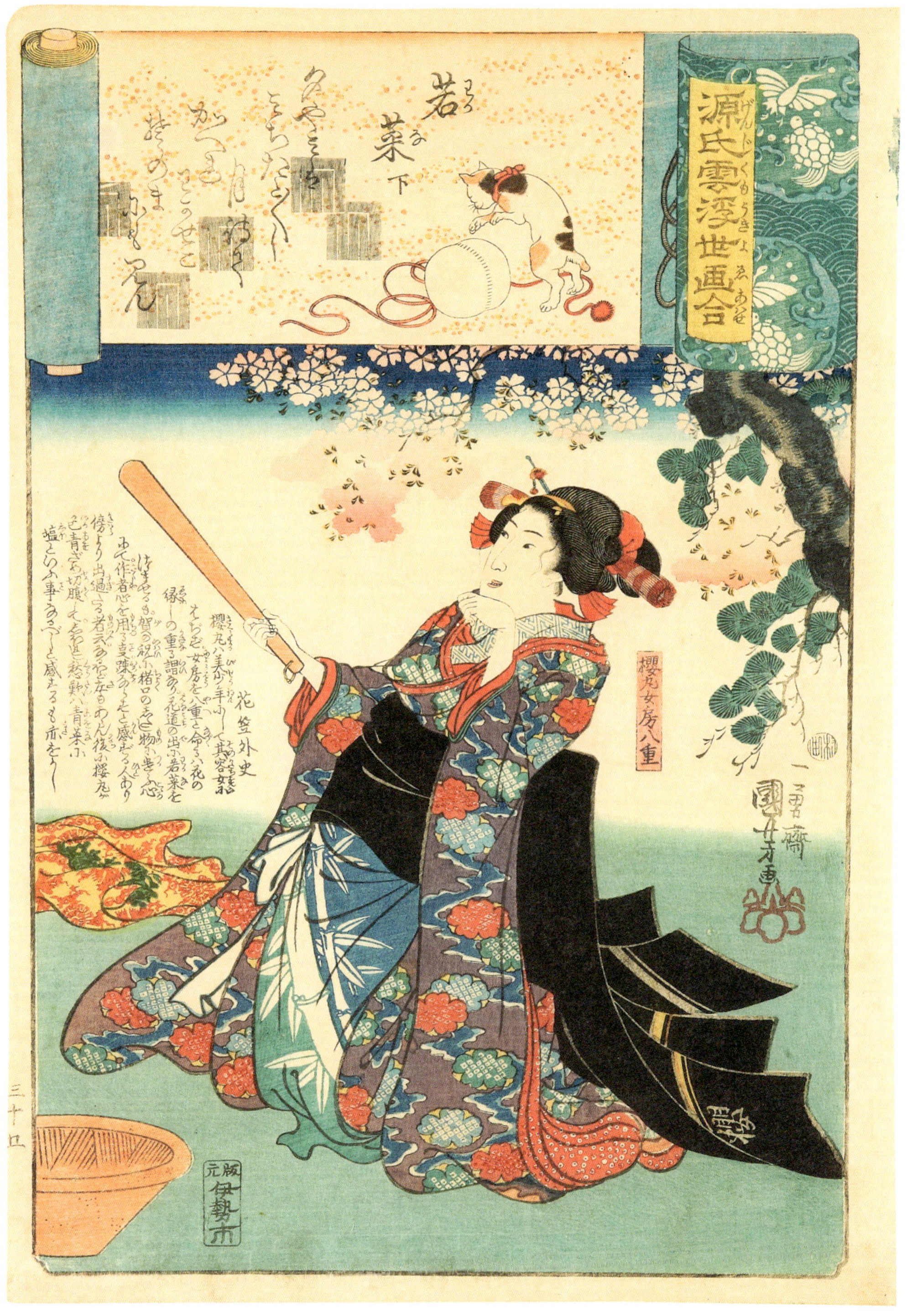
若
菜
下

源氏雲浮世画合

櫻戸女房八重

花笠外史

一勇齋
國芳画

版元
伊勢市

三十四

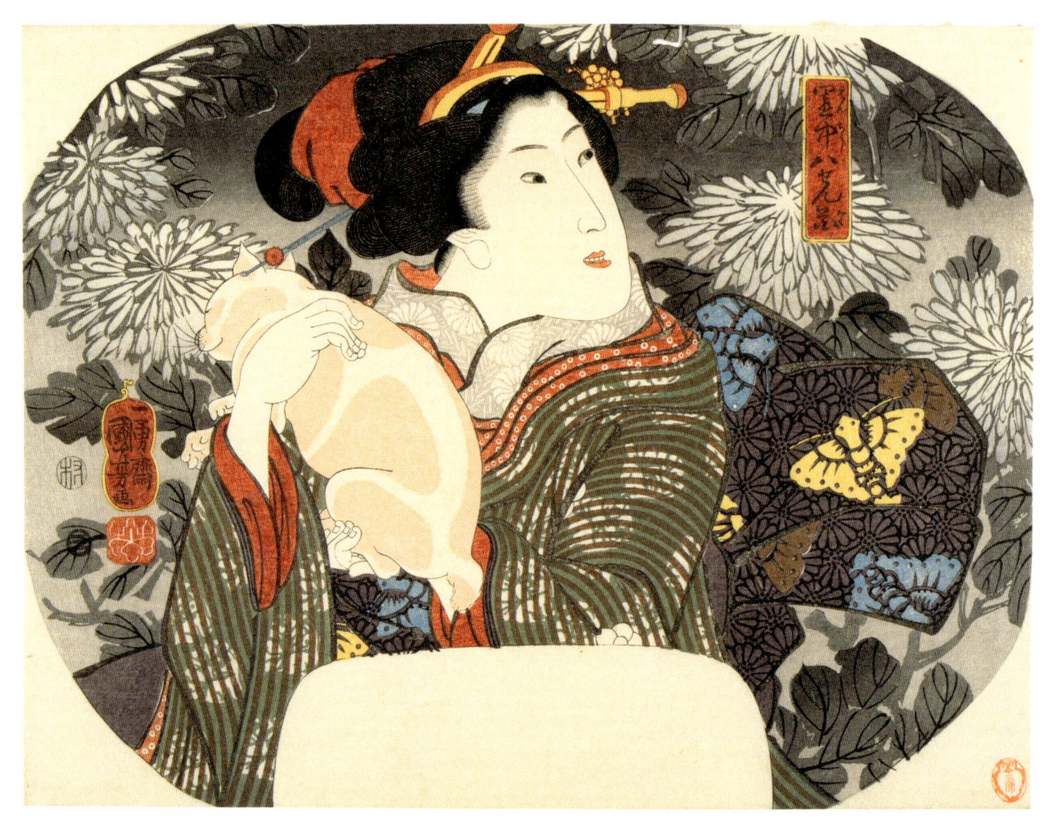

22 園中八せん花 菊 えんちゅうはっせんか きく

　中国、唐時代の詩人である杜甫に「飲中八仙歌」という有名な詩がある。それをもじって「園中八せん花」、つまり庭に咲く8種の花を描いた団扇絵のシリーズで、この一枚は菊。黒、深緑、赤などからなる色調が美しい。

　やんちゃぶりが目立つ国芳の猫だが、この猫は、たぷっとした体を女性に預けて、すやすやと眠っているようにも見える。丸さと柔らかさと少しどっしりした感触が伝わってくるようで、この重量感はオス猫か、などと邪推したくなる。薄茶色のぶち模様が優しい感じを醸し出すが、体の丸み、立体感を表すのに一役買っている。

Selection of Eight Beautiful Flowers in the Garden: Chrysanthemum

"Eight Immortals of the Wine Cup," a famous poem by Tang Dynasty poet Du-Fu, inspired a series of fan designs portraying instead "eight flowers blooming in a garden," of which this is the chrysanthemum. In black, deep green and red, the colors are exquisite.

Kuniyoshi's cats are notable for their mischief-making, but this one is flopped limply on its mistress, seemingly fast asleep. Rounded, soft and a little hefty, this weightiness leads one to suspect it is a tomcat. The tawny brown patches give the cat a certain gentleness, but also show the curves and dimensionality of its body.

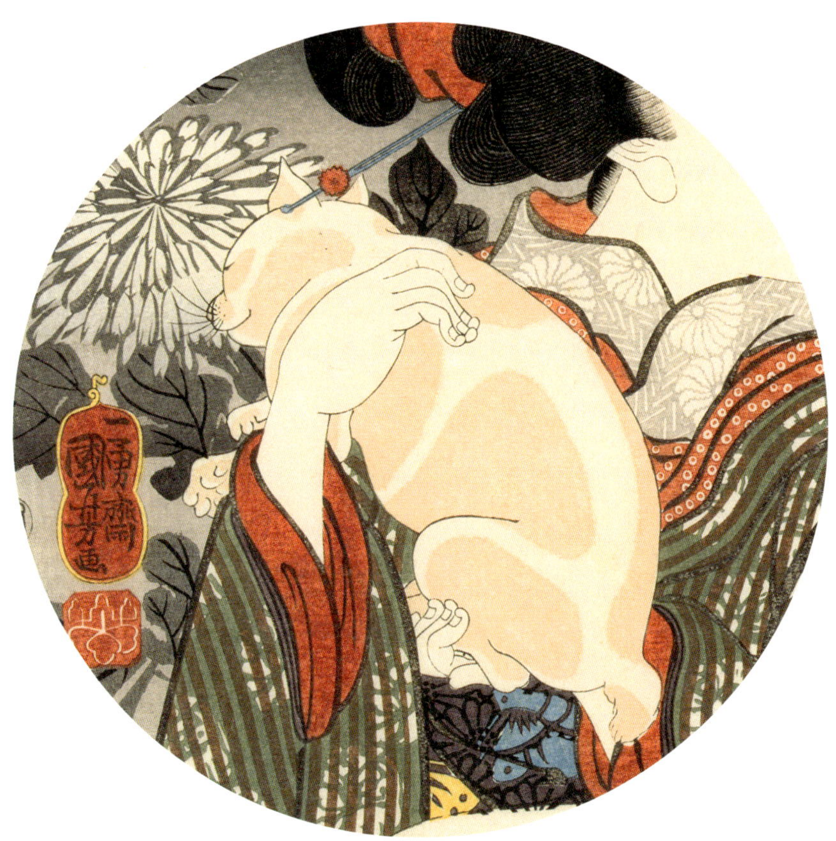

23 猫と遊ぶ娘　ねことあそぶむすめ

　団扇絵だが、右の縁に黒い枠と布が表されている。鏡の枠とカバー、つまり、鏡に映ったところという趣向である。ということは、この娘は、ただ猫と遊んでいるだけではない。猫にも、「ほうら、どうしたどうした」とばかりに、オモチャにされる自分の姿を見せている。現代人でもやりそうな猫遊びだが、道理で猫はご機嫌ななめのようだ。

　国芳の猫としては、かなり大きい描写である。本書の5章以降にも大きく描かれた猫が登場するが、それらは擬人化され、人間の顔と混淆されている。すると、普通の猫を大きく描いたものとしてはなかなか貴重で、国芳が捉える猫のディテールを存分に味わうことのできる一枚と言える。

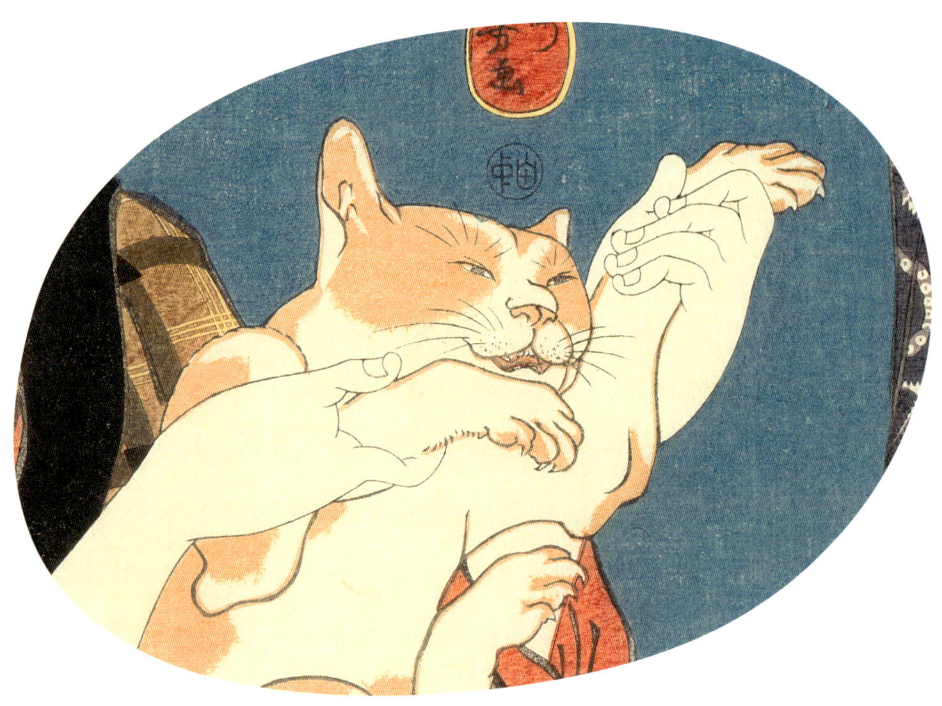

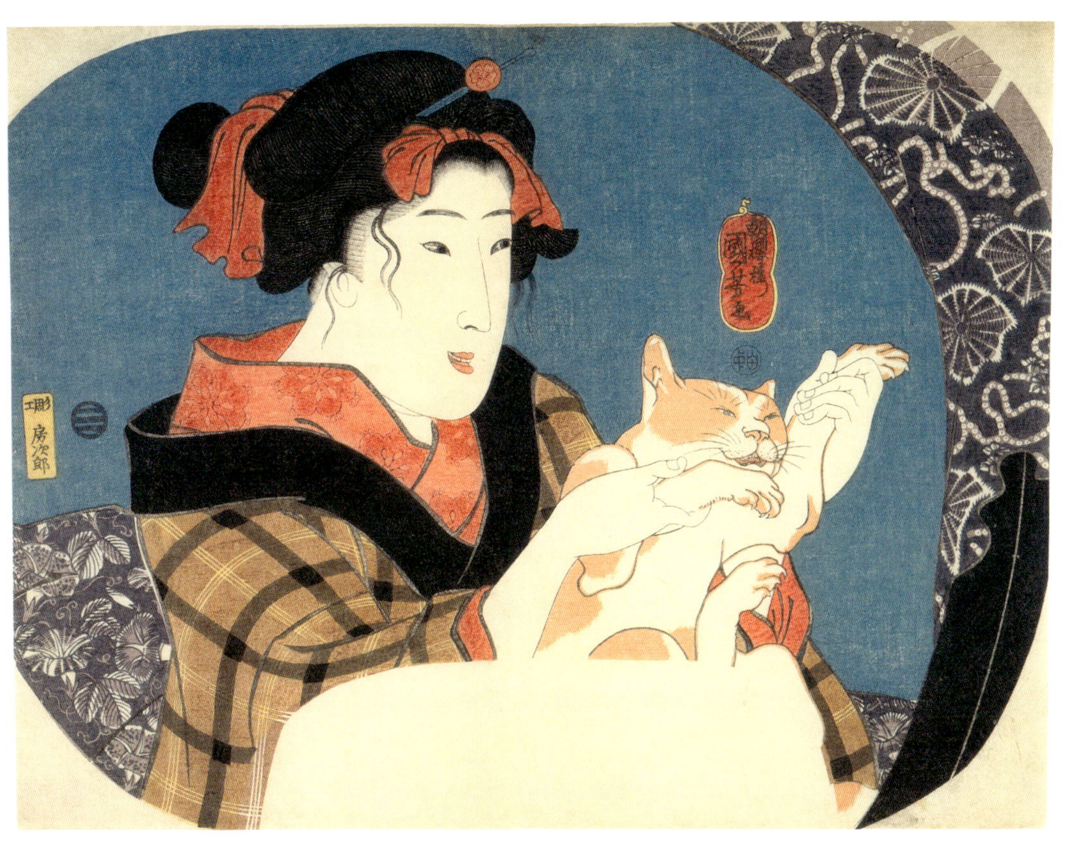

Girl Playing with a Cat

The black frame and fabric on the right edge indicate a fan design, in this case a mirror frame and cover, i.e. an image reflected in a mirror. Meaning that the girl is not simply playing with her cat: the cat in turn is also showing itself being used as a toy. We would still tease a cat in a similar manner today, and truth be told this cat is rather enjoying it.

This is quite a large depiction of a cat for Kuniyoshi. Similarly large images appear in chapters five through seven, but mix human and feline features. So here we have a precious example of an ordinary cat rendered large, and a print offering ample opportunity to savor Kuniyoshi's eye for feline detail.

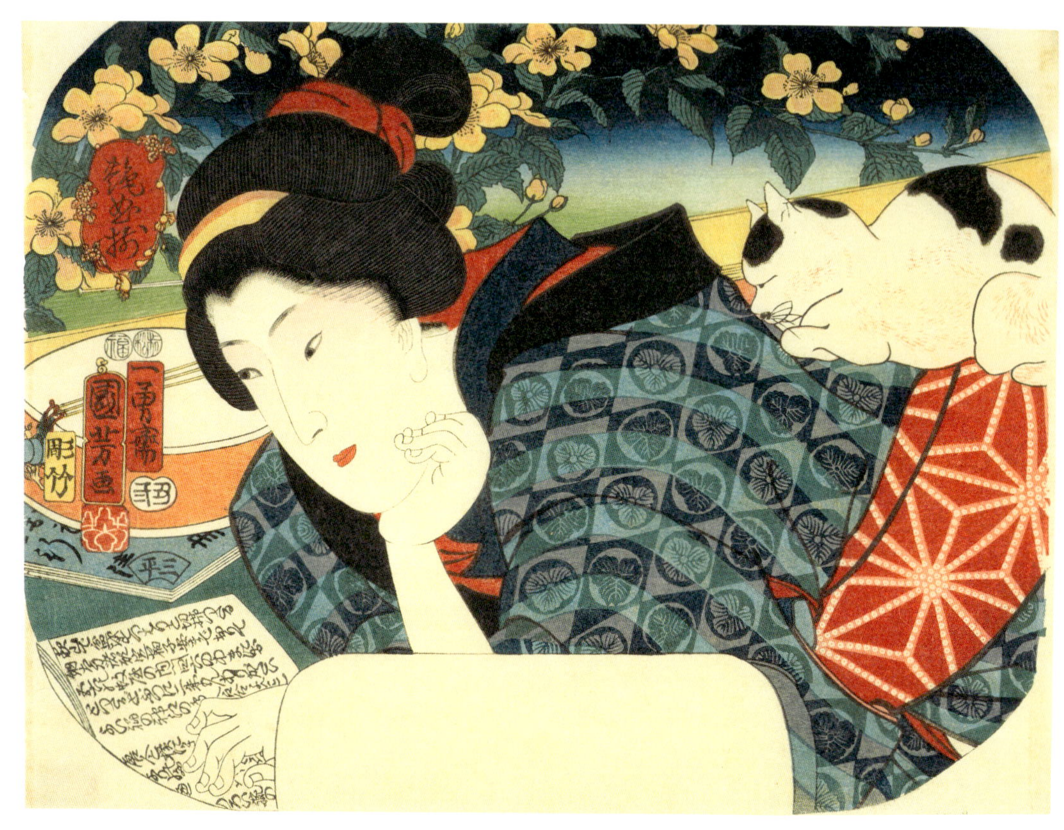

24 艶曲揃　えんぎょくぞろい

　黄色の山吹の花をあしらった、とても美しい団扇絵。「艶曲揃」とタイトルにあるが、いささか色っぽい読み物に夢中の女性という、少し悩ましい情景なのである。涼をとるための団扇として、ふさわしい趣なのだろうかと、考えてしまう。

　それはさておき、猫はどっしりと乗っている。かなり重そうだが、女性は読みふけっている。猫の視線をたどると、まるで一緒に読んでいるかのようだが、決してそんなことはないだろう。国芳の猫としては珍しい顔立ちで、余計な話ではあるが、赤塚不二夫の『天才バカボン』が連想されてならない。

Women Reading Kabuki Lyrics

A stunning fan picture featuring yellow Japanese roses, and slightly disturbing scene of a woman dreamily absorbed in risqué reading material. Perhaps though, it makes the perfect picture for a fan designed to cool.

In any case, puss is very comfortably ensconced. He or she looks quite heavy, but the woman is too lost in reading to care. The cat's gaze seems to suggest it is reading over its mistress's shoulder, though this is of course highly unlikely. It has an unusual face for one of Kuniyoshi's cats, calling to mind, albeit irrelevantly, Fujio Akatsuka's *The Genius Bakabon.*

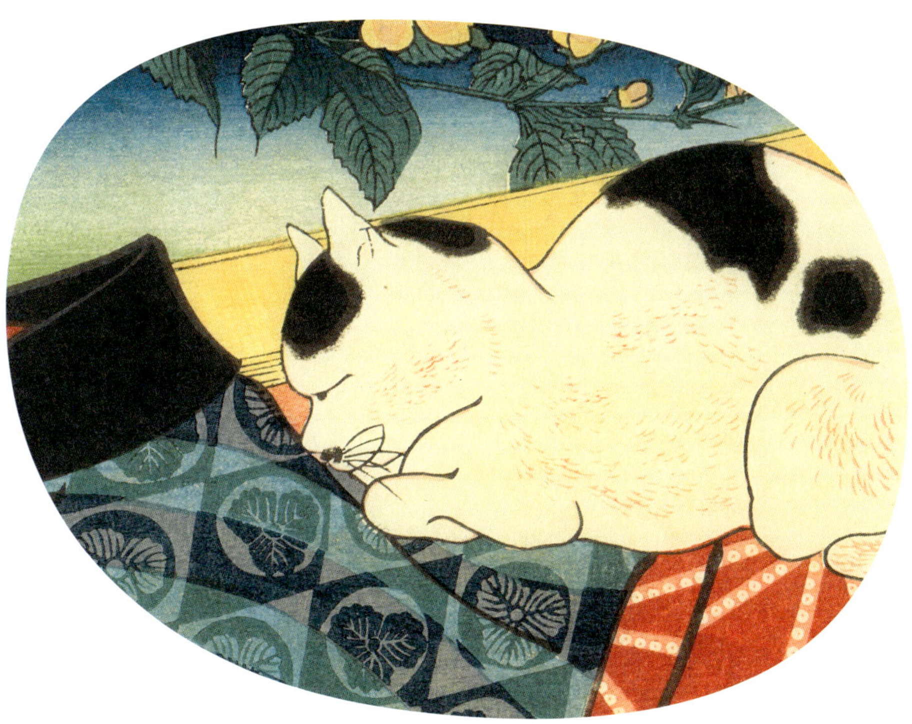

25 絵兄弟やさすかた　えきょうだいやさすがた

　辞書によると、「どら猫」は盗み食いなどをする図々しい猫や野良猫。「虎猫」は、虎のような柄の猫。言葉が似ているせいか、どうも二つのイメージは重なることがある。

　平安時代の武将、源頼政に、弓を海中に入れたら餌も付けていないのに鰹が釣れたという話がある。この図は、それと、鰹節のにおいに誘われてきた猫を重ね合わせたのかもしれない。

　国芳の猫には「虎猫」が少ない。それだけに、ちょっとした悪役としての性格も際立っている。女性は首根っこを押さえ、手で叩こうとしているが、そんな切羽詰まった状況下でも鰹節を離さない猫こそが見どころ。あらわなお尻も、必死な様子を物語る。

Graceful Sibling Pictures

According to the dictionary, a *dora-neko* is a cunning or stray cat that does things like steal food. A *tora-neko* meanwhile is a cat striped like a tiger (*tora*). It would seem the two sometimes coincide.

Legend has it that when the Heian general Minamoto Yorimasa shot an arrow into the sea he caught a bonito fish, despite not using bait. This illustration may overlay this story with the image of a cat lured by the smell of dried bonito.

This is a rare *"tora-neko"* among Kuniyoshi's cats, and for this reason alone stands out as a bit of a ruffian. Holding it down by the nape of its neck the woman tries to swat it, but the figure of the cat determined not to let go of the bonito even under these dire conditions is the highlight of the picture. The cat's exposed rear is another sign of its desperation to hang on to the fish.

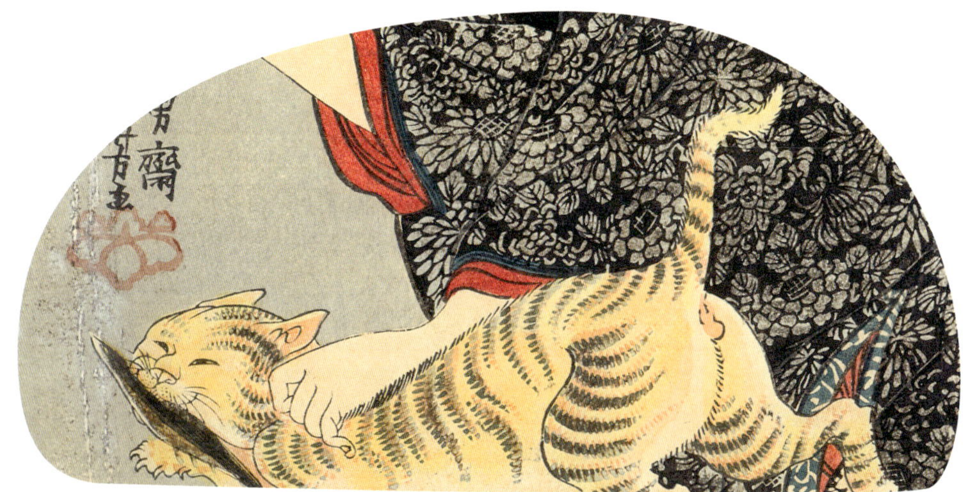

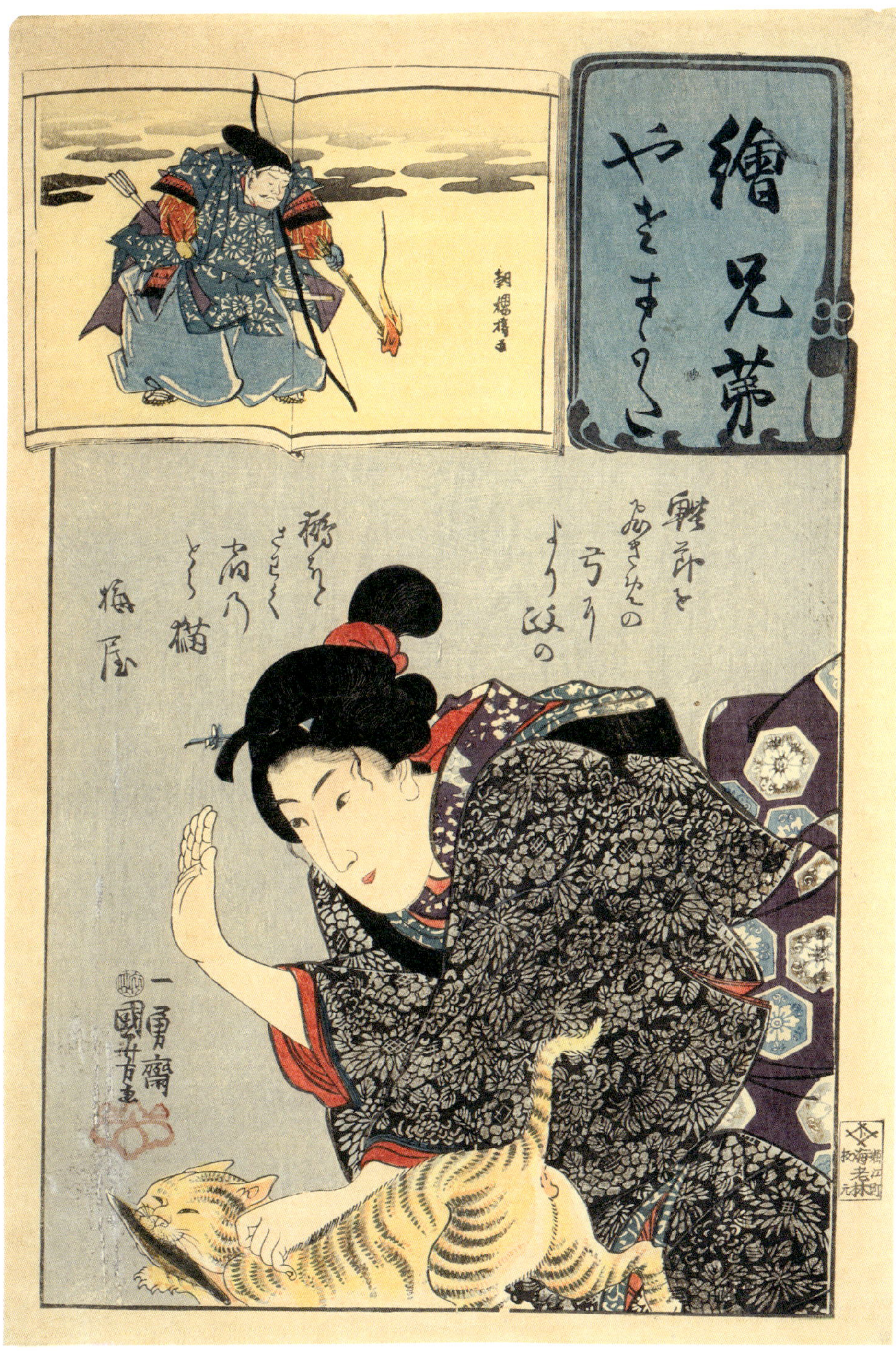
繪兄弟
やきまつる

朝畑樵画

雛許を
ふきふれんの
弓り
より政の

稅りと
さらゝく
南り
とら猫

梅屋

一勇齋
國芳画

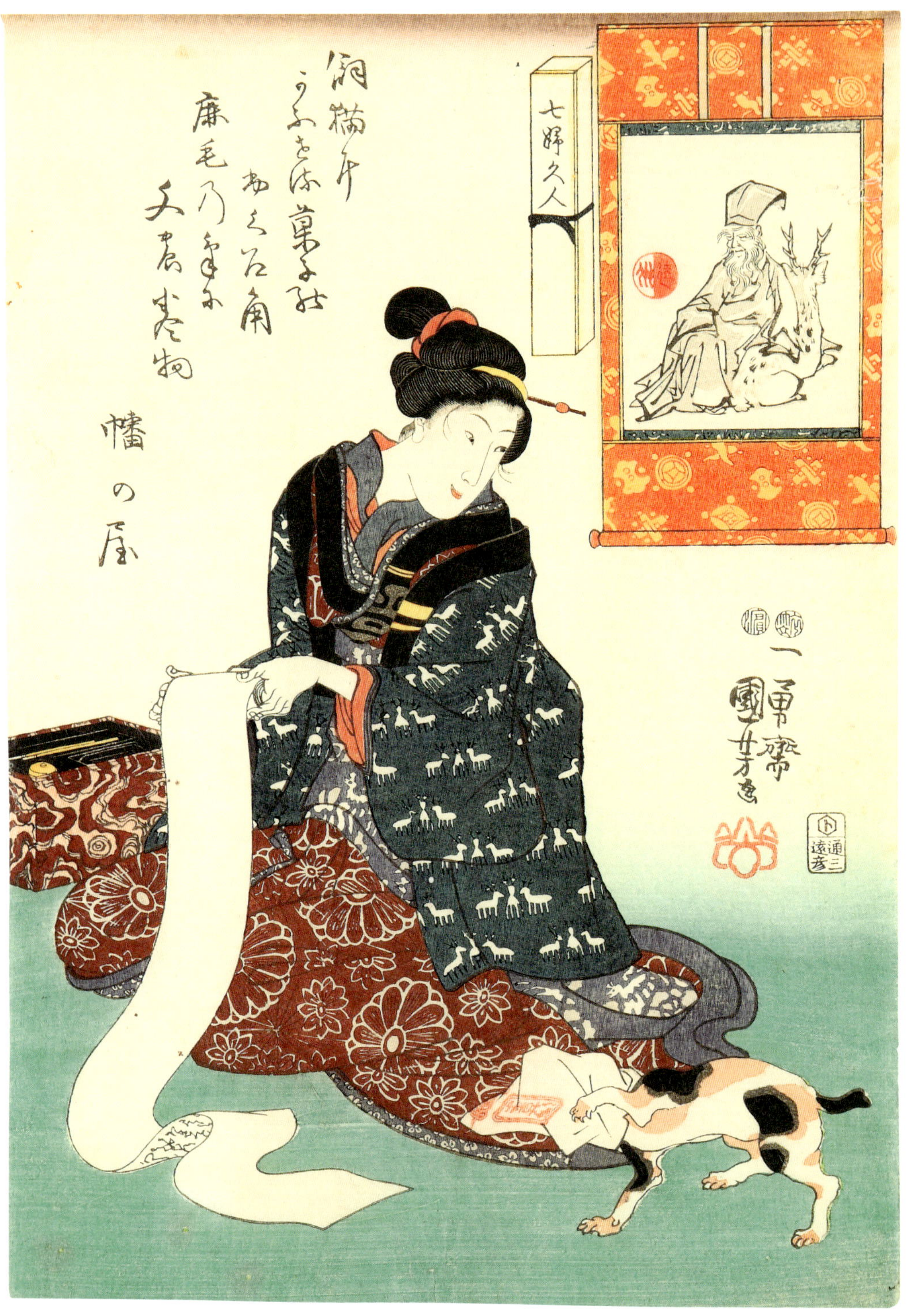

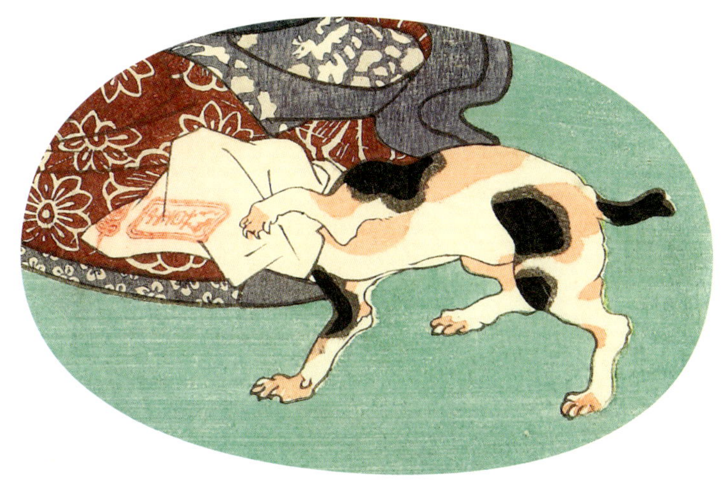

26 七婦久人 寿老人 しちふくじん じゅろうじん

　猫は自立心が強く、プライドも高い。それだけに人は猫で遊びたくもなる。この猫は、お菓子の袋を頭からかぶせられている。飼い猫は、時折置いてある袋に自主的に突入するから、この場合もそうなのかと思うところだが、画中の歌は「飼猫にかふせる菓子のふくろ角　鹿毛の筆に文の巻物」。つまり、女性がかぶせたのである。しかし、理由もなくいたずらしたわけではないのかもしれない。文を広げたくても、猫が飛びついてきてはどうにもならない。

　七福神にかこつけた美人画のシリーズで、この図は「寿老人」。寿老人は鹿を連れている神さまだが、鹿の生えたての柔らかい角は「袋角」と呼ばれる。お菓子の袋はそれに引っ掛けている。

Women Compared with the Seven Gods of Good Fortune: Juro-jin

Cats are proud, independent creatures: one reason humans like them as playmates. Here puss has suffered the indignity of having an empty sweet bag placed over its head. Pet cats occasionally stick their heads into bags voluntarily, so one assumes this to also be the case here, however the verse, "Sweet bag antlers placed over puss's head, writing a scroll with a deer-hair brush" suggests that the woman actually put the bag there. Not without reason though: there's no point unrolling her text if a cat is going to jump on it.

This print in a series of bijinga inspired by the seven gods of good fortune features the deity Juro-jin. Juro-jin is accompanied by a deer, and the soft, newly sprouted antlers of a deer (i.e. the velvet) are known as *fukurozuno*, literally "bag horns."

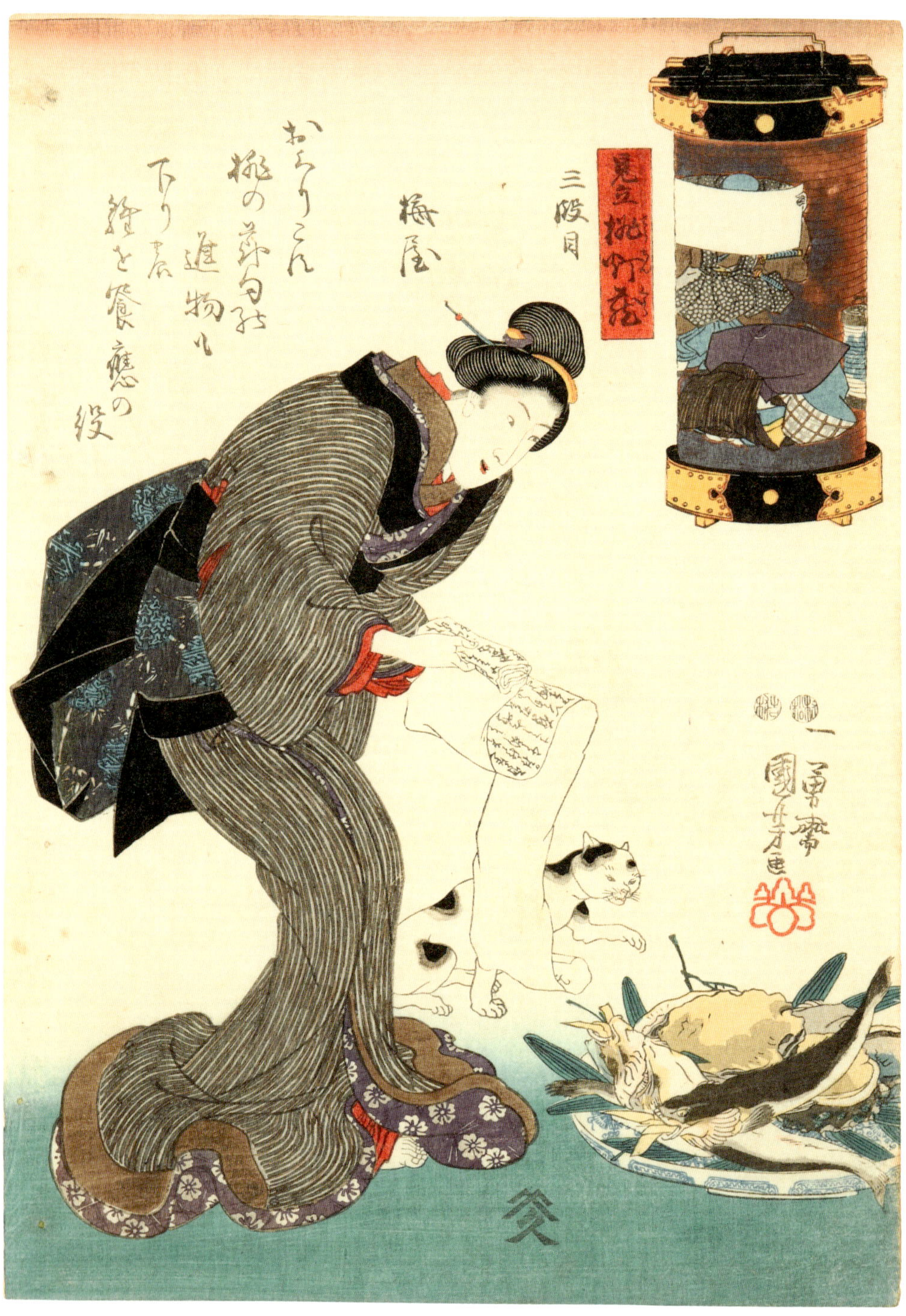

見立挑灯蔵
三段目
梅屋
おもりえん
挑の弟句子
進物ハ
下り君
経を食應の
役
一勇斎
國芳画

27 見立挑灯蔵 三段目 *みたてちょうちんぐら さんだんめ*

　歌舞伎の「仮名手本忠臣蔵（かなでほんちゅうしんぐら）」の場面に見立てた美人画。右上の提灯（ちょうちん）の中には、ある武士が賄賂（わいろ）を贈り、取り次ぎの者がその目録を読み上げる場面が表される。それを、江戸時代の一般家庭の日常に置き換え、描いている。

　桃の節句に届けられた進物。女性は目録を手に、嬉しそうである。しかし、最も喜んでいるのは猫。魚とアワビを見つけ、近寄ってきたが、前足の片方がもう出てしまっている。顔も意欲十分。こうなるともう、「忠臣蔵」も美人画も、どうでもよい感じである。

Parody of the Chushingura in Lanterns: Act Three

Bijinga inspired by a scene from the kabuki play *Kanadehon Chushingura* (The Treasury of Loyal Retainers). The lantern at top right shows a samurai passing over a bribe, and the middleman reading out a list of what the bribe consists of. This scenario is transplanted to everyday life in an ordinary Edo period household.

Gifts have been delivered for Girl's Day, and grasping a list of them in her hand, the woman looks delighted. The happiest of all however is the cat. Spying fish and abalone, it approaches, one of its front paws already outstretched. The expression on its face is also a ready indicator of its ambitions, which seem to eclipse both *Chushingura* and *bijinga*.

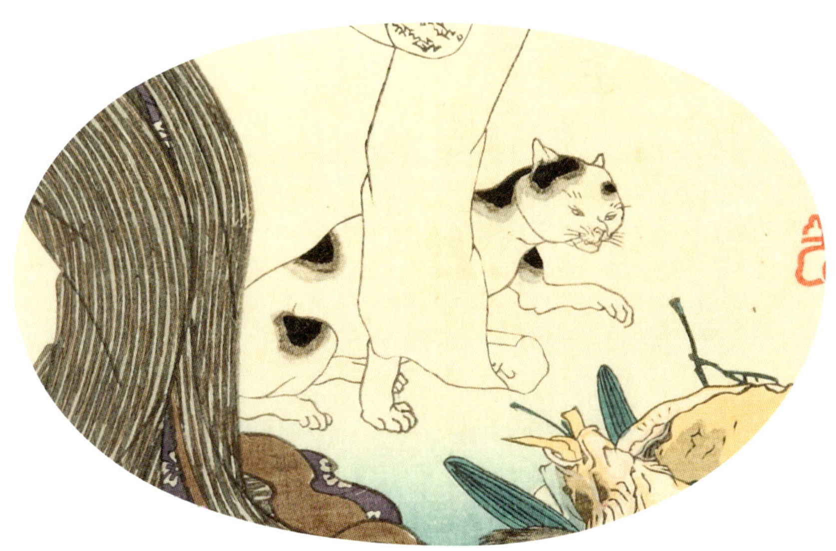

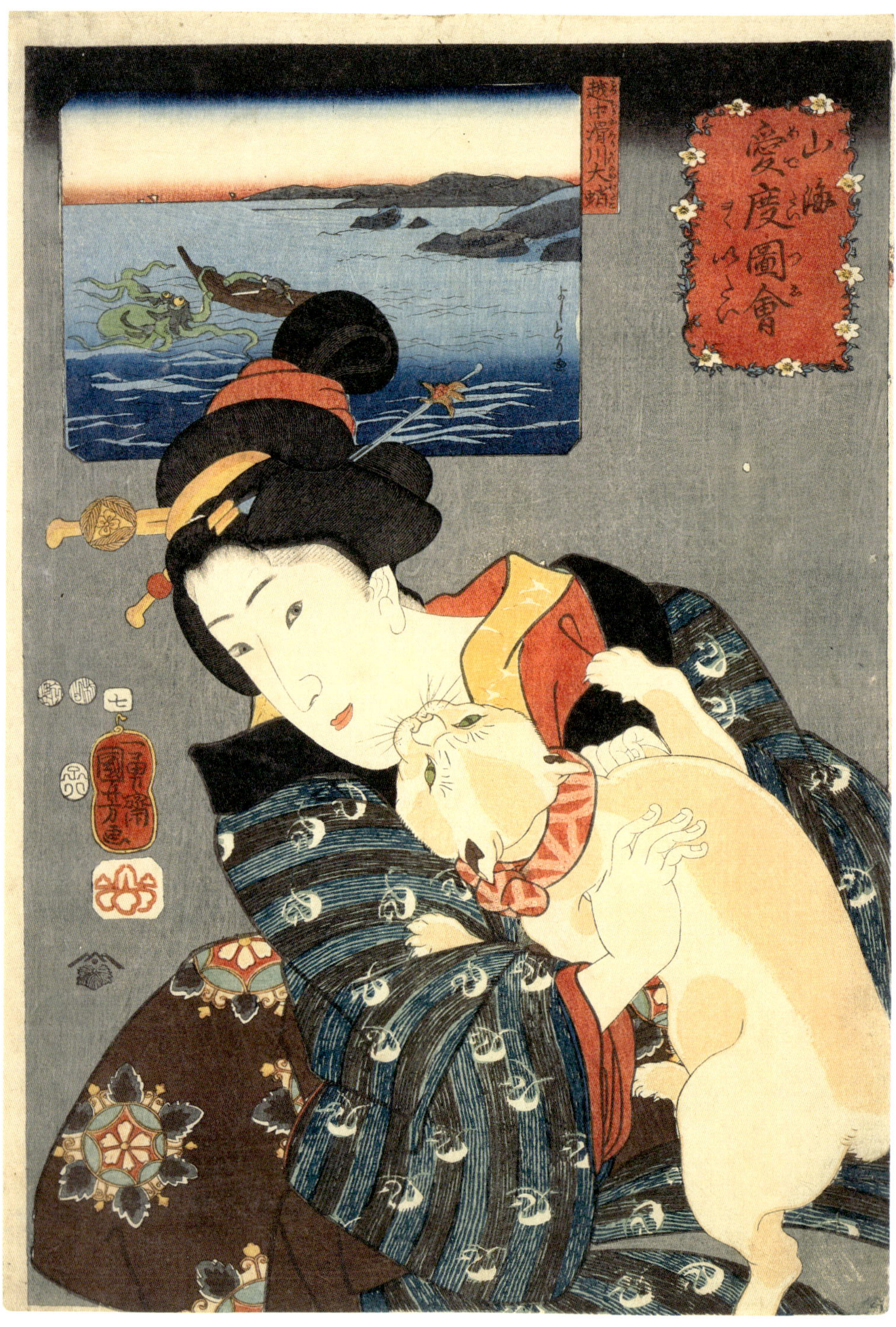

62

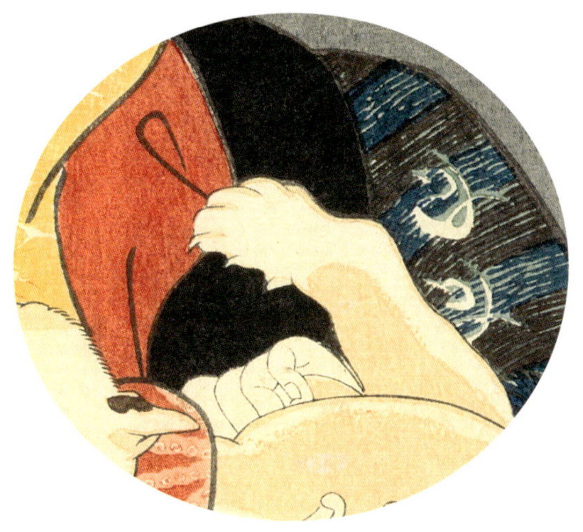

28 山海愛度図会 ヲヽいたい　越中滑川大蛸

さんかいめでたいずえ　おおいたい　えっちゅうなめりがわのおおだこ

「山海」は日本各地、「愛度」は「愛でたい」ということで、各地の名物と愛すべき様子の女性の絵をセットにしたシリーズ。江戸時代は、現代と同様、人々が日本各地の名物や風物に興味をもった時代だから、こんなアイディアも生まれたのである。

この図に登場する名物は、越中、今の富山県の滑川にいるという大蛸。舟に乗っている人間をも襲うという怪物らしい。そして、女性に爪を立てる猫。かわいい飼い猫も、扱いが悪ければこんな風に暴れるものである。「おお痛い」と言いながらも、女性は余裕ありげに、猫に愛情のこもった視線を向けている。

Auspicious Pictures of Land and Sea:
Ouch! – Giant Octopus at Namerikawa, Etchu

"Land and Sea" refers to locations around Japan, combined with "auspicious" in a series featuring regional specialties and women in adorable situations. The idea comes from the fact that like today, people in the Edo period were intrigued by the renowned products and natural features of different places.

Featured here is a giant octopus said to live in Namerikawa, Etchu, i.e. present-day Toyama Prefecture. This monster was even said to attack people on boats. Juxtaposed we have a cat unsheathing its claws at the woman. Even the cutest pet will react like this if mishandled. Note that though she says "Ouch!" the woman is gazing indulgently and lovingly at her feline companion.

29 うろたへた小猫盆画へ屎をたれ うろたえたこねこ ぼんがへくそをたれ

　数々の国芳の作品の中でも、猫への愛が並々ならぬことを物語る一点。「うろたへる」は「まごまごと歩き回る」の意味だろう。「盆画」は、板の上に砂で絵を描くもの。子猫が盆画に乗って、失敬してしまっている。用を足す場所を探していた子猫。盆画を見つけて、砂だけにいい按配だとばかりに、しでかしてしまったのだろう。

　猫との暮らしにこんな騒ぎはつきもの。子猫が困っているおかしさ、そして胸がきゅんとなる愛おしさ。国芳のまなざしは、現代の猫好きと何ら変わらない。

Urotaeta koneko bonga e kuso o tare
(A wandering kitten does its business in the sand picture)

Of Kuniyoshi's many works, this is one that truly speaks of his peerless cat-loving proclivities. *Urotaeta* in this case probably means to wander about in a flurry. A "bonga" (lit. "tray picture") is a scene rendered in sand on a board. A kitten has got into the bonga and is soiling it. Looking for somewhere to do its business, the kitten has no doubt found the picture, and judging the sand to be the perfect solution to its dilemma, done the deed.

Such dramas are part and parcel of life with a cat. The hilarious yet heartwarmingly cute figure of the poor desperate kitten shows Kuniyoshi's eye to be no different to that of cat lovers today.

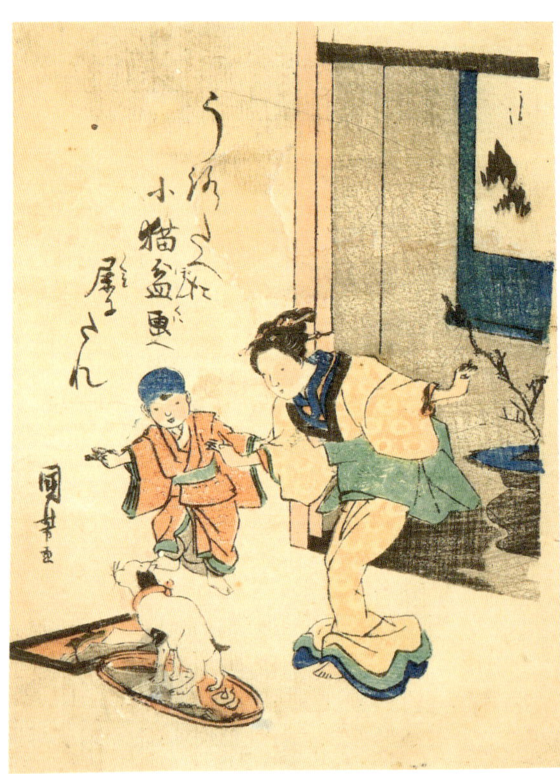

II

国芳の
「ねこ」以外の
お仕事

Kuniyoshi's
'non-cat'
work

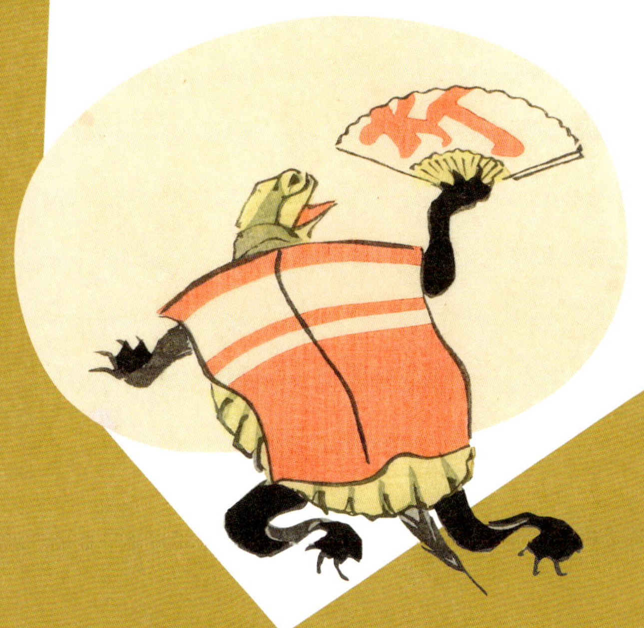

　徳川幕府が統治した 17 世紀から 19 世紀にわたるおよそ 260 年が、江戸時代。この時代に、庶民による庶民のための美術として生まれたのが、浮世絵だった。もともと日本の美術には長い歴史があり、たとえば歴史の教科書にも、平安時代や鎌倉時代の美術が挙げられている。ただ、それらは宮廷や寺社など特定の世界の人々のもの。ようやく江戸時代になって、広く庶民も美術を楽しむことができるようになったのである。幕府の政策によって、都市や経済が発展したことも大きかった。

　さて、国芳の活躍は江戸時代後期、19 世紀前半のこと。その頃の江戸の人口は世界一とも言われる。人々の楽しみである浮世絵や絵本なども、数限りなく売り出されていた。江戸で染物業を営む家に生まれた国芳は、浮世絵師となるべく、歌川豊国の弟子となり修行を積んだ。そして画家として名をあげたのは、三十代のはじめ。中国の長編小説『水滸伝』の登場人物を描いたシリーズで、一躍人気絵師となった。

　浮世絵には、手描きの肉筆画と木版画があるが、国芳の場合、木版画の仕事がほとんどである。国芳が原画を描き、専門の彫師が版木を作り、さらに専門の摺師が紙に印刷して、できあがる。また、そうして作られる商品の企画から販売までを統括するのが、版元である。版元から企画を持ち込まれ、せっつかれ、多くの弟子たちも抱えながら、せっせと筆を運ぶ。国芳は、そんな日常を送っていたのだろう。

　売れっ子の国芳だったが、四十代半ばで苦境に直面した。天保の改革と呼ばれる幕府の政治改革である。ゆらぐ世の中を建て直そうという方針のもと、庶民の娯楽も大きく制限され、浮世絵の中心商品だった役者や遊女の絵が禁止されたのである。ところが国芳は、それをアイディアと画才で乗り切った。いや、むしろその苦境が、国芳を前代未聞の新境地へと進ませたのである。

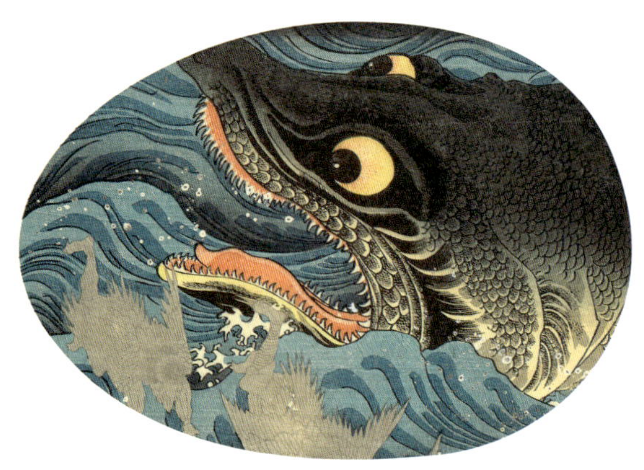

The approximately 260 years spanning the 17th to 19th century during which the Tokugawa shogunate governed Japan are known as the Edo period. The art form by the people, for the people that emerged during this period was ukiyo-e. Japanese art has a long lineage, and even history textbooks feature the art of the Heian and Kamakura eras, for example. But such art belongs to people of a specific world, such as that of the court, temple or shrine. It was only from the Edo period onward that the wider public gained access to the pleasures of fine art, due in large part to the urban and economic development achieved by the shogunate's policies.

For his part, Kuniyoshi was active in the later Edo period, that is, the first half of the 19th century. The population of Edo at this time is said to have been the largest of any city in the world. The ukiyo-e and picture books that gave pleasure to ordinary people were widely available. Kuniyoshi, born into a family of fabric dyers, became apprenticed to Utagawa Toyokuni with the intention of becoming an ukiyo-e artist, and undertook comprehensive training before finally making his name as a painter at around the age of thirty, acquiring overnight popularity with his portrayals of characters from Chinese novel *The Water Margin*.

Ukiyo-e consists of hand-painted renderings and woodblock prints, but in Kuniyoshi's case, prints dominate. Kuniyoshi would paint the original, a specialist carver would make the print block, then a specialist printer print it on to paper. It was the publisher who exercised overall control of products made in this way, from concept to sale. He would approach Kuniyoshi with a concept for a product, and Kuniyoshi in turn would quickly set to work with his brush, and the assistance of several apprentices. This was the pattern of his day-to-day work.

In his mid-forties and by now a household name, Kuniyoshi confronted the greatest challenge of his career: a series of political reforms enacted by the shogunate, known as the Tempo reforms. Under a policy designed to rebuild an unstable world, entertainments enjoyed by the masses were suppressed, and the pictures of actors and courtesans that formed the mainstay of ukiyo-e were banned. Kuniyoshi overcame this with a combination of brilliant ideas and artistic genius. In fact one could say that the crisis ultimately propelled his art into new, uncharted territory.

30 雪月花 月 _{せつげっか つき}

31 尾上菊五郎の玉屋新兵衛 関三十郎の鵜飼九十郎
_{おのえきくごろうのたまやしんべえ せきさんじゅうろうのうかいくじゅうろう}

この二つは、人気絵師になる以前のもの。後の作品のようなにぎやかさはなく、背景はさっぱりしているし、色も淡白である。それが初期の国芳の作風だったし、その頃までの浮世絵版画全般の雰囲気でもあった。

女性を描いたいわゆる美人画に、歌舞伎役者の絵。役者の絵は、ある演目が上演されれば、その内容に合わせて作られた。浮世絵師の日常とは、こうした絵をひたすら描き続けることだった。だからこそ、描写力で勝負するだけではなく、変わった趣向を取り入れもする。

《雪月花 月》では、窓から差す月明かりが描かれているが、西洋とは違い、この頃の日本では光や影を表現することは少なかった。壁にかかる額も、西洋風のもの。絵草紙屋_{えぞうしや}の店先でこれを見た人たちは、風変わりな絵だなと感じたはずである。

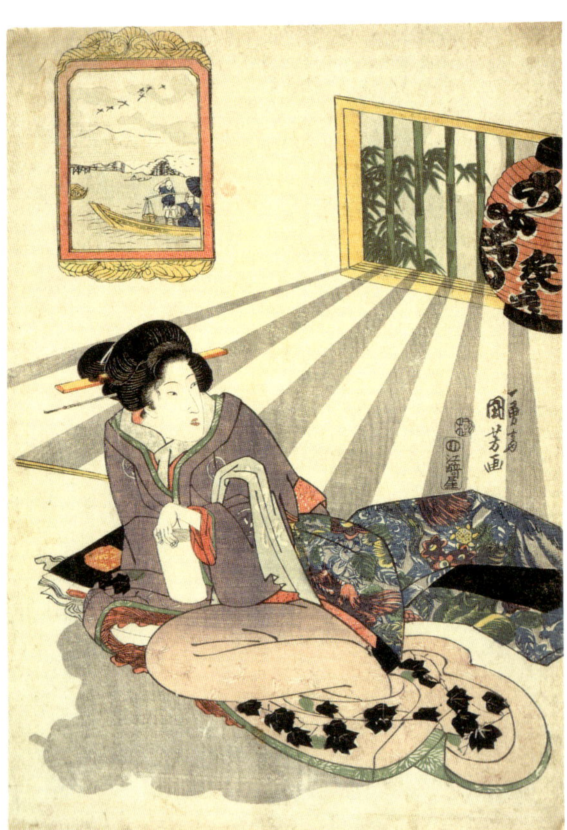

31 尾上菊五郎の玉屋新兵衛 関三十郎の鵜飼九十郎　　30

30 Snow, Moon and Flowers: Moon
31 Onoe Kikugoro as Tamaya Shinbei
and Seki Sanjuro as Ukai Kujuro

Two prints from before Kuniyoshi became popular. With uncluttered backgrounds and plain tones, they lack the busyness of his later work. This was Kuniyoshi's early style and also typical of the general look of ukiyo-e woodblock prints up to that time.

Shown here are a *bijinga* portrait, and picture of kabuki actors. The actor print was produced for the performance of a particular play, with relevant detail. The day-to-day existence of ukiyo-e artists consisted largely of churning out images such as these, hence they also incorporated unusual style elements and ideas, rather than relying solely on their descriptive powers.

Moon from an untitled series of *Snow, Moon and Flowers* depicts moonlight shining through a window. In contrast to the West, Japanese artists of this era rarely expressed light or shadow. The frame on the wall is also Western in style. People spotting this at their local printseller's must have found it rather unusual.

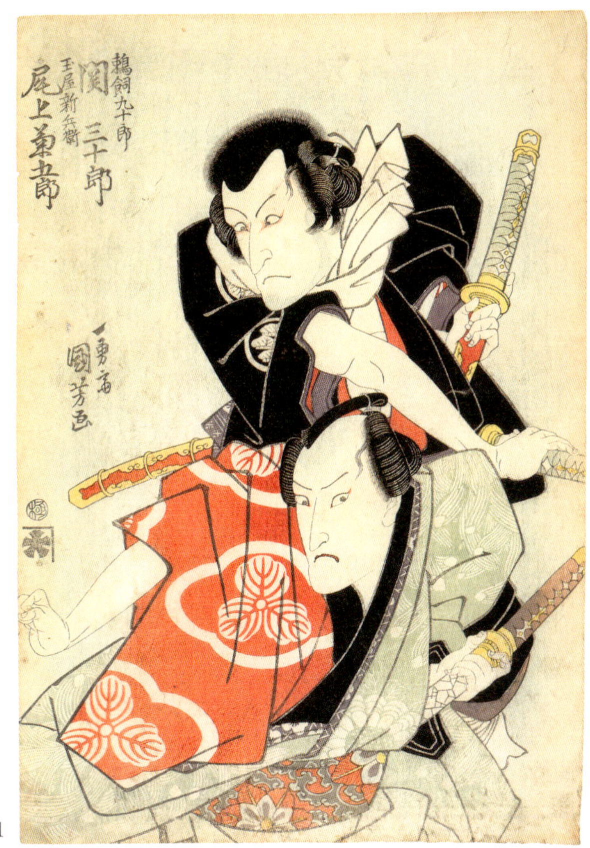

31

32 通俗水滸伝豪傑百八人之一個 活閻羅阮小七

つうぞくすいこでんごうけつひゃくはちにんのひとり かつえんらげんしょうしち

　国芳の出世作となった、『水滸伝』を題材にしたシリーズ。『水滸伝』は中国の明時代の長編小説で、事情があって社会からはじき出された英雄たちが、戦いをかさね、やがて「水滸」、つまり水のほとりに集結する物語である。

　国芳は、英雄の一人一人を一枚ずつの絵に仕立て、それぞれのキャラクターやエピソードの見せ場をわかりやすく打ち出した。

　この一枚は「活閻羅阮小七」。襲いかかる無数の矢を一枚の豹の皮で防いだ豪傑である。こんな激しい一枚もあれば、シリーズには、物静かな風情の理知的な姿の英雄もいる。しかし、そのどれもが、ダイナミックでカラフル。これ以前の作品と比べても、国芳の中で何かがはじけたことがわかるだろう。

One of the 108 Heroes of the Popular *Water Margin:* Living King Yama Ruan Xiaoqi

From the *Water Margin* series that made Kuniyoshi's reputation. A Ming dynasty novel, *Water Margin* features a band of heroic outlaws who fight a series of battles and eventually assemble on the "water margin," i.e. the edge of the water.

Kuniyoshi rendered the heroes individually, depicting their characters and pertinent episodes from the novel in an accessible way.

This is the great Living King Yama Ruan Xiaoqi, who repelled a rain of arrows using only a leopard skin. As well as such action paintings, the series includes quieter heroes of a more intellectual mien. All though are dynamic and colorful. Compared to his previous work, it is obvious that these prints marked a dramatic explosion of creativity in Kuniyoshi.

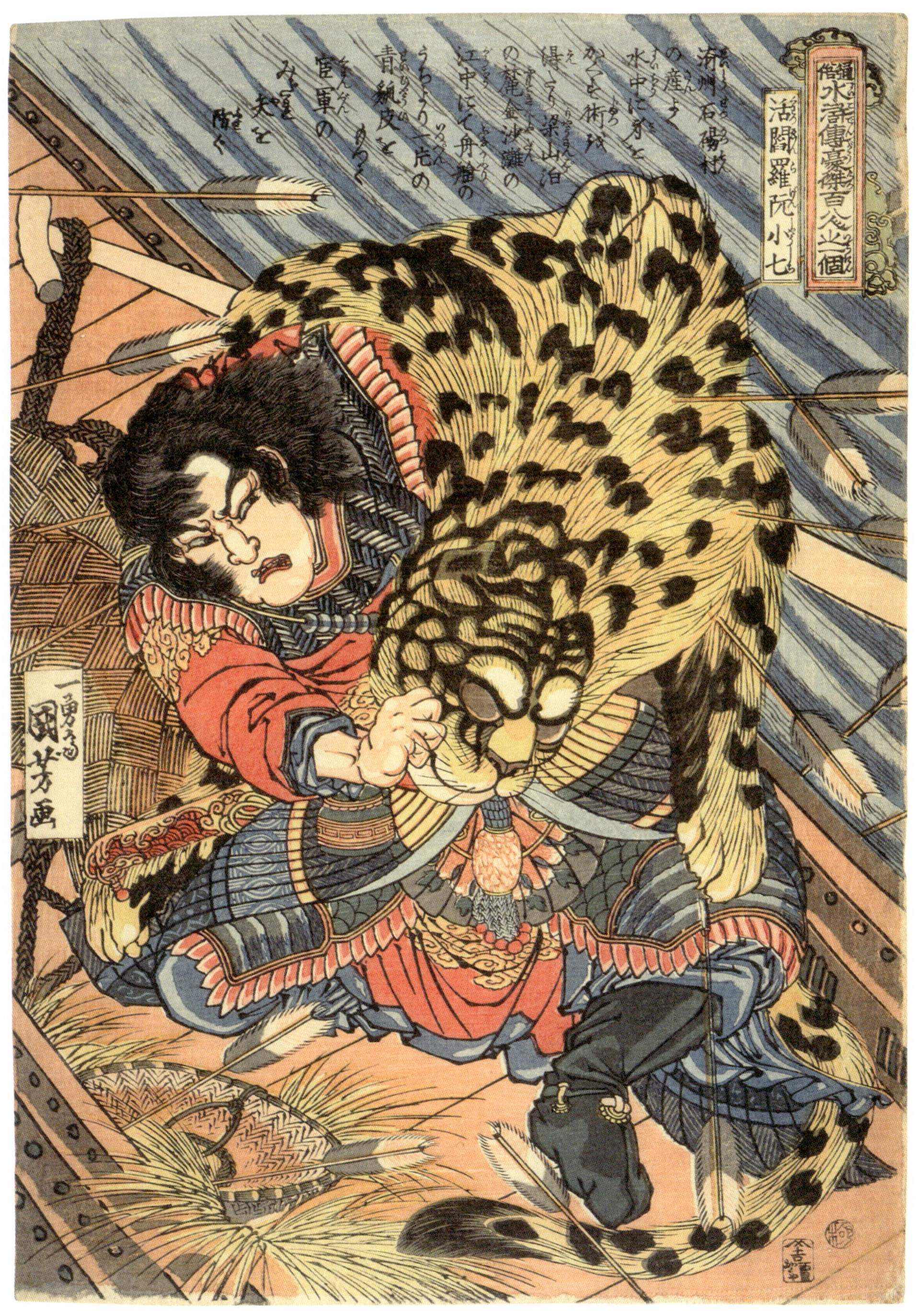

通俗水滸傳豪傑百八人之一個
活閻羅院小七
一勇斎 國芳画

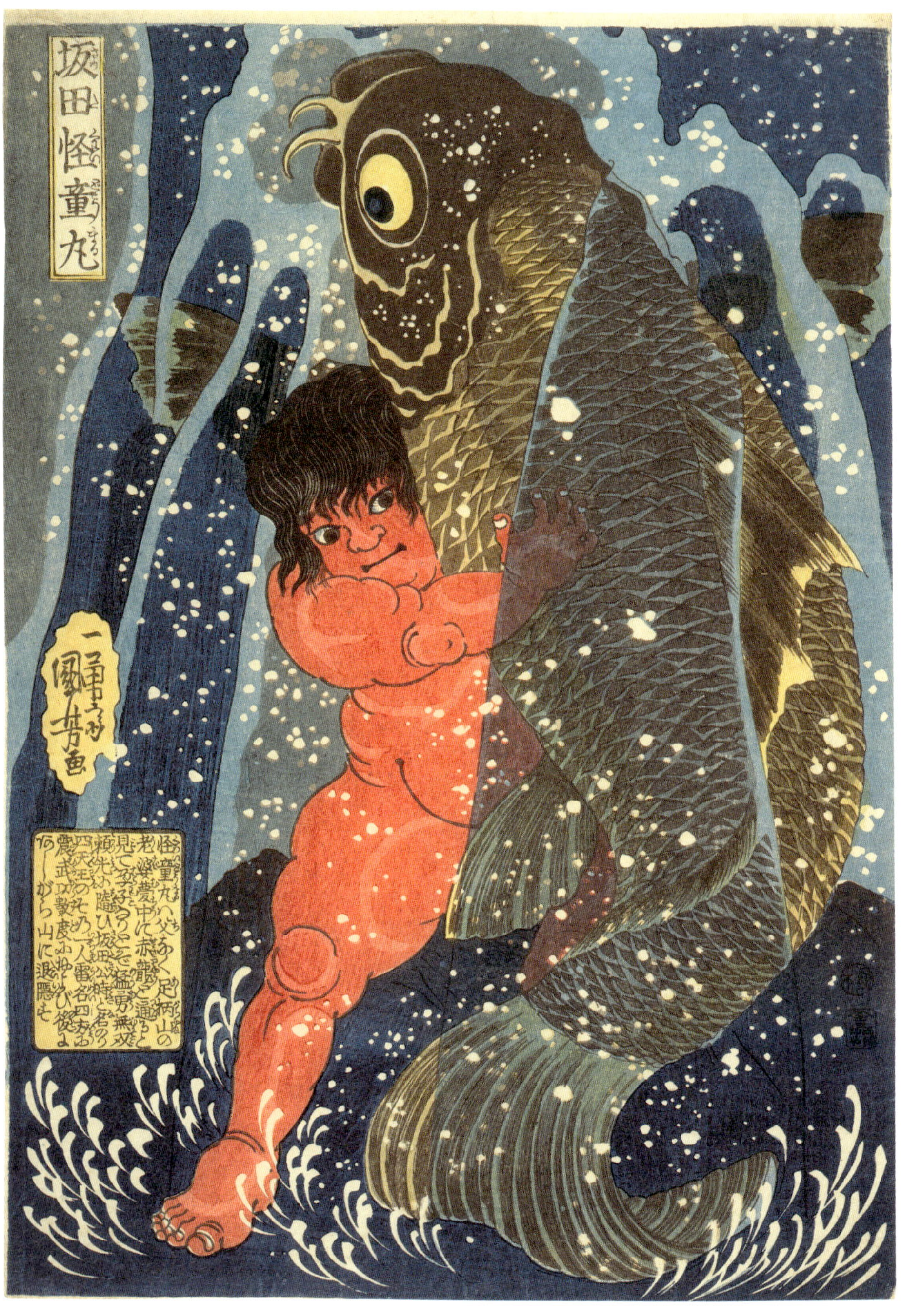
坂田怪童丸
一勇齋
國芳画
怪童丸は父あく足柄山の
老婆養ひ中にて恭龍と通り
見てもびらうごとく猛男無双
瓶洗い臨時ひ坂田公時とも名のり
震武坂田製度ふか地名四天王の
四天王のそめ人怪名四天王
がら山に退隠そ

33 坂田怪童丸 <ruby>さかたかいどうまる</ruby>

　足柄山の金太郎、後の坂田金時である。老婆が夢の中で竜から授かった子だと書かれている。自分より大きい鯉を捕まえようとする姿には激しい気性が感じられ、いかにも強そうだが、実にかわいい。
『水滸伝』のシリーズで確立された、登場人物がその強い色や形と一体となり、画面を所狭しと大暴れするスタイル。それが、さらなる傑作を生み出したのである。怪童丸と鯉以外、特に背景はない。水流は、もはや抽象化された観念の世界である。

Sakata Kaidomaru

This is Kintaro of Mt. Ashigara, later known as Sakata Kintoki, who, it is written, was the child of an old woman, conceived in a dream by a dragon. The sight of the lad trying to catch a carp bigger than himself indicates a feisty disposition, and great strength, but actually he is also rather sweet.

Complementing the strong colors and forms, figures established in the *Water Margin* series riotously filled the canvas, in turn with this print spawning an even greater masterpiece. Apart from Kaidomaru and fish, there is no background to speak of. The current has been relegated to the realm of the abstract.

34 東都橋場之図 とうとはしばのず

　国芳は、一時期、風景画に夢中になった。考えてみれば、景色というのは、四角い枠の中に収まっているわけではない。山、空や雲、面白い形の木々、きれいな町並み。それらを無理矢理押し込めて一枚の絵にするのが、風景画である。遠近法という、日本にはなかった西洋の特殊技術を知ったことが、国芳を駆り立てた。

　私たちが、カメラを手に良い構図を探すのと同じように、国芳は江戸の町を探索した。そして、この絵のようなカラフルで楽しい名作の数々が誕生したが、全画業に照らせば少数である。絵は、「探す」ものではなく、やはり作るものだ、という気持ちになったのかもしれない。

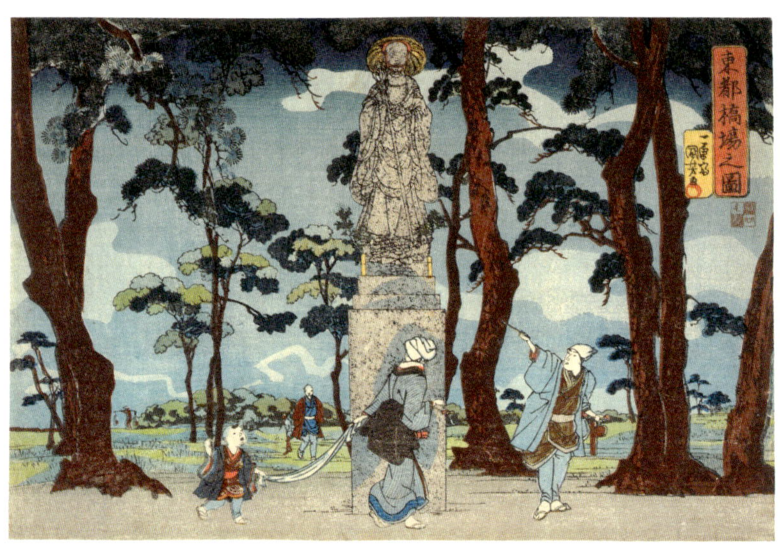

The Eastern Capital: Picture of Hashiba

For a time Kuniyoshi focused on landscapes. Scenery by nature is not confined to a square frame. Mountains, sky and clouds, interesting-shaped trees, tidy streetscapes: forcing them all into a single picture is what landscape painting is about. Kuniyoshi was spurred on by his encounter with perspective, a specialized technique hitherto unknown in Japan.

Just as we set out camera in hand in search of good composition, Kuniyoshi scoured the streets of Edo to produce these and many other delightful, colorful masterpieces. Very few, however, in light of his oeuvre. Perhaps he began to feel that pictures are indeed made, rather than "found."

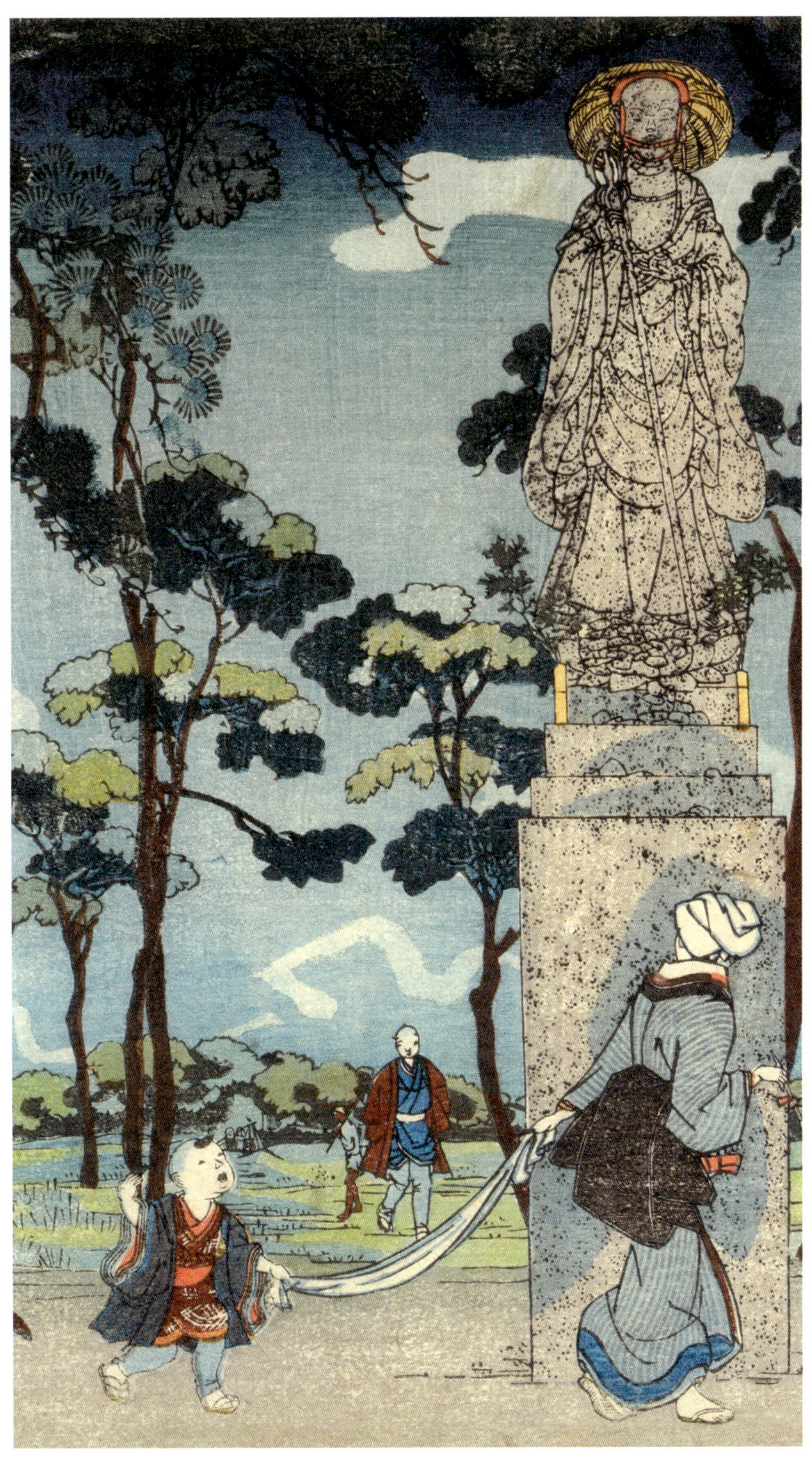

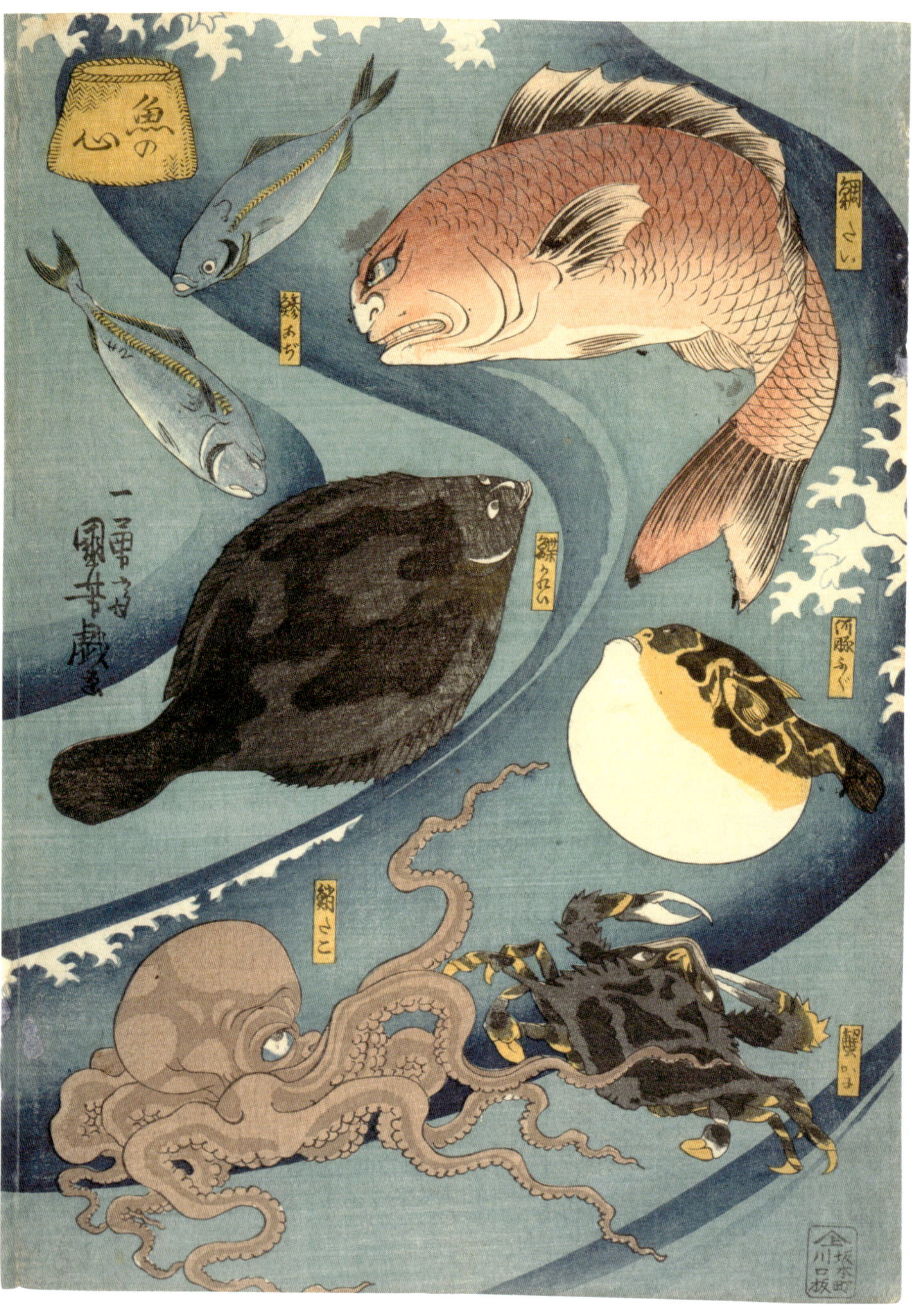

魚の心
鯛 たい
鯵 あぢ
鯵 あぢ
鰈 かれい
河豚 ふぐ
一勇斎國芳戯画
鮹 たこ
蟹 かに
坂本町
川口板

35 魚の心 うおのこころ

　天保の改革で歌舞伎役者や遊女の絵が禁止されたことで、考え出したものの一つが、この「人面魚」。それぞれが役者の似顔絵になっている。江戸時代、色々な魚が泳ぐ図は、伊藤若冲や渡辺崋山ら何人かの画家が描いているが、恐らく朝鮮の絵画からきたアイディアだろう。

　見る人が見ればわかる、というより、当時、浮世絵がたくさん出回った有名な役者たちの顔なのだから、多くの人がすぐに誰の顔か、わかったのではないだろうか。それでも検閲をくぐり抜けたのである。必死の作戦が成功したのか、許容範囲のユーモアか、当時の実況やニュアンスは、私たちには計り知れない。

Actors as Fish

When pictures of kabuki actors, courtesans and such were banned under the Tempo reforms, one response was these "fish with faces." Each is a caricature of an actor. In the Edo period, several painters including Ito Jakuchu and Watanabe Kazan produced illustrations of swimming fishes, probably an idea from Korean painting.

One suspects it was not so much a case of being in the know as instant recognition by most, these being famous actors of whom numerous ukiyo-e were then in circulation. Still they managed to slip under the censor's radar. Whether this was due to a desperate strategy paying off, or the humor being deemed within tolerable limits we cannot know, the true circumstances and subtle nuances of that time being unfathomable to us today.

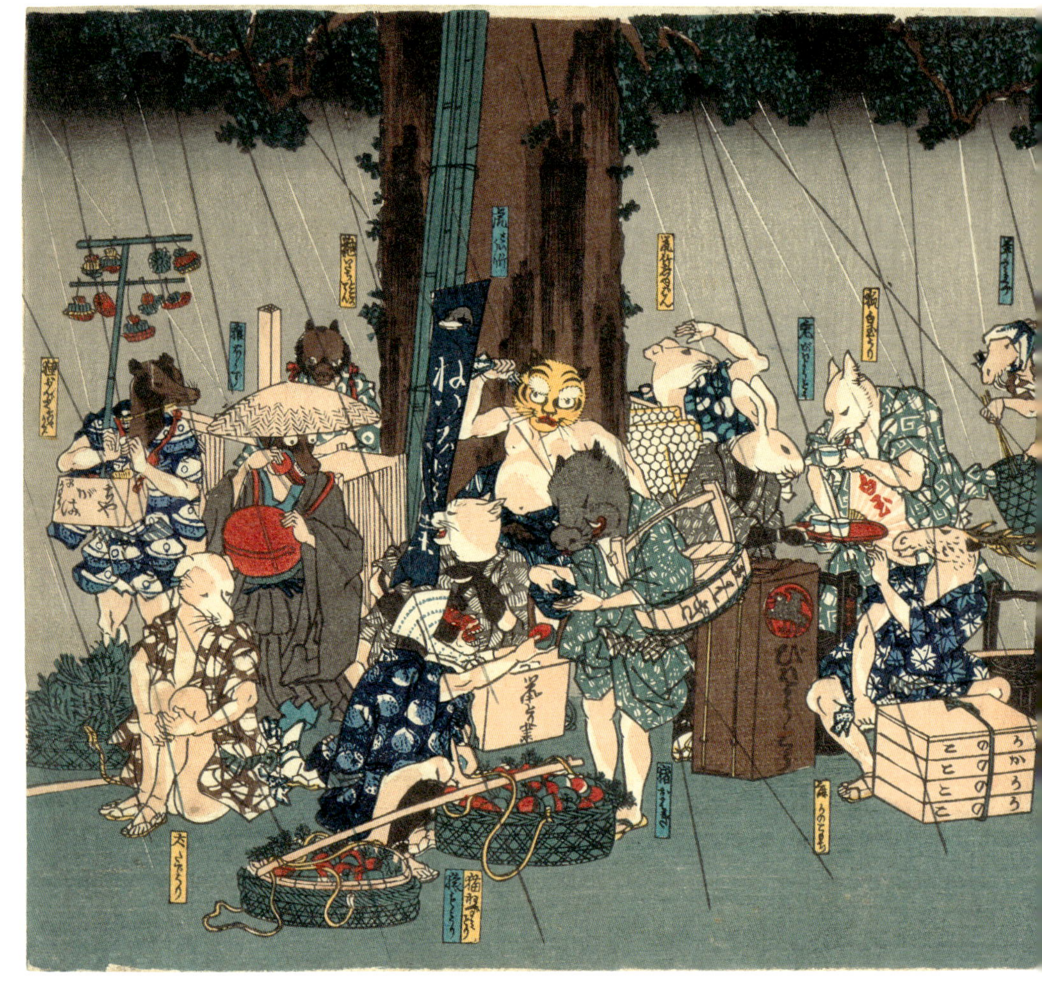

36 道外獣の雨やどり　どうけ けもののあまやどり

　天保の改革による取り締まりは、魚に役者の似顔を当てはめるような、きわどい絵ばかりでなく、さまざまな楽しい絵を生み出すことにもつながった。役者絵や美人画といったお決まりの商品だけではない、老若男女を喜ばせる世界が広がったのだから、結果として、改革は浮世絵界を魅力的にしたとも言えるだろう。

　急に降り出した雨。動物たちが次々と木の下にやってくる。みんな仕事の最中だったようだ。画中の字によると、虎の生業は「とい竹」売り。虎は竹林にいるものだというのが、当時の日本人のイメージだから、である。もちろん猫もいる。ねずみとりの薬を商っているらしい。

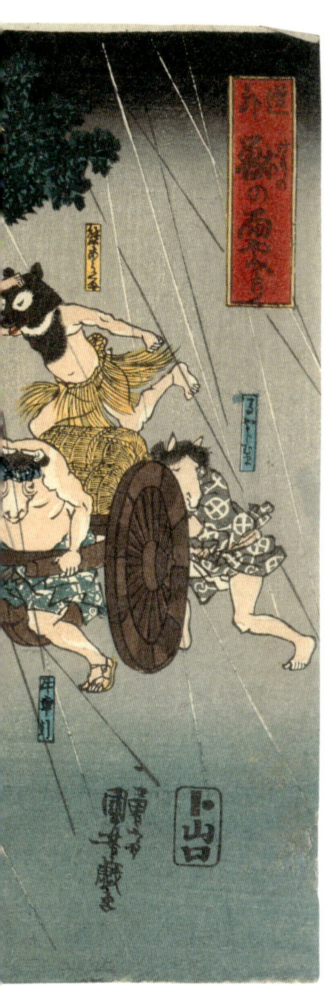

Fool Beasts Taking Shelter From the Rain

The restrictions imposed by the Tempo reforms led not only to such bizarre creations as piscine caricatures, but all sorts of paintings in a lighter vein as well. Forcing ukiyo-e to expand from the stock images of actors and beauties to works everyone could enjoy, ultimately the Tempo reforms only served to boost its allure.

A sudden downpour sends animals scurrying to shelter under a tree. All seem to have been at work. According to the text, the tiger's natural calling is that of a seller of bamboo pipes, not surprising as the Japanese then saw tigers as creatures living in bamboo forests. Of course there is a cat too, in this case, it would seem, trading in rat poison.

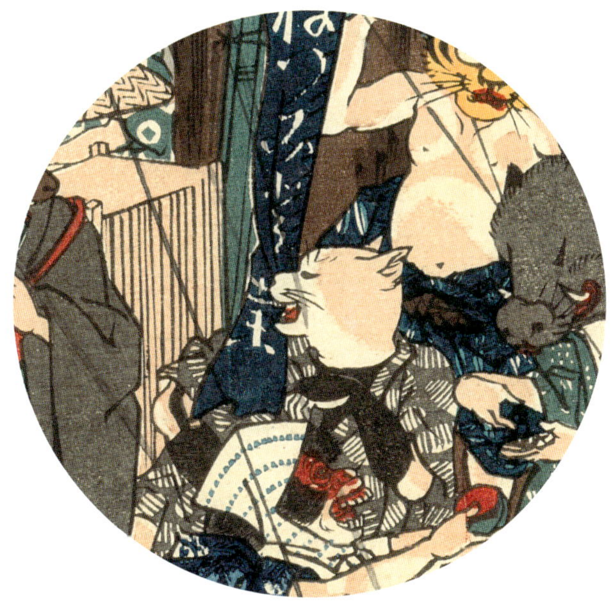

37 かゑるづくし <かえるづくし>

歌舞伎ファンならば、格好良い見得や決めのポーズは、見逃せないポイント。もちろん天保の改革以前には、本物の役者たちのその瞬間が、商品化されていた。そして、取り締まり後、ファンの心を満たしてくれたものの一つがこれ。みな実際の芝居で役者たちが見せる、名場面である。

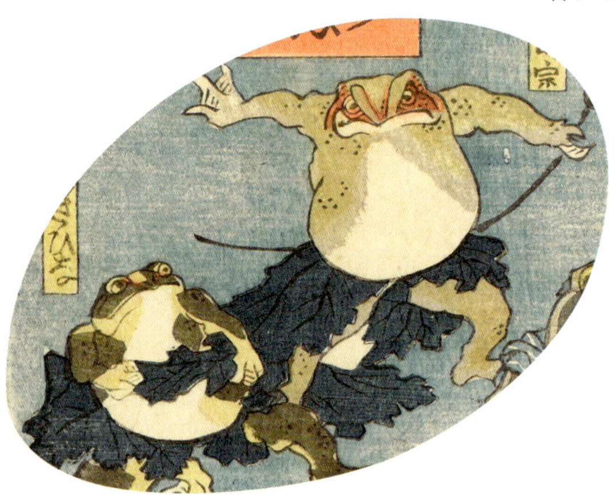

実におかしいが、どれもこれも見事な形である。いや、見事だからおかしいのだろう。ある日、芝居見物に行った家族がこんな絵を買ってきたら、留守番をしていた人も吹き出したに違いない。そして、これを見ながら大まじめに役者のまねなどしたら、家中大爆笑だろう。

Frogs Playing Various Roles

For fans, dazzling displays and classic poses are unmissable elements of kabuki. Obviously, until the Tempo reforms, the look and poses of real actors were commodified. Following the clampdown, this type of print is one of the things that satisfied the souls of kabuki fans. These are all standard scenarios acted out in real plays.

While highly humorous, each one also is a splendid example of a kabuki form. Perhaps it's that very perfection that makes them so funny. If a family member who'd gone to the theatre one day bought a picture like this, those waiting at home would have found them hilarious too. And if it were used to gravely mimic the actors, the whole house would have rung with laughter.

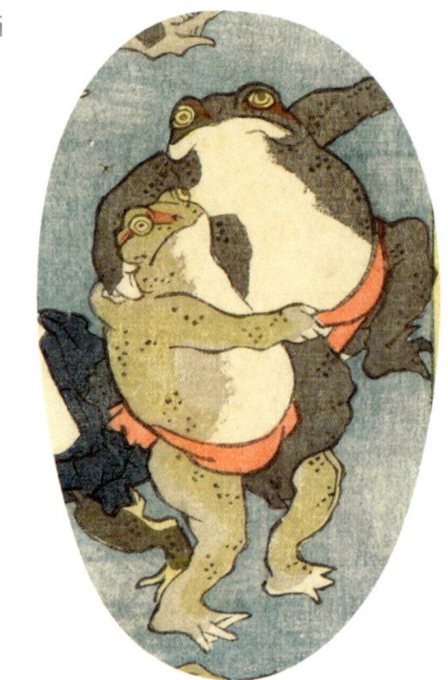

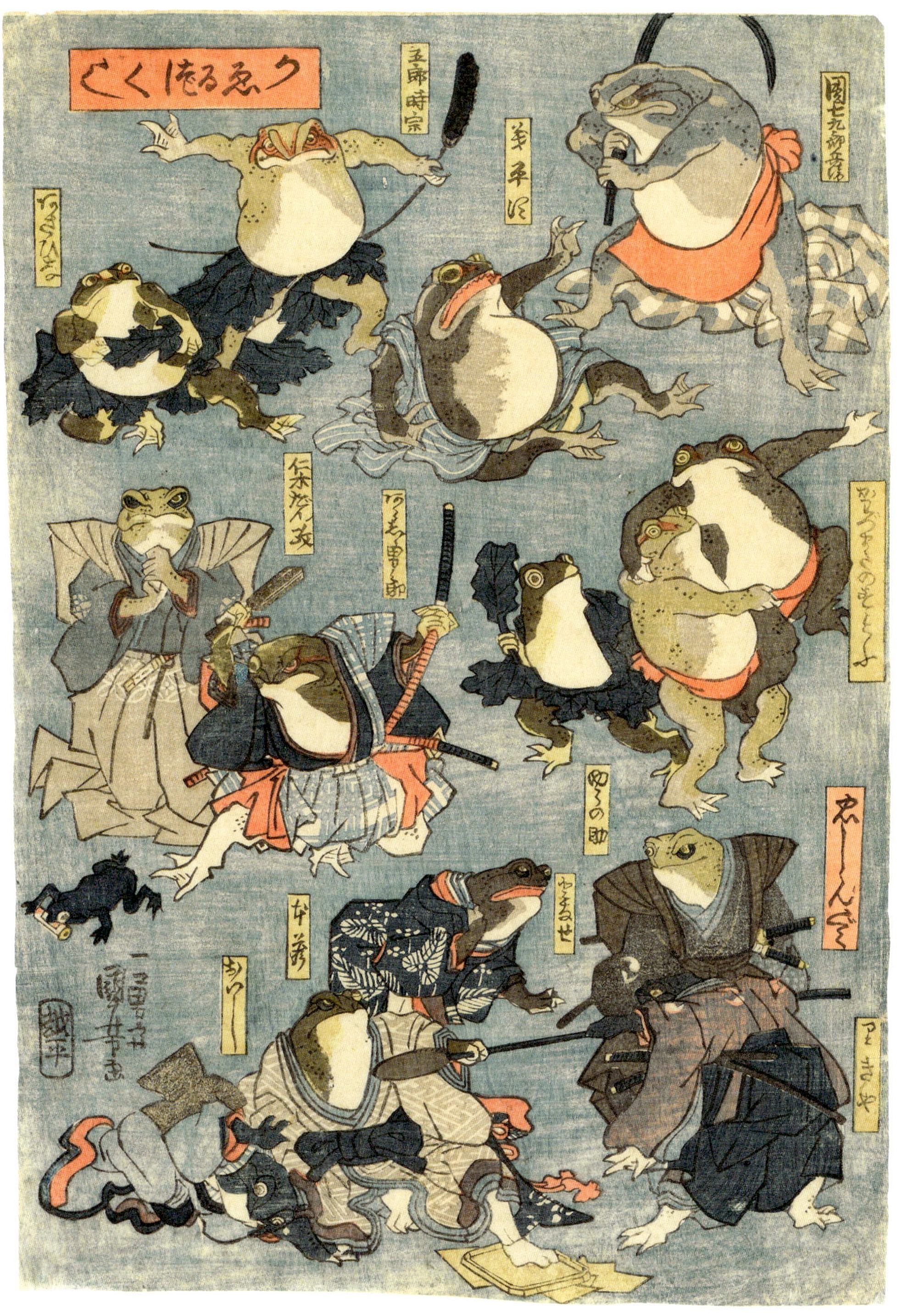
うらるくご
五郎時宗
半平に
國七九御
いせいびの
仁木だい玄
つも曹弁
からづきのそくろよ
ぬらの助
やまぜ
たーんざく
な菱
も 〴〵や
一勇斎
國芳画
歳平

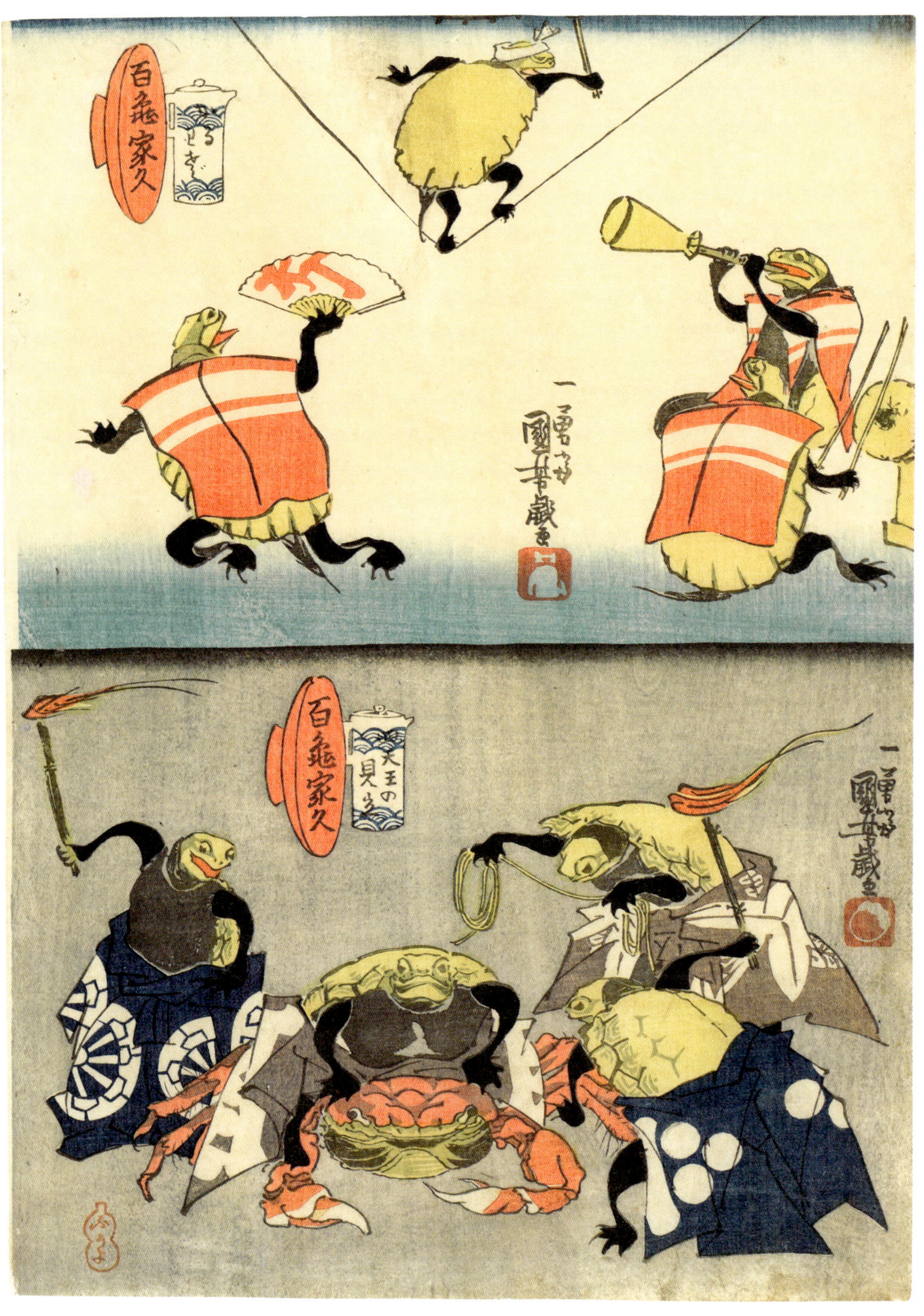

38 百亀家久 かるわざ・四天王の見立

　亀が色々を演じるシリーズ。上下で図柄が違うので、二つの趣向が楽しめる。タイトルの「百亀家久」は、妖怪たちが練り歩く百鬼夜行をもじったもの。「家が久しく」というのは、長寿のおめでたい亀に引っ掛けた駄洒落である。亀は鮮やかな黄色で、それがライト感覚の笑いに一役買っている。

　上は、綱渡りの芸。この頃、江戸では見世物が盛んで、曲芸もその一つだった。鉢巻き姿で必死にバランスをとる亀。その様子を見守り、調子を合わせながら、太鼓を叩き、盛り立てる仲間たち。猫形の印にも注目。

　下は、平安時代の武将、源頼光の四人の家来たちである。妖怪の土蜘蛛を退治する場面のはずだが、やっつけているのは蟹。

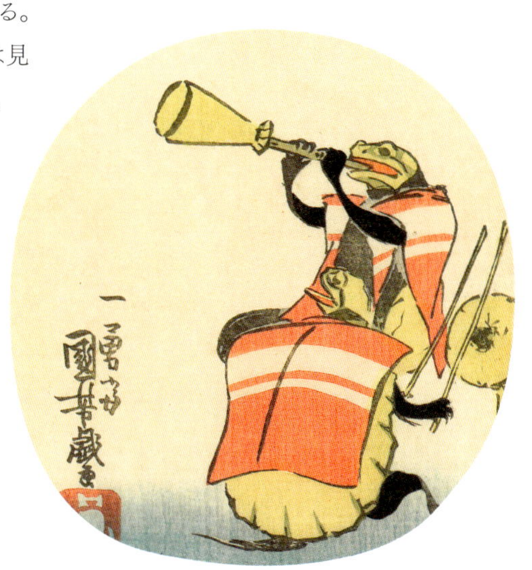

One Hundred Turtles of Good Luck (Hyakki yakyu): Acrobatics / Representation of the Four Great Retainers

One of a series featuring turtles in various roles. The picture is split, offering double the interest. *Hyakki yakyu* is a play on *Hyakki yagyo* (Night Parade of One Hundred Demons), a pun and reference to the turtle's status as a symbol of longevity. The vibrant yellow of the turtles lightens the mood and adds to the joke.

The top picture shows tightrope walking. Entertainments of all sorts were popular in Edo around this time, acrobatics being one type. A turtle wearing a headband tries desperately to keep its balance, while his comrades watch and beat drums accordingly to ramp up the tension Note also the cat-shaped stamp.

Below are the four retainers of Heian period general Minamoto no Yorimitsu. This is supposed to show them vanquishing a giant demon spider, but instead the creature being attacked is a crab.

39 金魚づくし 玉や玉や　きんぎょづくし たまやたまや
40 きん魚づくし ぼんぼん　きんぎょづくし ぼんぼん

　勇ましい武者絵で評価される国芳だが、見逃せないのが「かわいいもの好き」という点。このシリーズには、役者などのモデルは存在しない。金魚が人間のすることをしているという、想像の世界である。

　「たーまやー、たーまやー」と売り歩くシャボン玉売りは、夏の風物詩。たまらず子供たちが駆け寄り、くっついて歩くわけだが、ここでは金魚だけでなく、カエルになりかけたオタマジャクシや亀の親子も一緒である。手を伸ばす亀の子の、何といたいけなことか。

　もう一点の「ぼんぼん」とは、お盆に子供たちが手をつないで歌って歩く風習のこと。ここにも、まだしっぽの残るカエルの子が紛れ込んでいるが、ちゃんと金魚に仲良くしてもらっている。

　国芳は、背中に彫り物をするなど威勢のいい人だったが、こんな作品を本気で描いているところをのぞいてみたいものである。

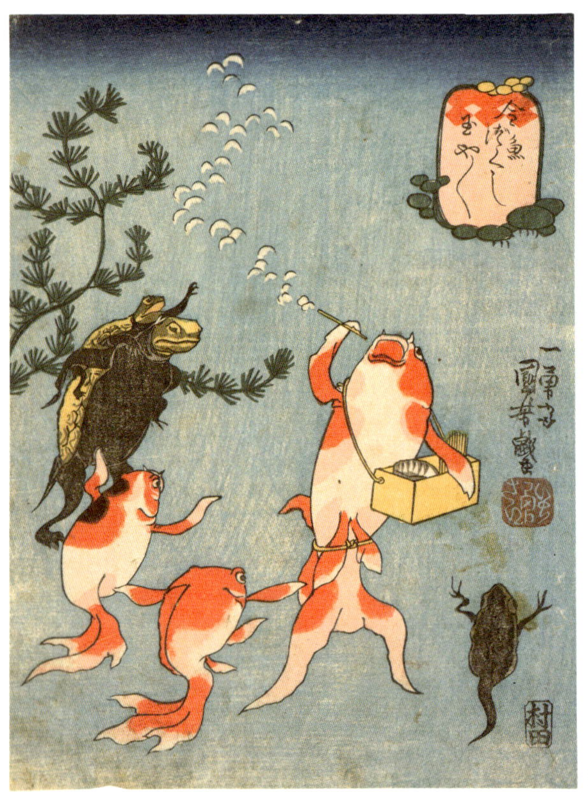

39

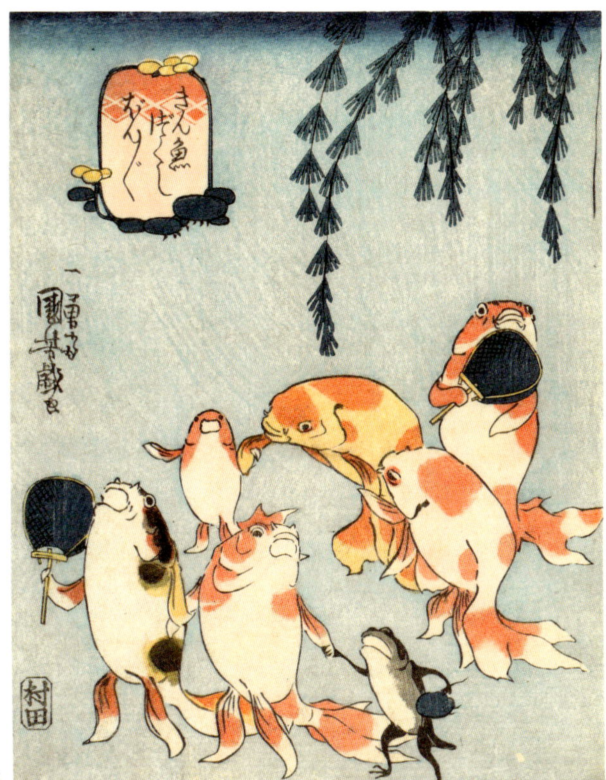
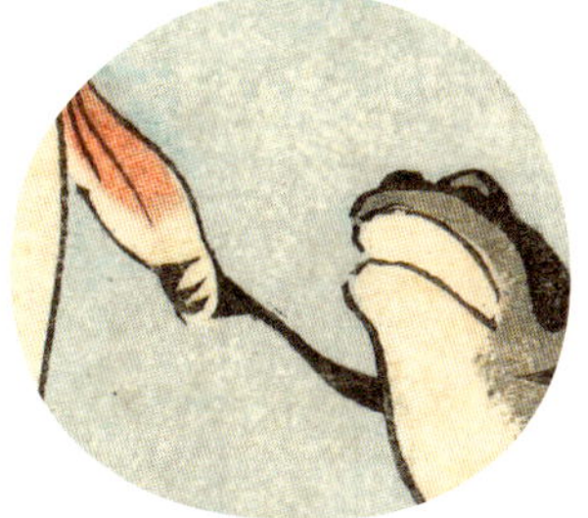

40

39 Set of Goldfish: Blowing Soap Bubbles
40 Set of Goldfish: Singing 'Bonbon' Song

Kuniyoshi was acclaimed for his courageous warriors, but his love for the cute and quirky should not be overlooked. This series has no models, actors or otherwise. It is an imaginary world in which goldfish do human things.

The bubble mix seller with his call of "Sooap bubbles, sooap bubbles" was a summer staple. Unable to resist, children have come running and are trailing behind him. Here we have not only goldfish but a tadpole halfway through its transformation to frog, and a turtle and its young. Note especially the dear little turtle, hand eagerly outstretched.

The other print, Bonbon, refers to the custom of children joining hands and walking along singing at the Obon festival. Here too, a tadpole still with tail has worked its way into the fun, and is getting on famously with the goldfish.

Tattooed back and all, Kuniyoshi must have cut quite a daunting figure, but just imagine watching him devotedly at work on paintings like these.

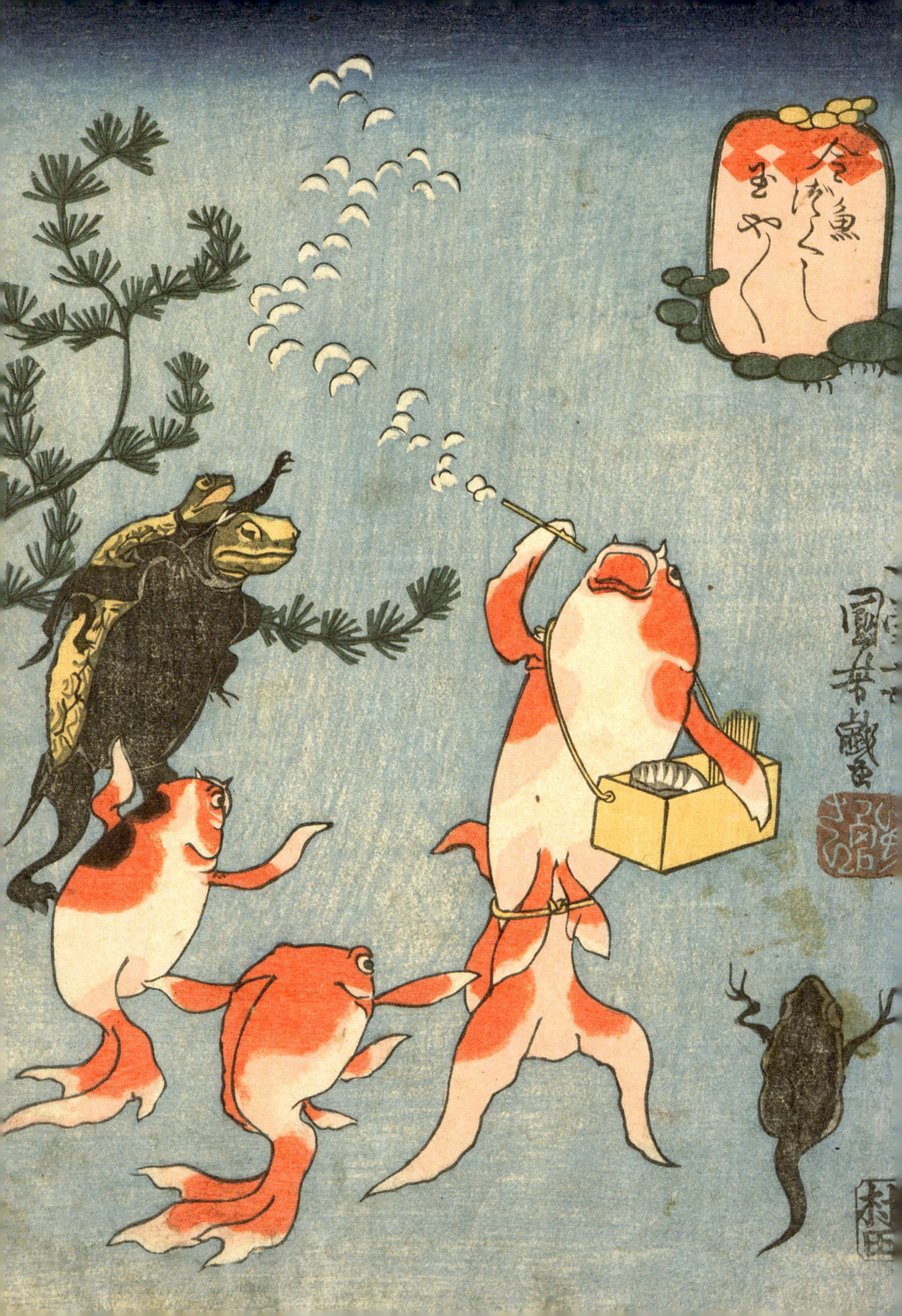
今ぎよ魚づくし
たまや

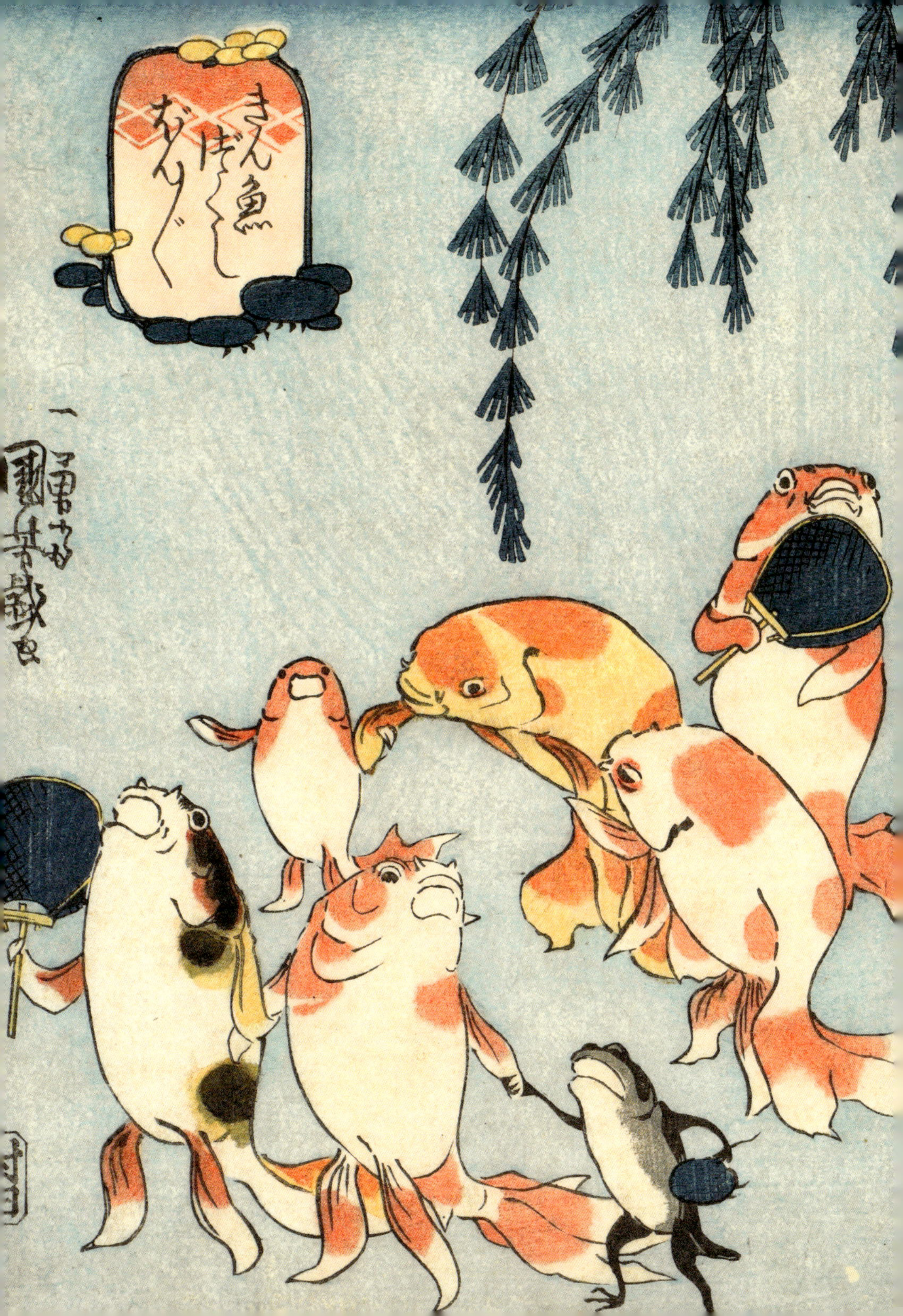
きん魚
ばくし
をりく
一勇斎
國芳戯画

41 みかけハこハゐがとんだいゝ人だ みかけはこわいが とんだいいひとだ

　国芳が五十代を迎えた頃、幕府の取り締まりの厳しさも一段落した。しかし、いったん湧き出した国芳のアイディアの泉は、もはや止めようもなく、ただの役者絵や美人画や武者絵の名手に戻ることはできなかった。この絵は、そんなおかしな絵の創作家としての代表作。

「大勢の人が寄ってたかって、とうと、いい人をこしらえた。とかく人のことは人にしてもらわねば、いい人にはならぬ」と書いてある。人の世界の精神論だが、人の情けのありがたさをまじめに説いているのか、ふざけた絵と組み合わせることで茶化しているのか、真意は今ひとつわからない。顔もさることながら、実は、手がそれ以上に面白い。

He Looks Fierce but He's a Really Great Man

As Kuniyoshi turned fifty, the shogunate's restrictions relaxed a little. But the wellspring of his ideas, once tapped, could not be capped, and there was no going back to simply being a renowned painter of actors, beauties and samurai. This is one of the most notable examples of his more "out-there" output.

The text translates roughly as "Many came together to eventually make a good person. After all, it is only people who understand other people." A reference to the realm of human spirit, but it's impossible to tell Kuniyoshi's true intention: is he seriously holding forth on the virtue of human compassion, or poking fun by teaming it with a jokey illustration? The face is interesting enough, but in fact the hand is even more so.

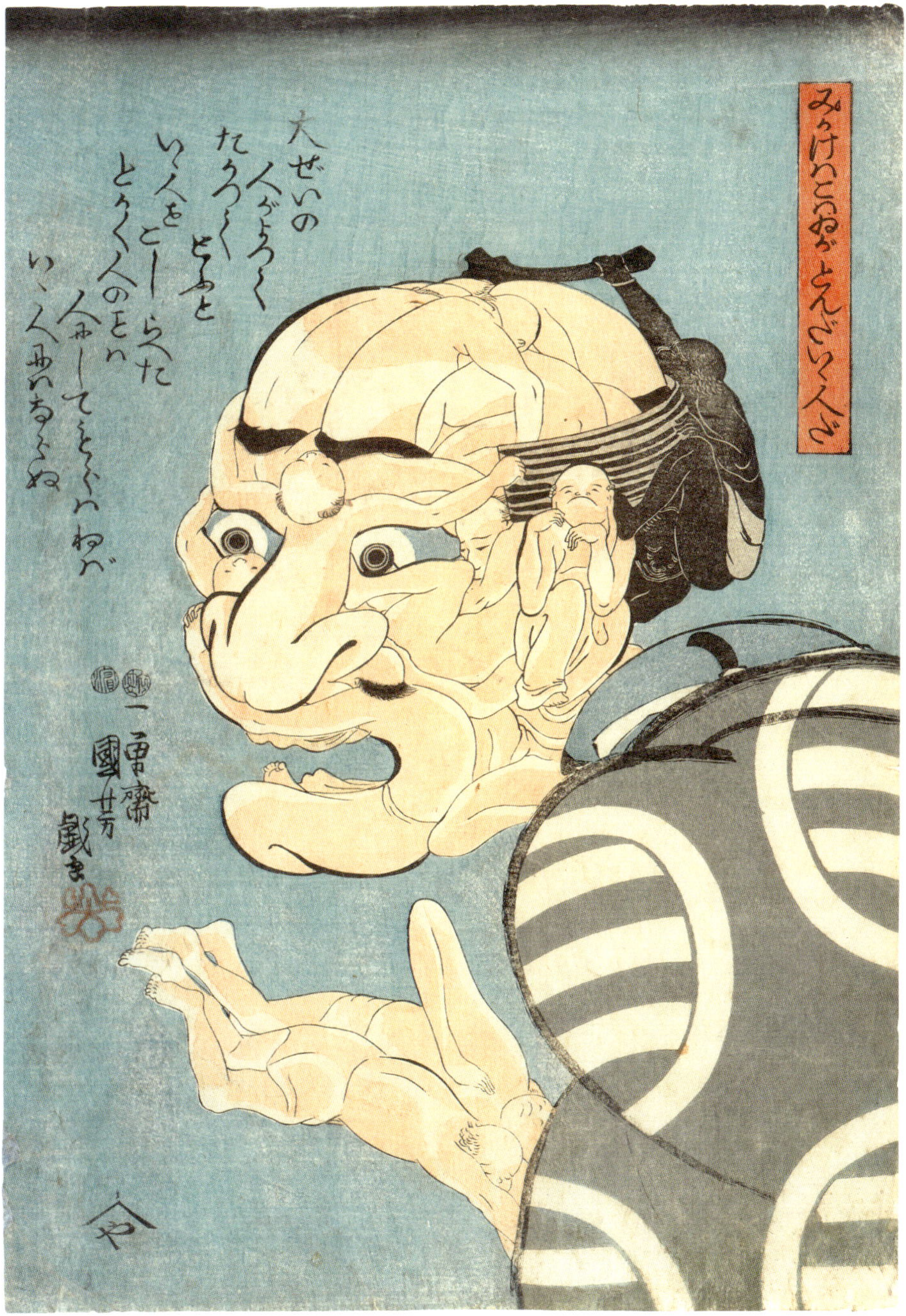
みかけハこハゐがとんだいゝ人だ
一勇斎国芳戯画

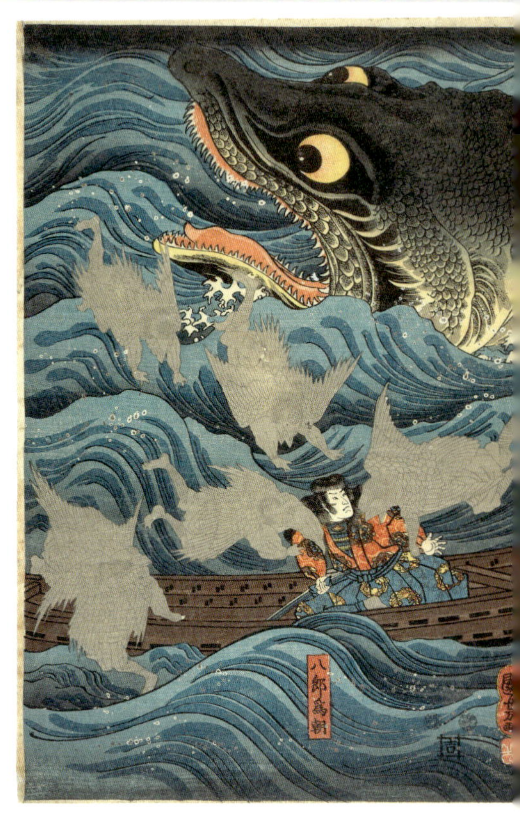

42 讃岐院眷属をして為朝をすくふ図

さぬきいん けんぞくをして ためともをすくうず

　嘉永年間、五十代の国芳は、造形家として絶頂期を迎える。浮世絵という商品には大きさの定型があったが、3枚で一つの作品とする方法を、国芳は思う存分利用した。この絵も、ただダイナミックなだけではない。ワニザメと舟、二つの長いものから作られる構図は絶妙で、次の瞬間の動きまで目に浮かぶようだ。

　曲亭馬琴の小説『椿説弓張月』の一場面。都落ちしていた平安時代の武将、源為朝は、都を目ざすが暴風に見舞われる。妻は海を鎮めようと入水、幼い息子を乗せた舟とは離ればなれになり、為朝は、もはやこれまでと自害しようとする。それを都の法皇、讃岐院の使いの烏天狗が助ける。そして画面上半分は、実は別の場面。息子と家来を乗せた舟は、はぐれた後に大破するが、海をさまよう二人の前に突如ワニザメが現れ、彼らを救った。つまり、二つの異なる場面を一画面にまとめ上げたのである。

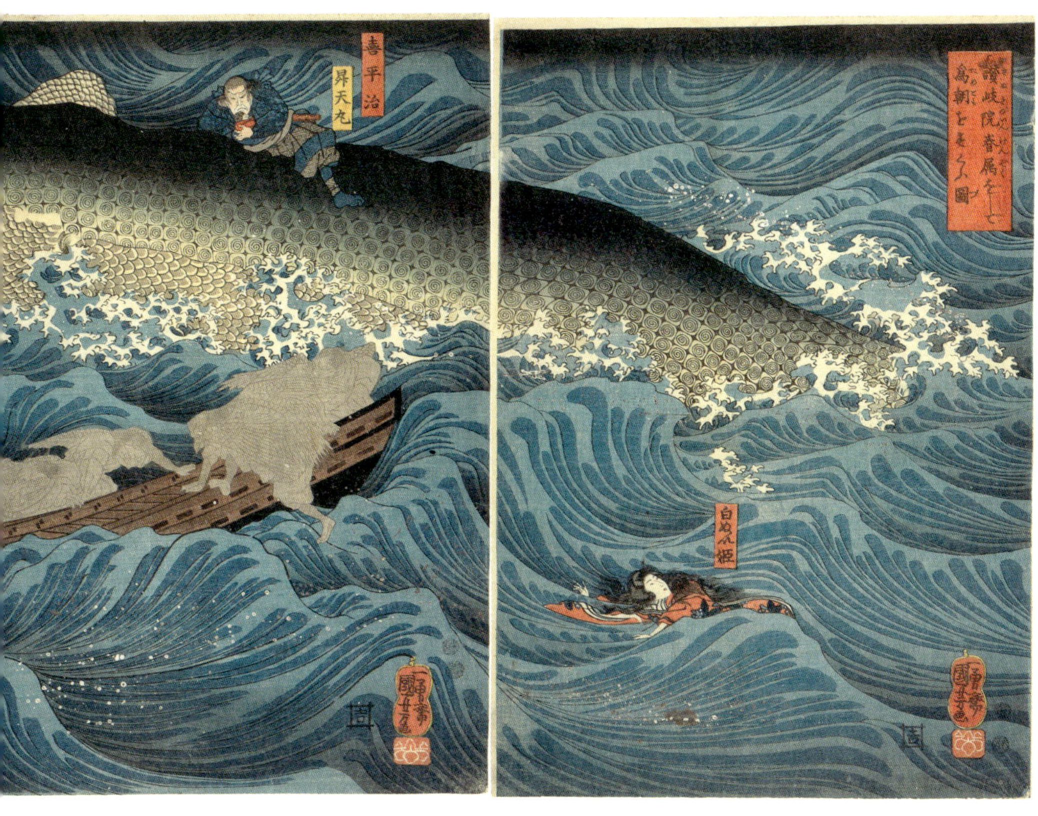

Tametomo Rescued by Tengu Sent by Sanuki-in

Kuniyoshi reached his zenith as a designer in his fifties, during the Kaei era. As a product ukiyo-e had a standard format, but Kuniyoshi frequently used a method employing three prints to create a single work. This painting is not only dynamic; the composition consisting of two long things – the man-eating shark, and the boat – is exquisite, allowing the viewer to visualize the next movement.

A scene from Kyokutei Bakin's novel *Strange Tales of the Crescent Moon*: having fled the capital, Heian general Minamoto no Tametomo is determined to return, but encounters a violent storm. In an attempt to appease the seas his wife drowns herself, and becoming separated from the boat carrying their young son, the despairing Tametomo tries to take his own life. He is saved by crow *tengu*, servants of the retired emperor Sanuki-in. The top half of the picture is actually another setting: the shark surfacing to rescue Tametomo's son and retainer when the boat carrying them is damaged after becoming separated, leaving the pair lost on the waters. Thus two different scenes are brought together in the one print.

版画の輝き

　庶民に買える値段だった浮世絵版画。国芳の水滸伝や、有名な歌川広重の東海道五拾三次といった「シリーズもの」なども次々に販売された。そうした商品を手にする楽しみは、さしずめ現代のトレーディングカードにたとえてみたくもなるが、それだけでは、浮世絵版画の魅力を理解したことにはならないだろう。

　当時の暮らしを想像してみよう。最小限の色で染められた着物をまとい、ふだん使う食器は、もちろん華麗な色絵などではない。居住空間は、主に木や紙や墨の色で成り立っている。

　そんな時代、絵草紙屋の店先に並ぶ色摺りの版画は、人々の目にどんな風に映っただろう。一枚の紙に、その時代に使うことのできる、あらゆる絵の具の色が注ぎ込まれている。特に国芳の頃などは、色どうしを複雑に重ねるなどして、さらに幅広い表現も追求されている。版画の一枚一枚は、まるで色彩の宝石箱のように見えたに違いない。

　今、ご自分のいる部屋をぐるりと見渡していただきたい。現代の暮らしには、何とたくさんの色が溢れかえっていることか。

The glamor of prints

Ukiyo-e woodblock prints were affordable for ordinary people. Even serial works like Kuniyoshi's *Water Margin* and Utagawa Hiroshige's famous *Fifty-Three Stations of the Tokaido* were fast sellers. It's tempting to liken the pleasure of holding such a picture in one's hand to that of today's trading cards, but to do so would be to miss some of what exactly made ukiyo-e so appealing.

Imagine if you will how people lived back then. Garbed in clothing dyed in an austere color palette, dining off dishes that generally were not decorated with flamboyant designs. Living spaces were largely composed of the colors of wood and paper and ink.

How did the multicolored prints displayed in the local bookseller's look to the people of this time? Poured into each sheet of paper were all the colors of paint then available. By Kuniyoshi's day especially, in the quest for an even broader range of expression artists were layering different shades in complex ways. To the people of the time, each print must have been a veritable treasure trove of color.

Now take a look around the room where you are right now, and see just how full of color our lives are today.

III

「ねこ絵描き」 のひみつ

Secrets of
a 'cat painter'

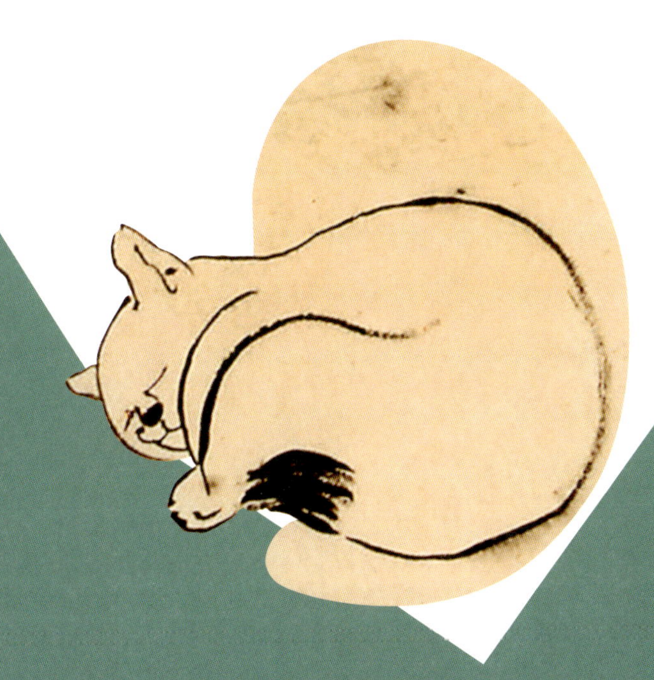

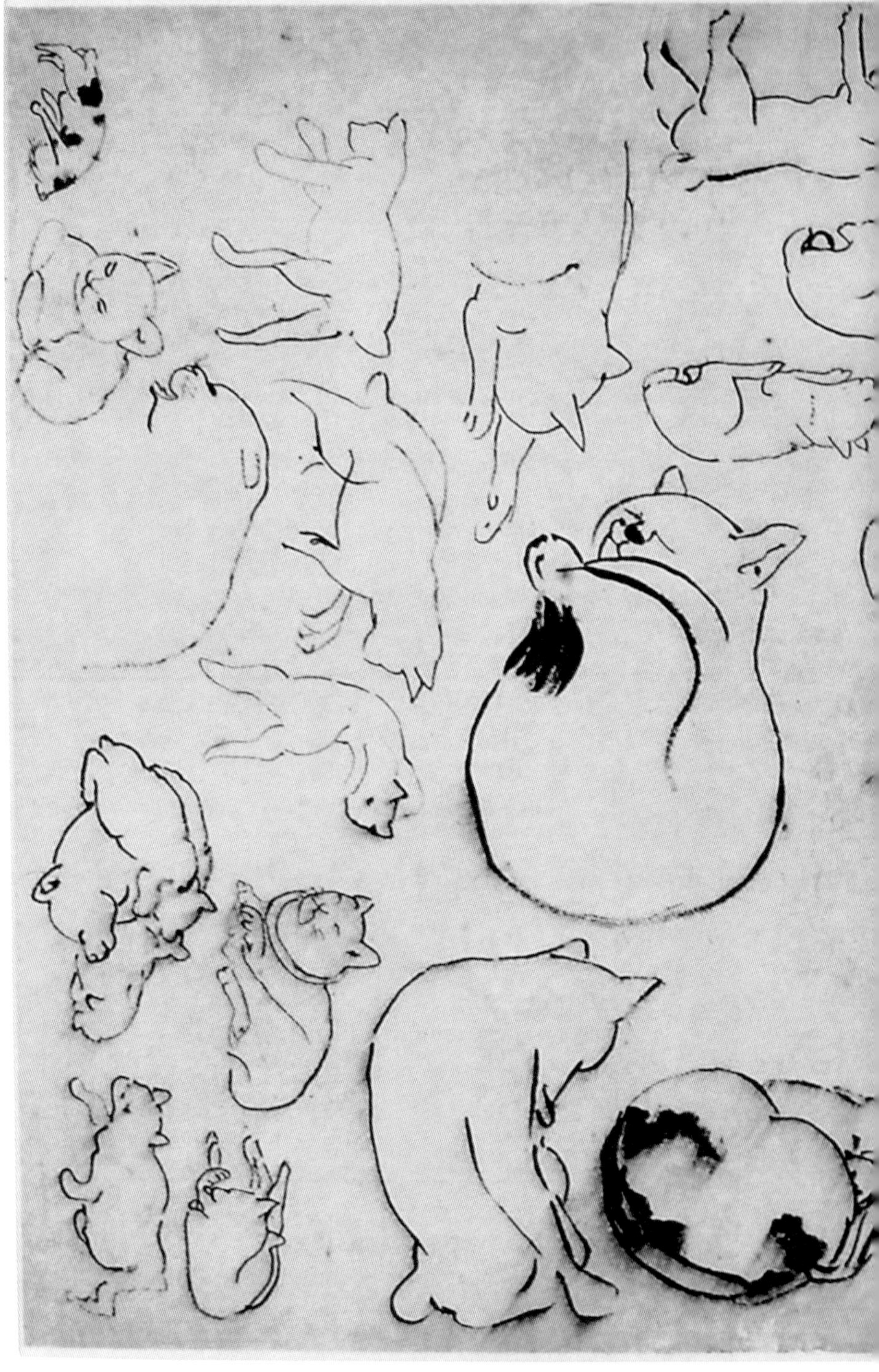

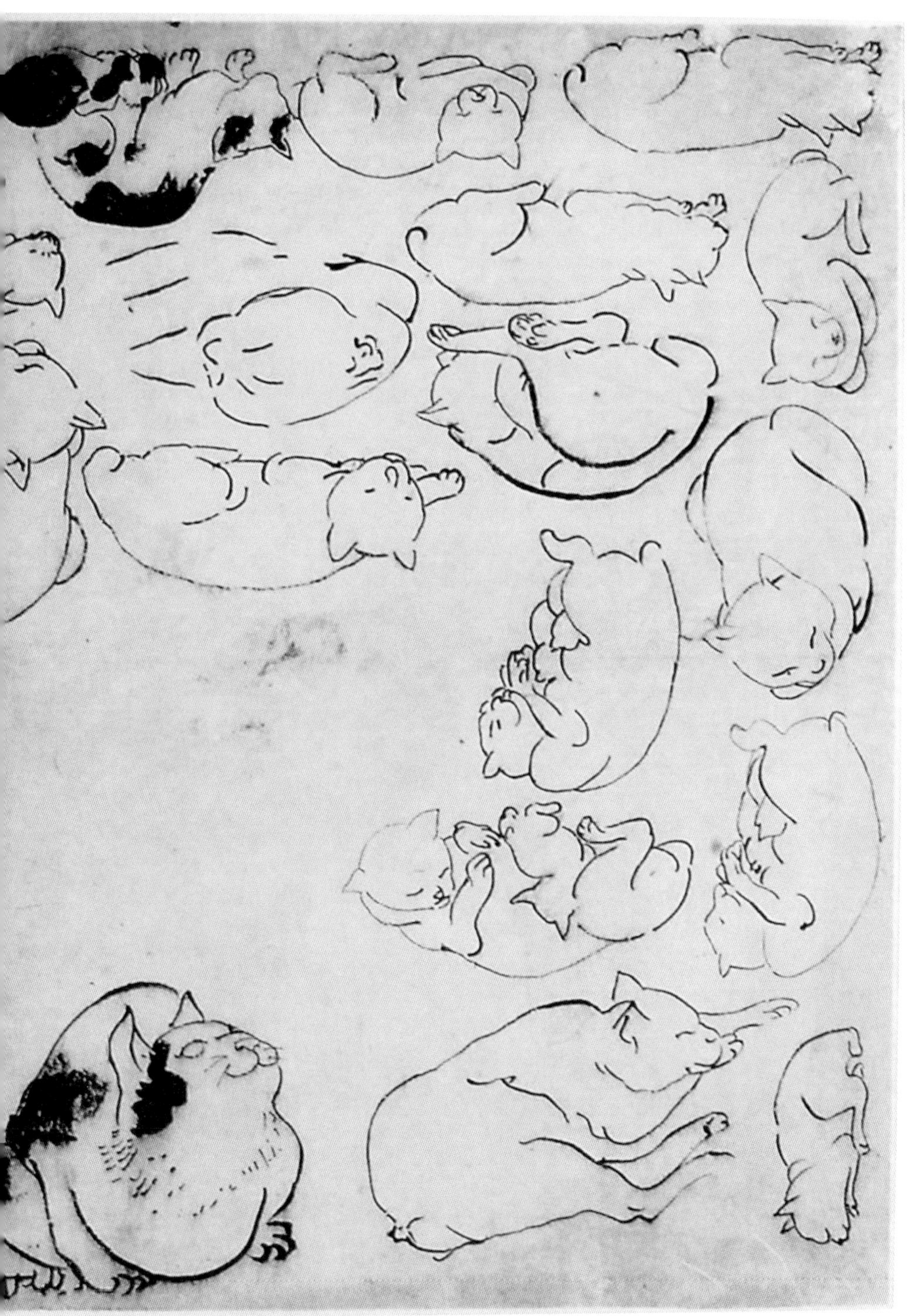

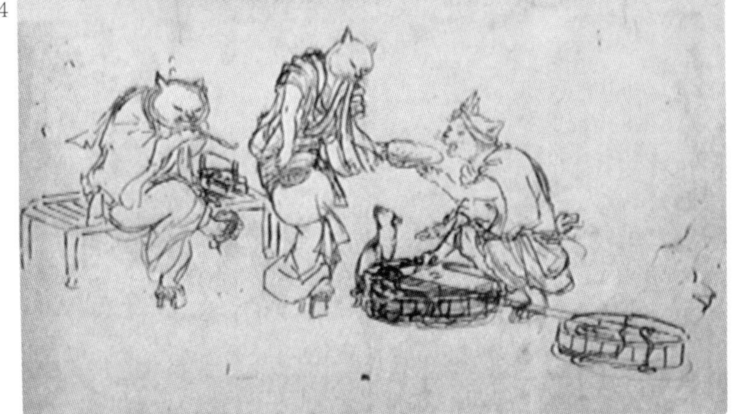

© National Museum of Ethnology Leiden, invnr 3010-3

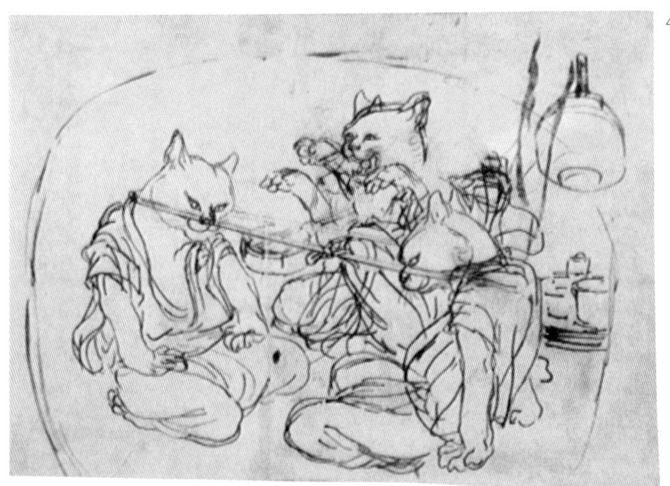

© National Museum of Ethnology Leiden, invnr 3513-605-39

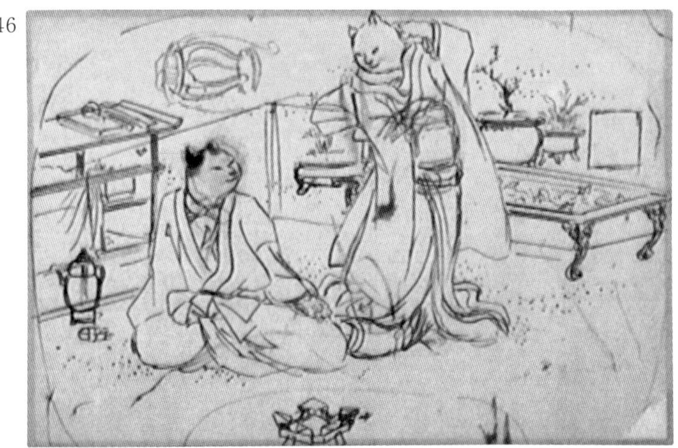

© National Museum of Ethnology Leiden, invnr 3513-570

　国芳の肉筆画は少なく、しかもほとんどが美人画である。これほど多くの猫たちを世に送り出した国芳だが、彼自身の生な筆から生まれた猫を見ることはできないのだろうか……国芳の猫に恋いこがれる者なら、誰もがそう思うだろう。

　実は、オランダのライデン国立民族学博物館に、そんなファン垂涎の資料が収蔵されている。国芳のさまざまな作品の下絵類の中に、猫の作品の構想を練るための下絵や、それより前の段階と思われる猫のスケッチの数々が含まれているのである。下絵やスケッチも「芸術の一部」として注目を浴びるようになった近代とは異なり、江戸時代には最終的な作品こそがすべて。下絵やスケッチは、他人に見せるようなものではなかった。まして大量の版画のための絵を次から次に描かなければならない浮世絵の場合、それらが後世に残ることは稀である。ライデンの資料はきわめて貴重であり、国芳の猫ファンにとっては、奇跡的な幸運である。

　たくさんの猫のスケッチが集められた一枚（43）は、日頃から描きためていたさまざまな姿のスケッチを一枚の紙に描き直した、いわばポーズ集といったところだろう。よく見れば、版画作品の中に、似たポーズを見い出すこともできるかもしれない。シンプルな線描で形の概略を表したに過ぎないが、猫の実態からエッセンスを濃厚に抽出したかのようで、見事というほかない。左上隅の黒ぶちの1匹など、小さな描写なのでうっかりすると見落としてしまうが、気づけば胸がきゅんとなること間違いない。どの描写にも、国芳の「家族」への愛が感じられる。

　また、作品のための下絵も魅力いっぱいである。ここでご覧いただくものの多くは団扇絵のための下絵だが、本書収録の《猫の源氏　賢木》（55）のものもある。比べてみると、下絵では、背景に部屋の中の様子がもっと描かれているが、完成作では雅びな雲の模様に変わっている。『源氏物語』だけに、典雅さを演出する方向に進んだのだろう。《猫のけん》（71）の別バージョンと思われる図もあるが、登場人物の動きが実に豊かである。

　ほかにも、猫たちが「首引き」の遊びに興じる一図や、猫世界の行商と買い手のやりとりを、なぜか普通の猫がちょこんと座って見守っている一図など、どれも魅惑の光景である。いつの日か、これらの完成作すべてに巡り会いたいものである

Few hand-painted works by Kuniyoshi remain, and most that do are bijinga. He gifted the world so many cats, yet to see them straight from his own brush would seem an impossible dream: at least that's what anyone mad about Kuniyoshi's cats would assume.

But some mouth-watering material for these fans is actually available, at the Museum Volkenkunde in Leiden, The Netherlands. Among sketches for various of Kuniyoshi's works, here one finds numerous concept drawings the artist used when percolating ideas for his cat paintings, and rougher sketches that would have been the prior step. Unlike these days, when drawings and sketches are the subject of growing attention as "part of art," in the Edo period the final result was all. Drawings and sketches were not for showing to others. This was especially so in the case of ukiyo-e, which required artists to produce reams of pictures for large numbers of prints. These preliminary renderings rarely survived for later generations. The Leiden material is extremely valuable, and a miraculous slice of good luck for fans of Kuniyoshi's cats.

The sheet crammed with several cat sketches (43) could be described as a catalog of poses; sketches of cats with various looks that Kuniyoshi drew from day to day, redrawn on a single piece of paper. A close study would no doubt reveal poses similar to these in his print works. Kuniyoshi does no more than use simple line drawings to show abbreviated forms, but therein seems to have distilled the essence of feline existence, and done so splendidly. Cats like the black pied example in the left top corner could easily be overlooked in such a small work, but when one does notice them, they are heart-rending in the extreme. Every portrayal exudes Kuniyoshi's love for his "family."

The drawings for Kuniyoshi's works also hold great appeal. Most of the drawings here were for fans, but there is also one for Cat Version of the Tale of Genji: Sakaki (55). Comparing the two we see that the sketches show more of the room in the background, but in the finished work this has changed to an elegant cloud pattern. Being The Tale of Genji, no doubt Kuniyoshi wanted to take the work in a more refined direction. There is also an illustration that is likely an alternative version of Cats Playing a Hand Game (71), and the movements of the figures are truly expressive.

Other works in the collection include cats amusing themselves with a game of kubihiki, a type of tug-of-war, and a picture in which for some reason ordinary cats are plonked down watching the to-ing and fro-ing between a cat-world peddler and shopper. All make charming scenes. I hope some day to encounter the completed versions of them all.

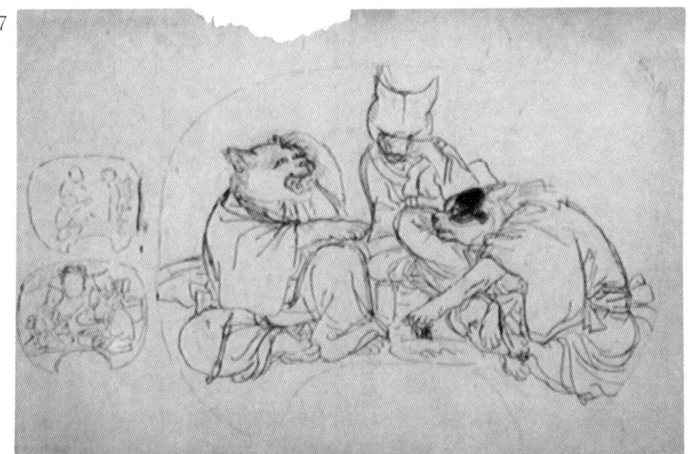

47

© National Museum of Ethnology Leiden, invnr 3513-571

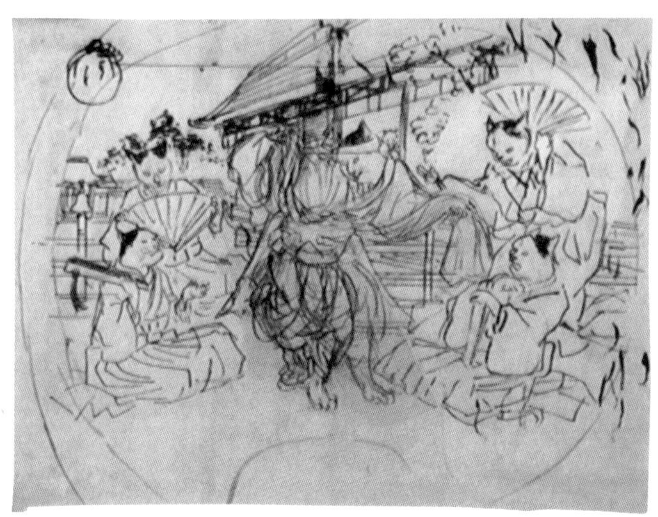

48

© National Museum of Ethnology Leiden, invnr 3513-603-14

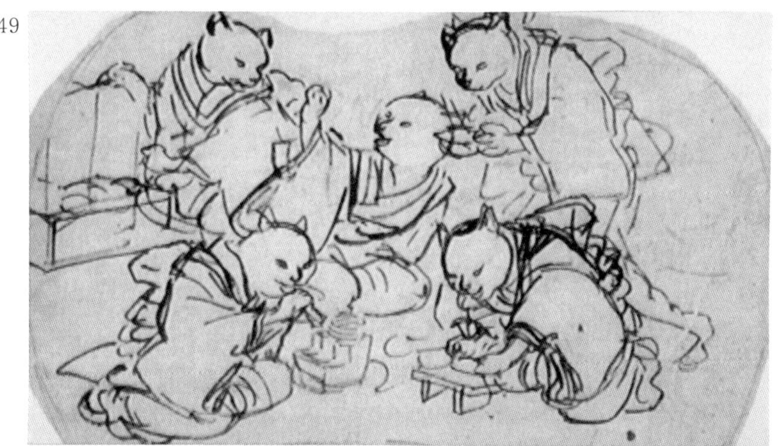

49

© National Museum of Ethnology Leiden, invnr 3513-568

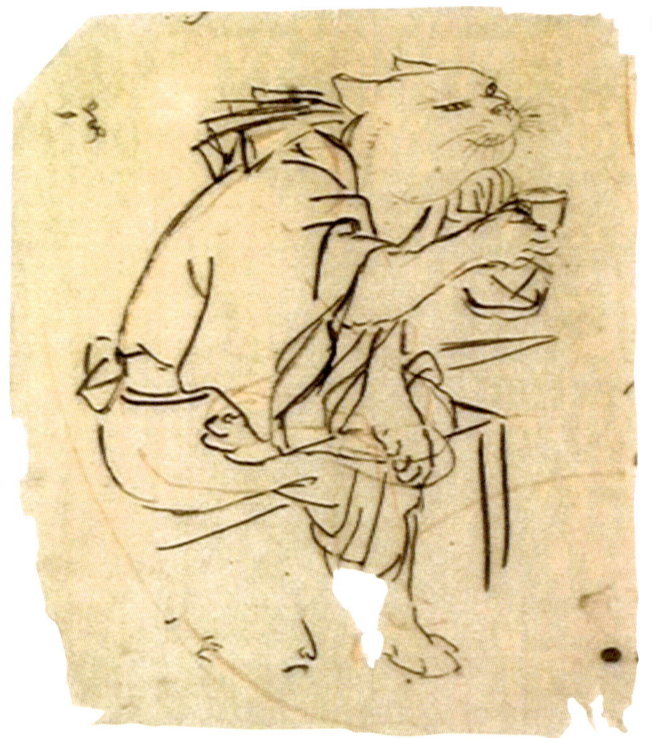

51

IV.

ねこさえいれば
満足という
同好の士のために

For like-minded folks

who need only

a cat to be happy

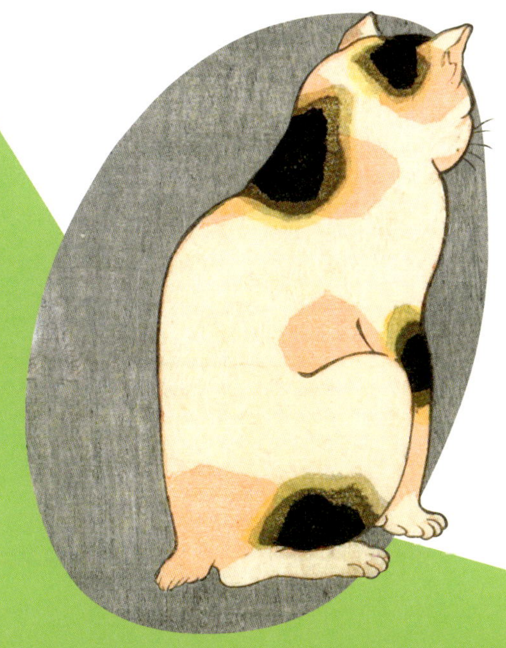

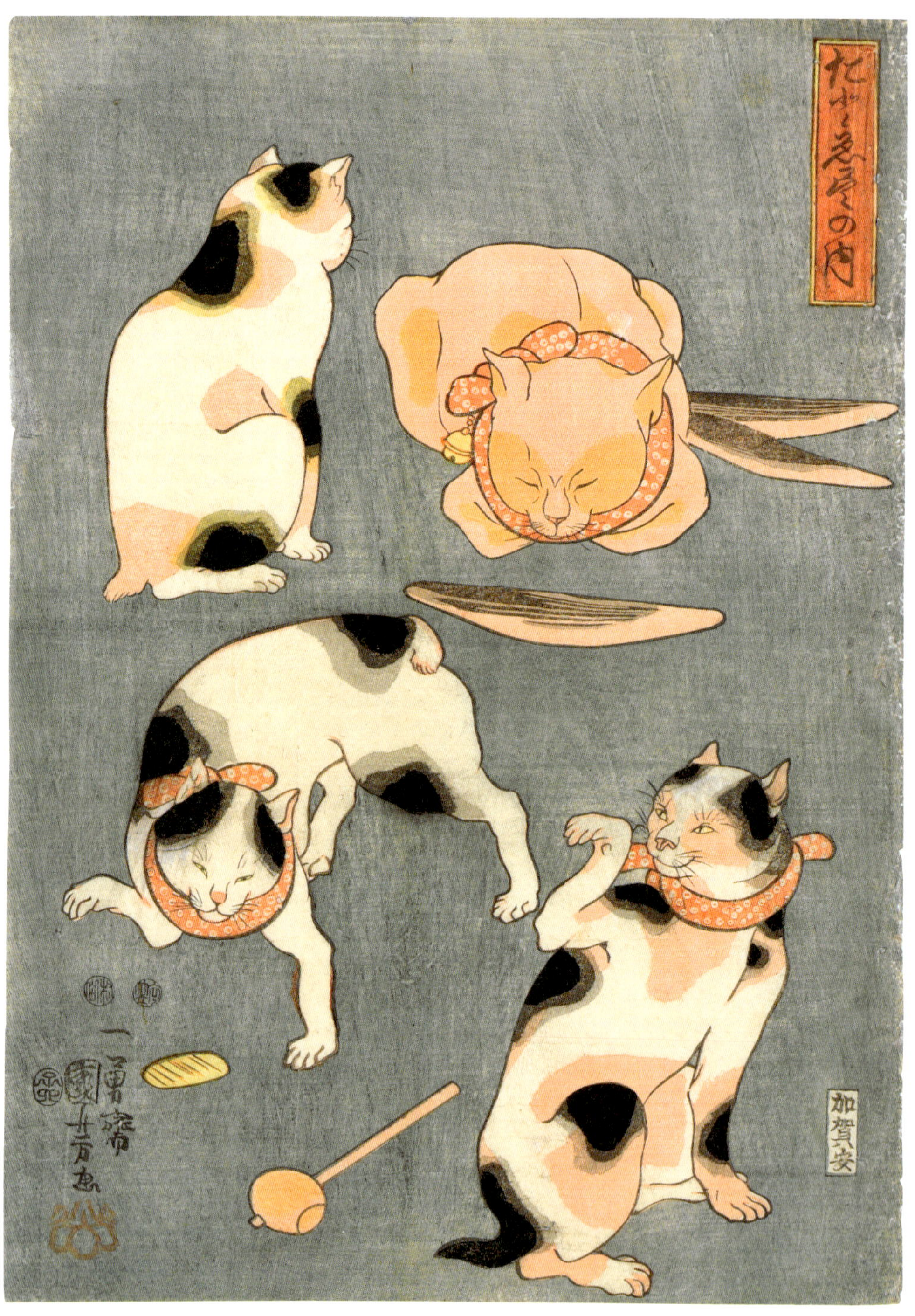
たぐゐ　ゑ　の内
加賀八安

52 たとゑ尽の内 _{たとえづくしのうち}

　猫の登場する色々なことわざや言い回しがある。たとえば「猫に小判」、「猫も食わない」。それだけ猫は、古くから人と近しかったわけである。

　そうした言葉を集めて、猫で表した作品。ところが絵の中に説明がないので、きわめて難解である。江戸時代の人たちにはちょっとした楽しいクイズだったのかもしれないが、現代人には、答えのわからないものばかりである。恥ずかしながら、私がすぐにわかったのは、上記の二つと猫舌だけ。猫背、猫の尻に才槌など、たくさんの言葉遊びの解読に、ぜひ挑戦していただきたい。

Proverbs Illustrated by Cats

Cats appear in many Japanese proverbs and sayings, eg "like gold coins to a cat" ("pearls before swine") and "even a cat won't eat it" ("wouldn't touch with a ten-foot pole"), a reminder of what a familiar presence cats have been in our lives since early times.

This work presents several such expressions in feline form. The problem is that in the absence of explanations, they are exceedingly hard to fathom. While in the Edo period this may have constituted a lighthearted pop quiz, today we struggle to decipher any of them. I confess the only ones I picked immediately were the two above, and *nekojita* (meaning someone sensitive to hot food/drink). But don't let that put you off trying to identify the many sayings here such as "cat's spine" (hunchbacked) and "taking a mallet to a cat's backside" (referring to something unsuitable).

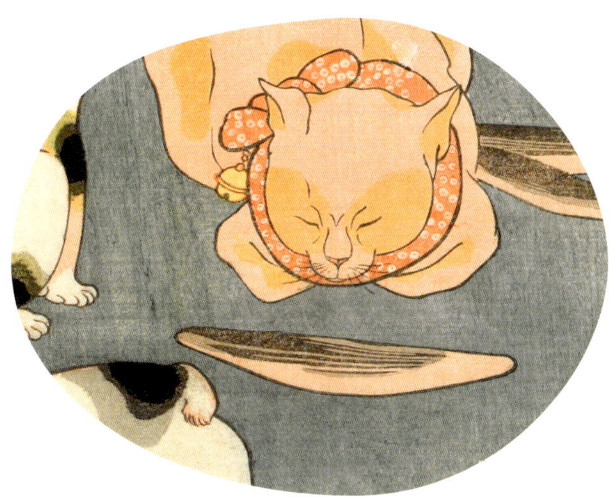

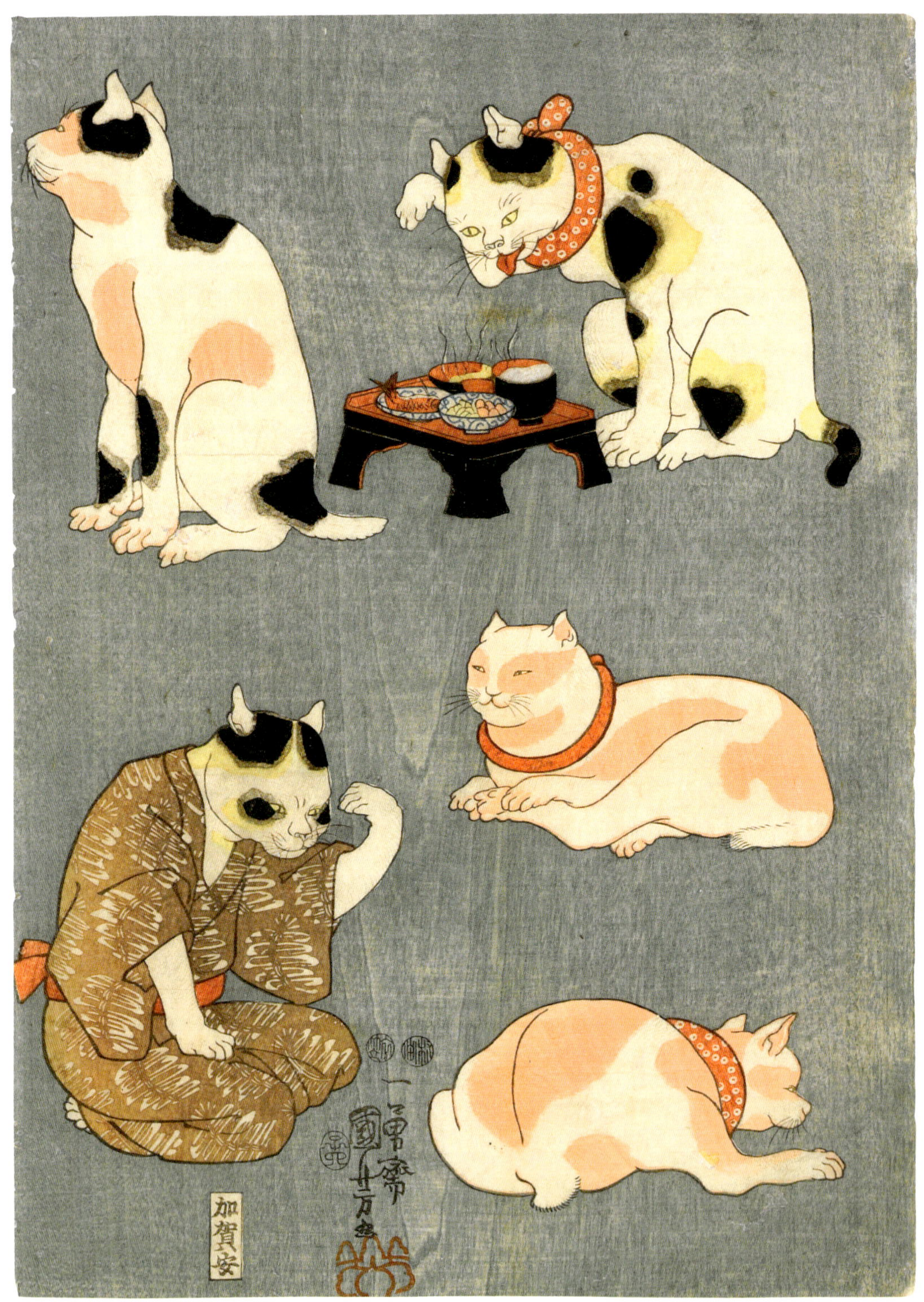

加賀安

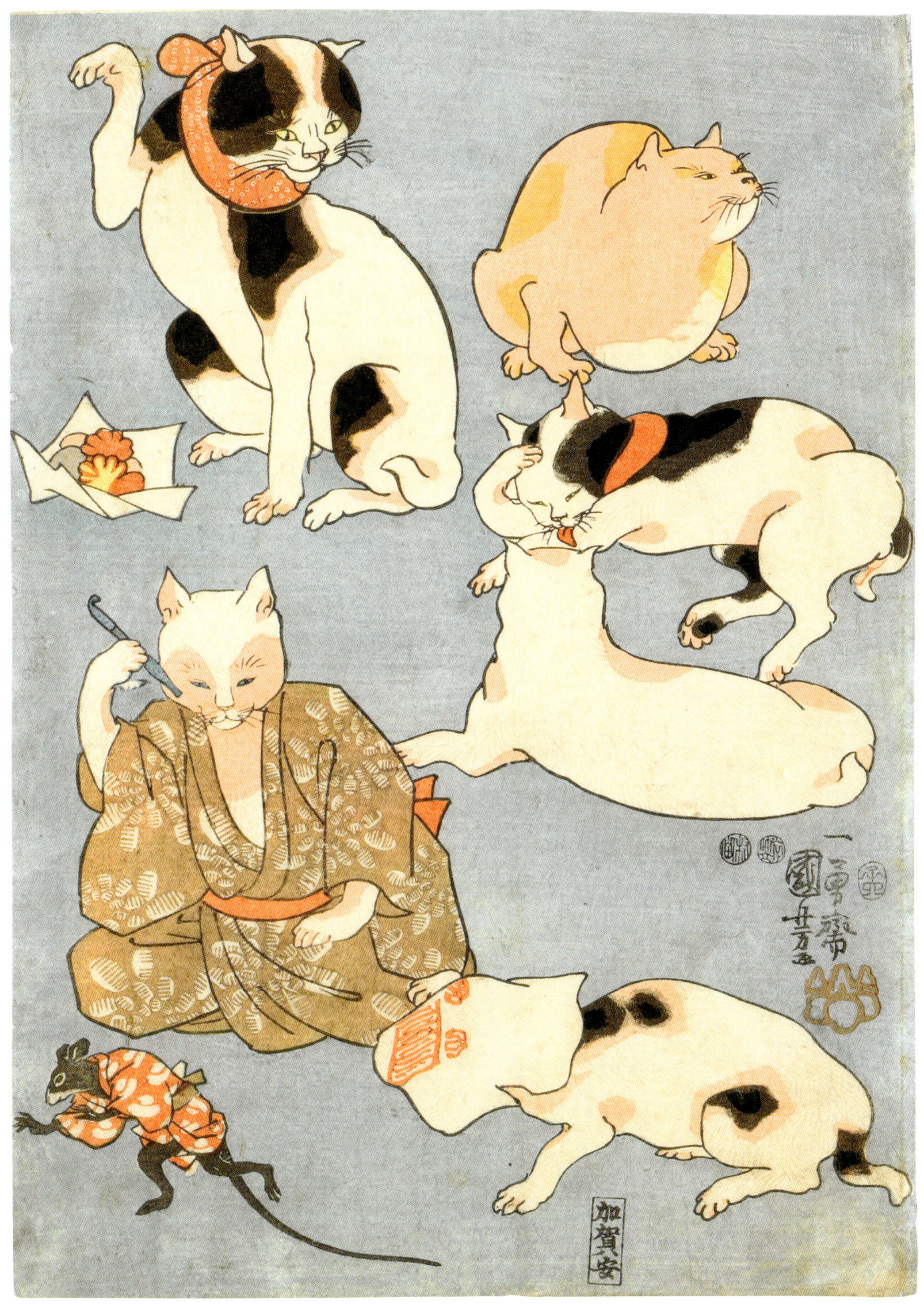

53 其まゝ地口猫飼好五十三疋 そのままじぐち みょうかいこうごじゅうさんびき

　江戸と京を結ぶ東海道。その53の宿場と猫の世界を、駄洒落で引っ掛けた作品。実際には起点の日本橋と終点の京を加えた55で、上・中・下の3枚に分かれている。

　それぞれ一つずつ拾ってみよう。「上」の最初の日本橋は、2本の鰹節にすり寄る猫。日本橋だから、「二本だし」。「中」の上段には張り子の猫がいるが、「はりこ」ならぬ鞠子の宿場。そして「下」の終点の京には「ぎゃう」とある。凄まじい形相の猫に捕まったねずみの悲鳴か、はたまた猫の雄叫びか。

　「うまいっ！」という駄洒落から、かなり苦しいものまでさまざまだが、ひとつとして同じような描写はなく、まるで国芳の猫の集大成のようだ。ただし、それは「リアル系猫」に限っての話。国芳のもう一つの本領が、次章以降に続々と登場する「人間系猫」なのである。

Cats for the 53 Stations of the Tokaido

The Tokaido was the route connecting Edo and Kyoto, and this work uses puns to link the 53 stations or post towns along the way with the world of cats. There are actually 55 stations including the departure point of Nihonbashi and end point Kyoto, divided into three prints.

Surveying each individually we find Nihonbashi in the right-hand print consisting of a cat edging up to two pieces of dried bonito. Thus the place name Nihonbashi becomes *nihon* (two) *dashi* (stock). In the top row of the middle section is a papier-mache (*hariko*) cat, a reference to the station at *Mariko*. Then in the left-hand print the final destination of Kyoto, or Kyo as it was known, is denoted by *gyo*. Is this the squeal of the mouse caught by a fearsome-looking feline, or the cat's throaty battle cry?

The puns range from clever to excruciating, but the renderings of cats are remarkable in their diversity, akin to a compilation of Kuniyoshi's cats. "Real cats" that is: his other specialty was the cats with human faces that appear in the following chapters.

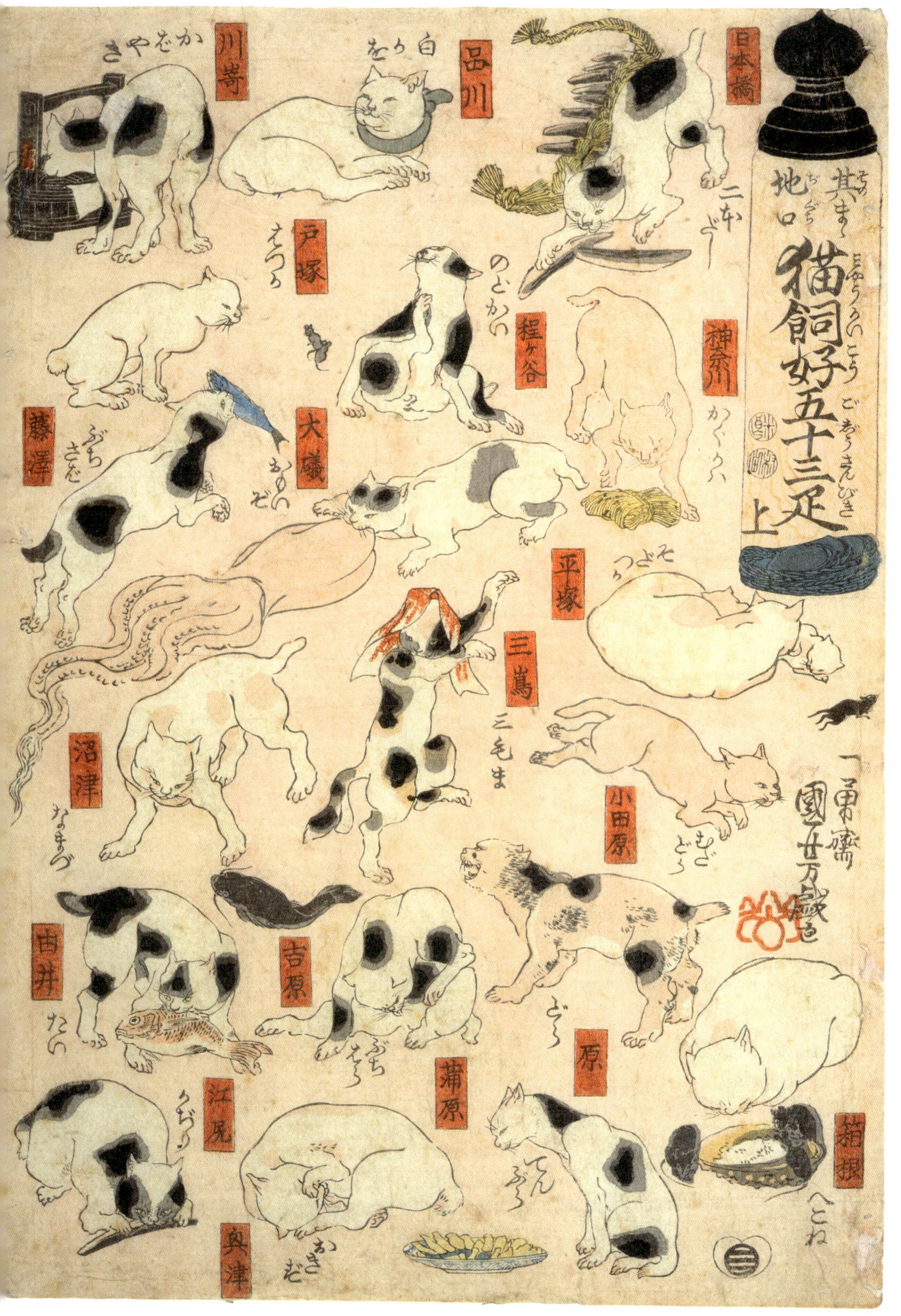

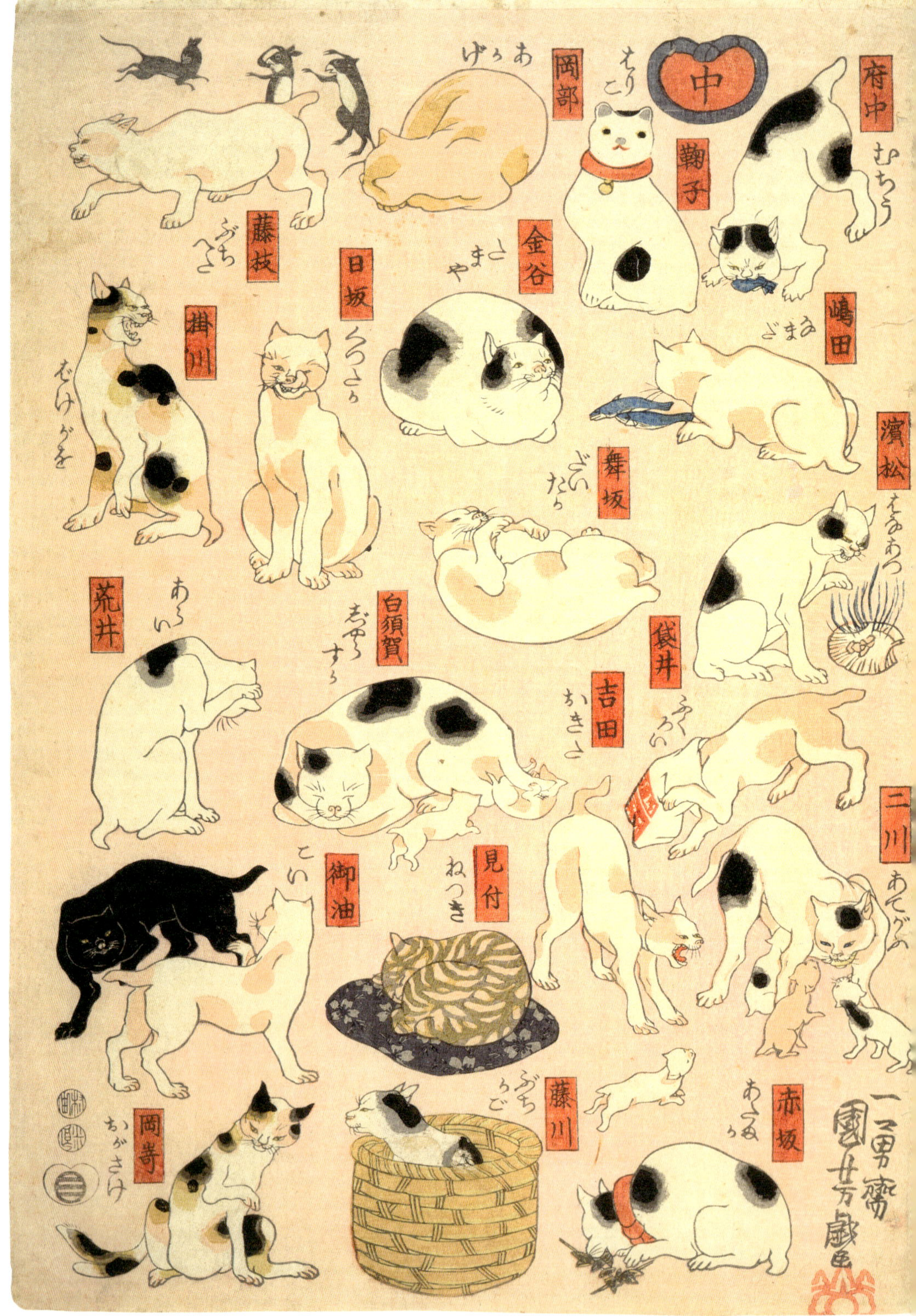
中
岡部
鞠子
府中
金谷
日坂
掛川
藤枝
嶋田
濱松
舞坂
荒井
白須賀
袋井
吉田
二川
御油
見付
藤川
赤坂
岡崎
一勇齋
國芳戯画

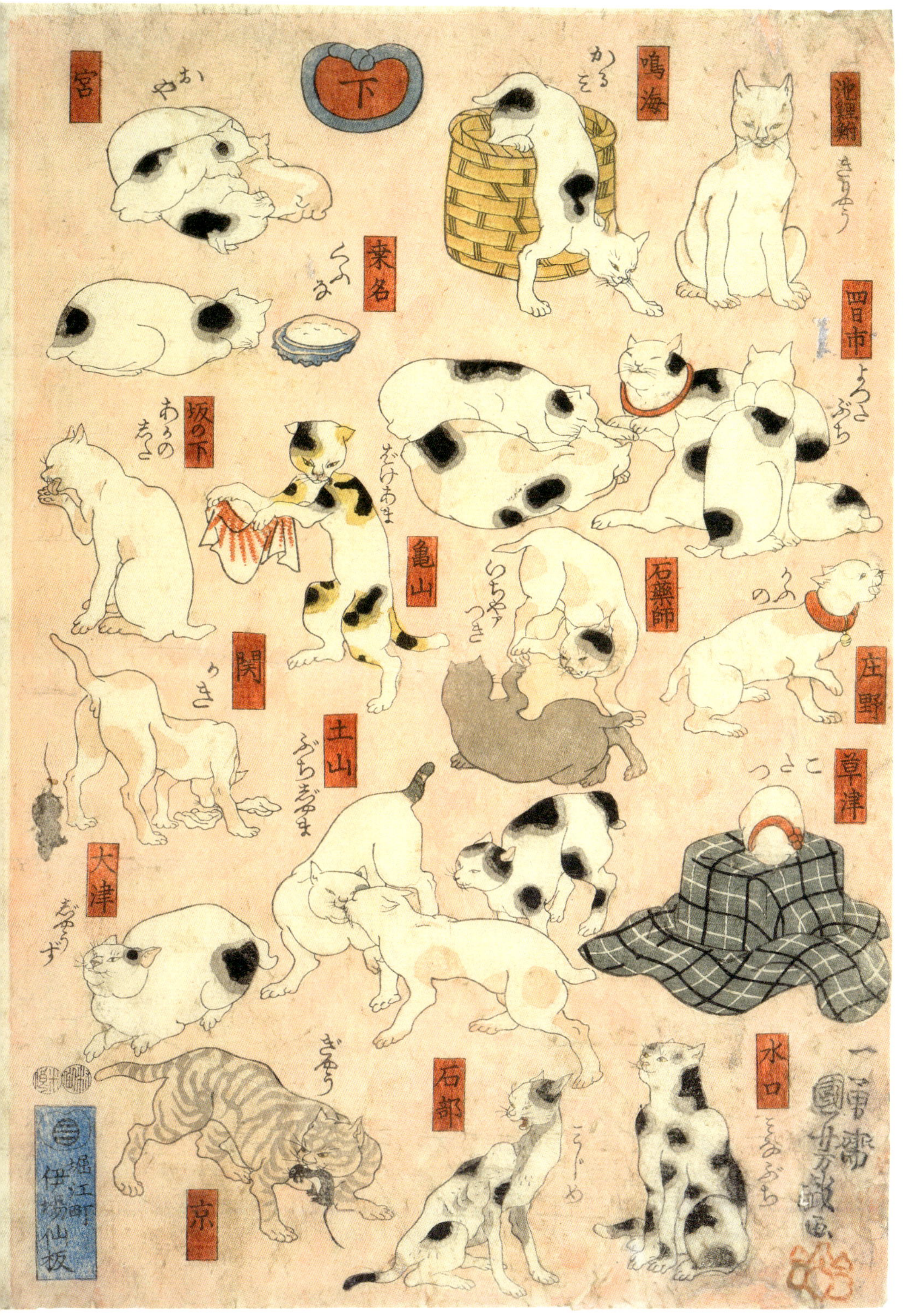

下
宮
やお
鳴海
かるそ
池鯉鮒
きりふう
桑名
らふも
四日市
よろさぶち
坂の下
あろのさ
おけあま
石薬師
亀山
いちやつき
のろ
庄野
関りさ
草津
つよこ
土山
ぶちぎま
大津
ぎやうず
水口
をろぶち
石部
うらめ
京
ぎやう
堀江町
伊場仙板
一勇斎國芳戯画

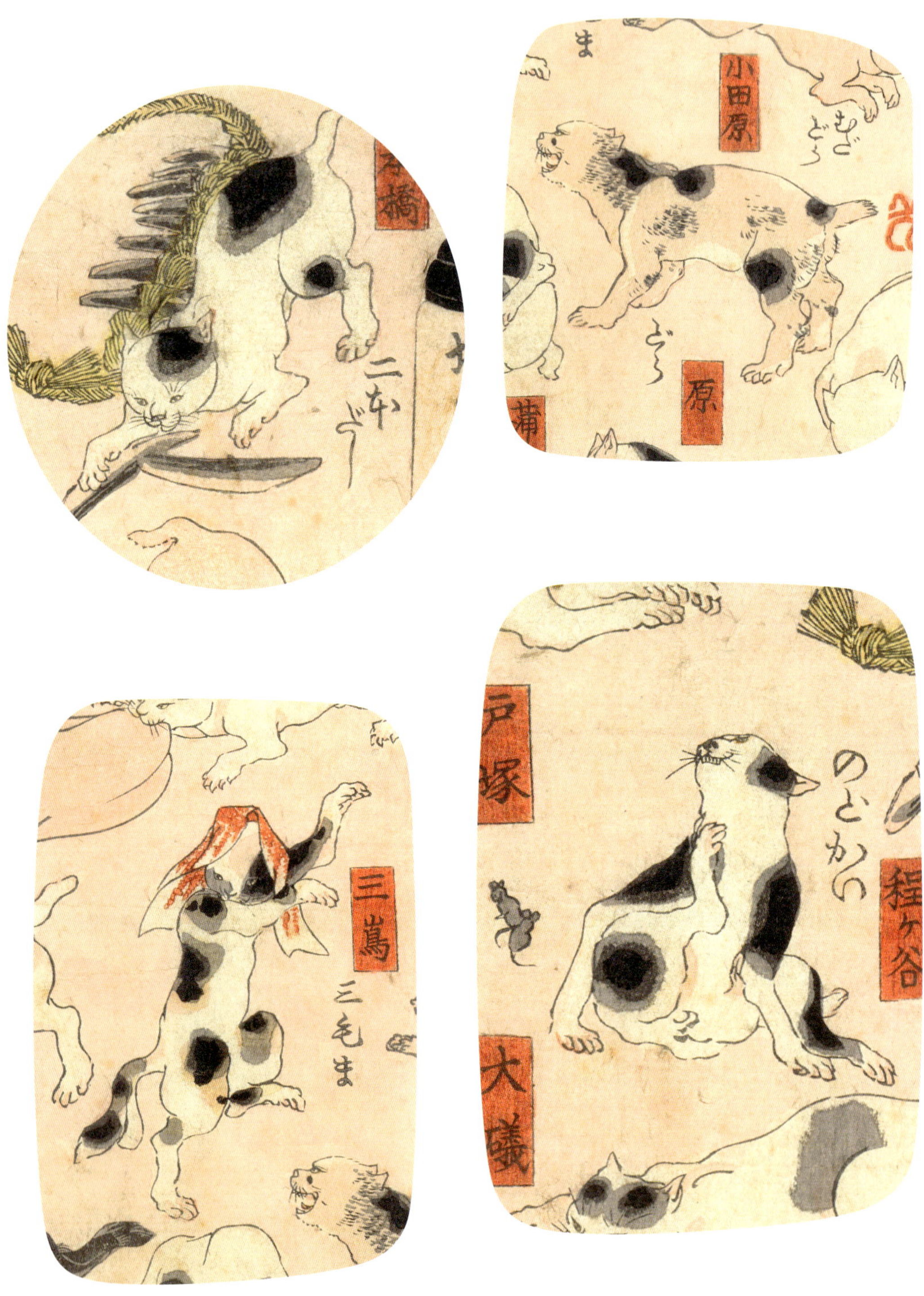
戸橋
二本どて

小田原
むさ
どう
どう
原
蒲

三嶌
こもま

戸塚
大磯
のとかの
程ヶ谷

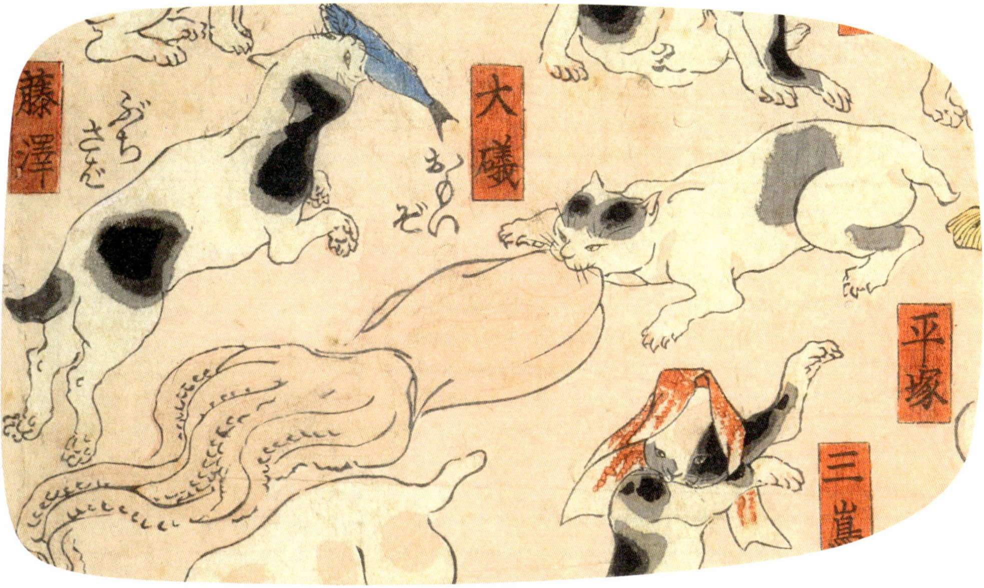

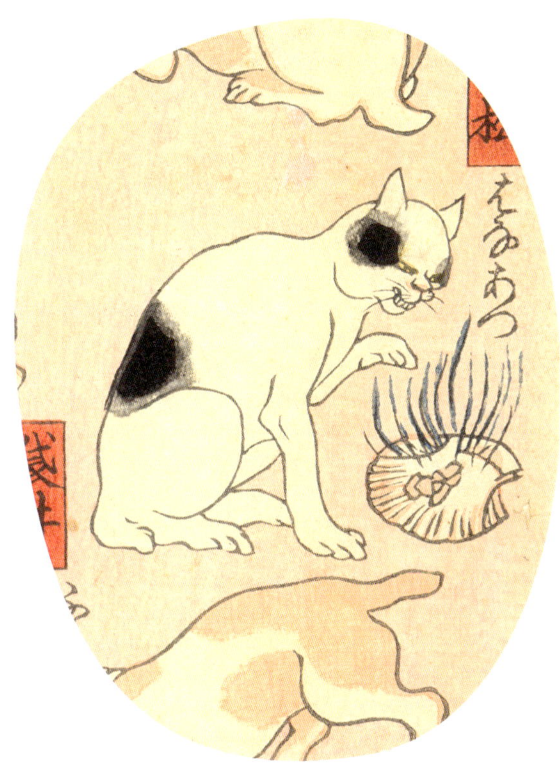

藤澤
ぶち
さご
大磯
おもひ
ぞ

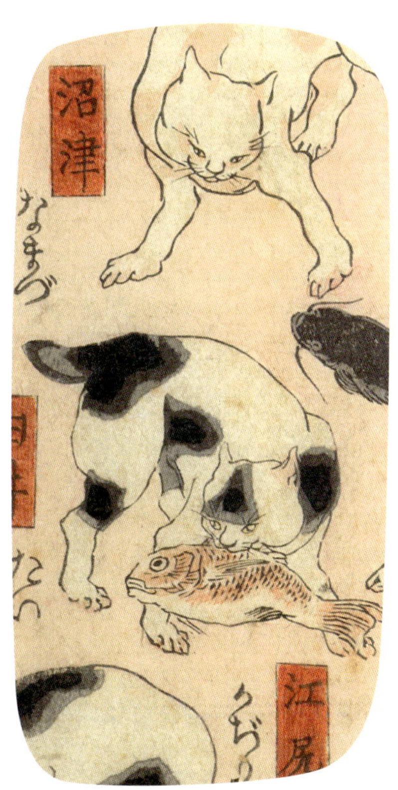

沼津
なまづ
江尻
ぐち

肉球をめぐって

　清少納言は『枕草子』で、猫の耳の中の複雑さについて書いている。たしかに猫と暮らしていると、人とは異なる体のありさまに驚いたり、不思議に感じたりすることがある。そのひとつが肉球。猫好きにとって、ぷくっとした肉球は欠かせないポイントである。肉球を押すと、ふだん収納されている爪が出てくるのが面白くて、つい遊んでしまうという飼い主の方も多いだろう。

　国芳の猫の描写は、現代の猫好きにとっても、かゆいところに手が届くようなもの。ところが不思議なことに、肉球の魅力を意識した描写が案外見られない。はっきり描かれたものは、《猫のけん》(71) や《猫のけいこ》(72) くらいだろうか。

　そんなことを考えながら、ふと、飼っていた猫のことを思い出した。以前は外と家を行き来していたものを、転居するのに合わせて完全な室内飼いにしたのだが、それからしばらくしてのこと。ガサガサで土色をしていた頃には想像もしなかった、透き通るようなピンク色の柔らかな肉球が出現して、それはそれは驚いた。「肉球好き」は現代人ならではの特権なのだろうか。

Paws for thought

In her *Pillow Book*, Sei Shonagon wrote of the complexity of the inside of a cat's ear. Living alongside cats, one can certainly be surprised and mystified at the ways in which they differ physically from humans. One such difference is the pads of their paws. To cat-lovers, those fleshy paws are an indispensable facet of a cat's charm. Many cat owners are doubtless fascinated by the way the claws, usually sheathed, emerge when the pad of the paw is pressed, and cannot resist playing with their pet's pads.

　Kuniyoshi's portrayals of cats do tickle the fancy of modern cat-lovers too. Intriguingly however, surprisingly few consciously focus on the appeal of the underside of the paws. *Cats Playing a Hand Game* (71) and *Cats Taking a Lesson* (72) are perhaps the only two in which the pads are clearly drawn.

　Pondering this, I was suddenly reminded of my own cat. Though previously he had come and gone between house and yard, on moving I decided to keep his entirely indoors. Some time after the move, much to my surprise these soft, translucent pink pads appeared, pads that were unimaginable when his paws were rough and dirty. Does this make the liking for the pads of a cat's paws an entirely modern privilege?

V

演出家国芳と千両役者ねこ、力を合わせる

Kuniyoshi as director
and cats as stars
join forces

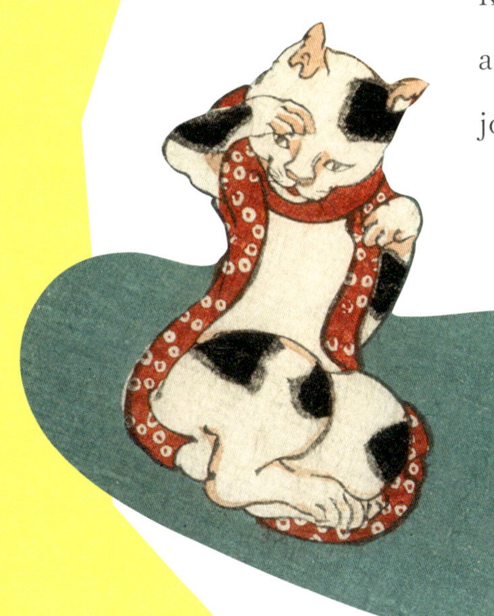

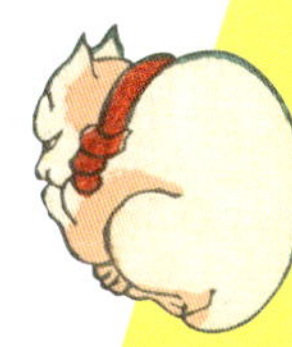

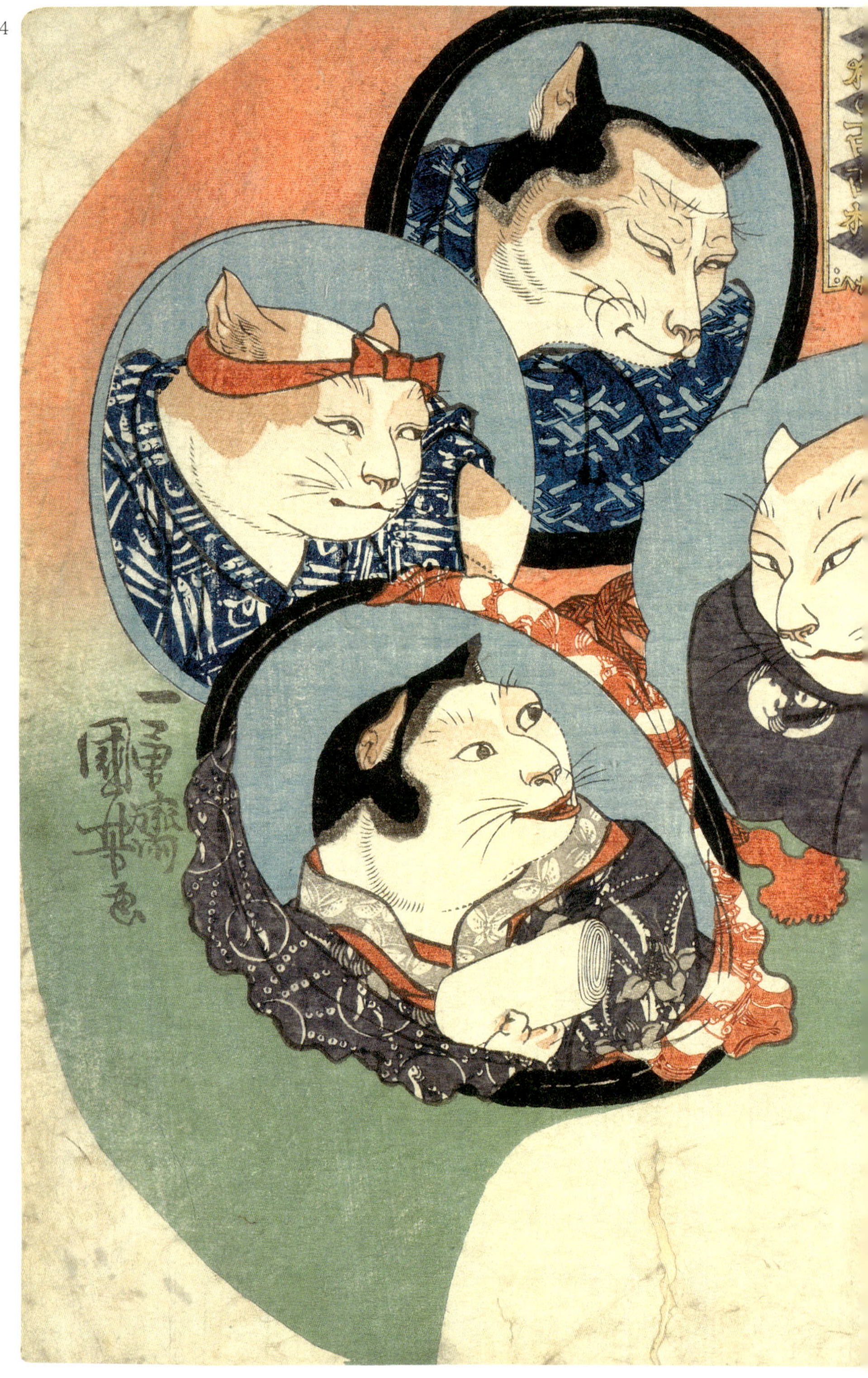

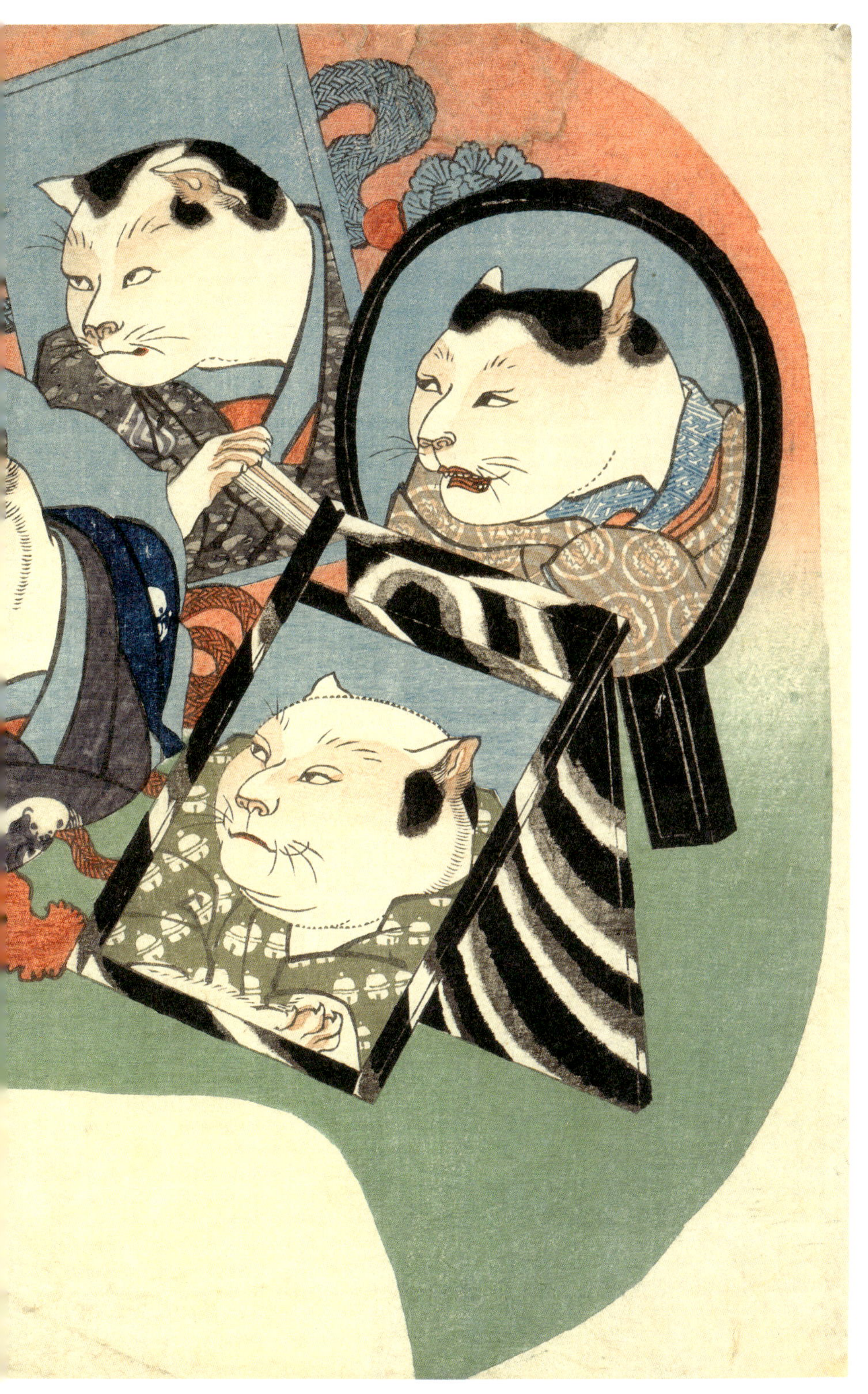

54 猫の百面相 ねこのひゃくめんそう

　猫の役者たちが演じるのは、「仮名手本忠臣蔵」の七段目。国芳は、猫のスターたちを綺羅星のごとく一枚の団扇絵に登場させた。含みのある表情、多弁なポーズなど、全員が際立ったキャラクターとさすがの貫禄を見せつける。主役はもちろん中央の大星由良之助。そこに役者たちの視線が集まるように配置され、次々に展開する物語をわくわくして見ているような気分になる。現代の大衆的な芝居のポスターを見たことでもあるのかと疑いたくなるような、うまい作りだ。

One Hundred Faces of Cats

A company of cat actors are performing the seventh act of the kabuki play *Kanadehon Chushingura*, feline stars arrayed on a fan like their cosmic equivalent. All meaningful expressions and eloquent poses, they exhibit remarkable character, and the dignified mien one would expect. The main role of course is that of Oboshi Yuranosuke in the center, positioned so that the other actors' eyes converge upon him, giving the viewer the sensation of watching a rapidly unfolding, thrilling story. A cleverly constructed work that could almost be mistaken for a poster for a popular present-day play.

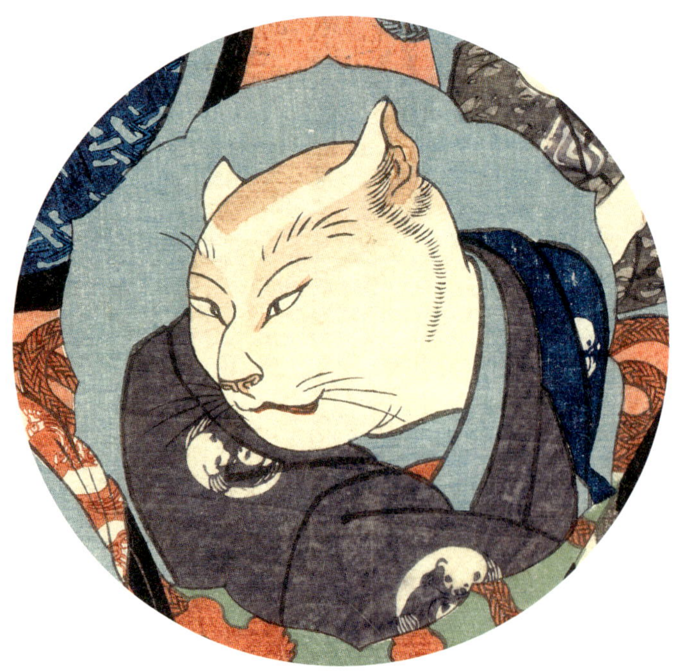

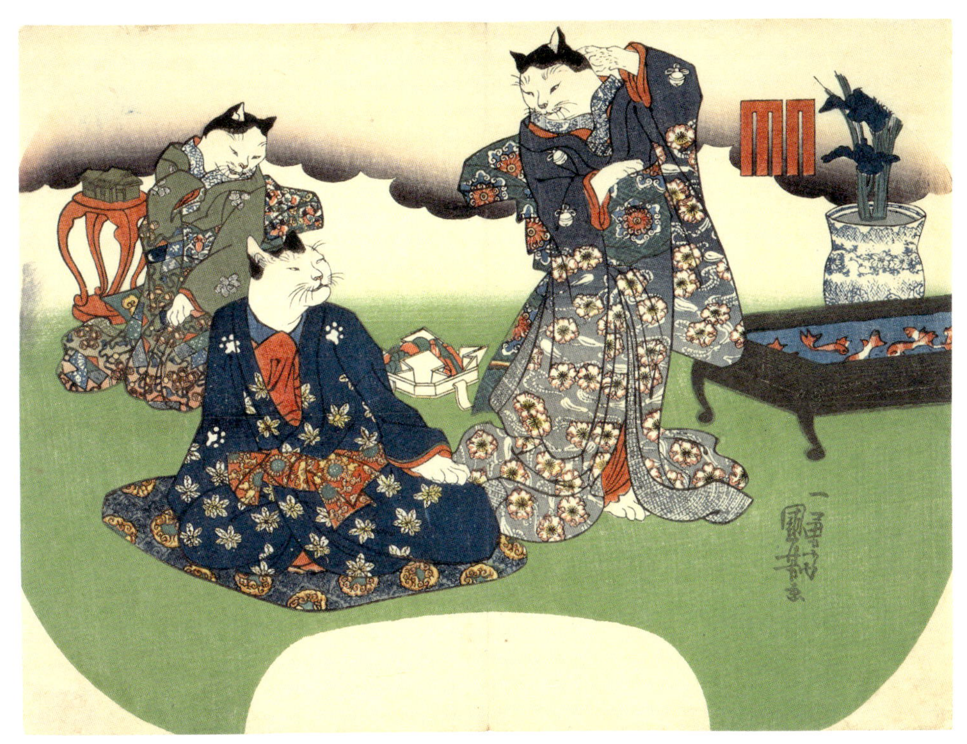

55 猫の源氏 賢木 ねこのげんじ さかき

　やけに雅びである。というのも、猫たちが演じているのは『源氏物語』。右上に描かれているのは、香道の遊び、源氏香のしるし。「賢木」の段であることを示している。

　力強く演じている「流行猫の戯」（56,57）と比べてみてほしい。立ち姿も座る姿もしなやかで優美である。表情もどことなく貴族然としていて、気どっている。着物の文様も見どころ。小判、鈴、猫の足跡もある。猫たちが室内でたくさんの金魚を飼っているのも、見逃せないところだ。

Cat Version of the Tale of Genji: Sakaki

Remarkable in its refinement, but then this is *The Tale of Genji*. Depicted at the upper right is a *Genjiko* pattern symbolizing a combination of incense fragrances, thus identifying this as the chapter "Sakaki."

In stark contrast to the robust performances in *Fashionable Cat Games* (56,57), here both sitting and standing cats are graceful and elegant, even their facial expressions haughtily aristocratic. The kimono with their gold coin, bell, and cat footprint patterns are a further highlight. And note that cache of juicy goldfish being kept as pets.

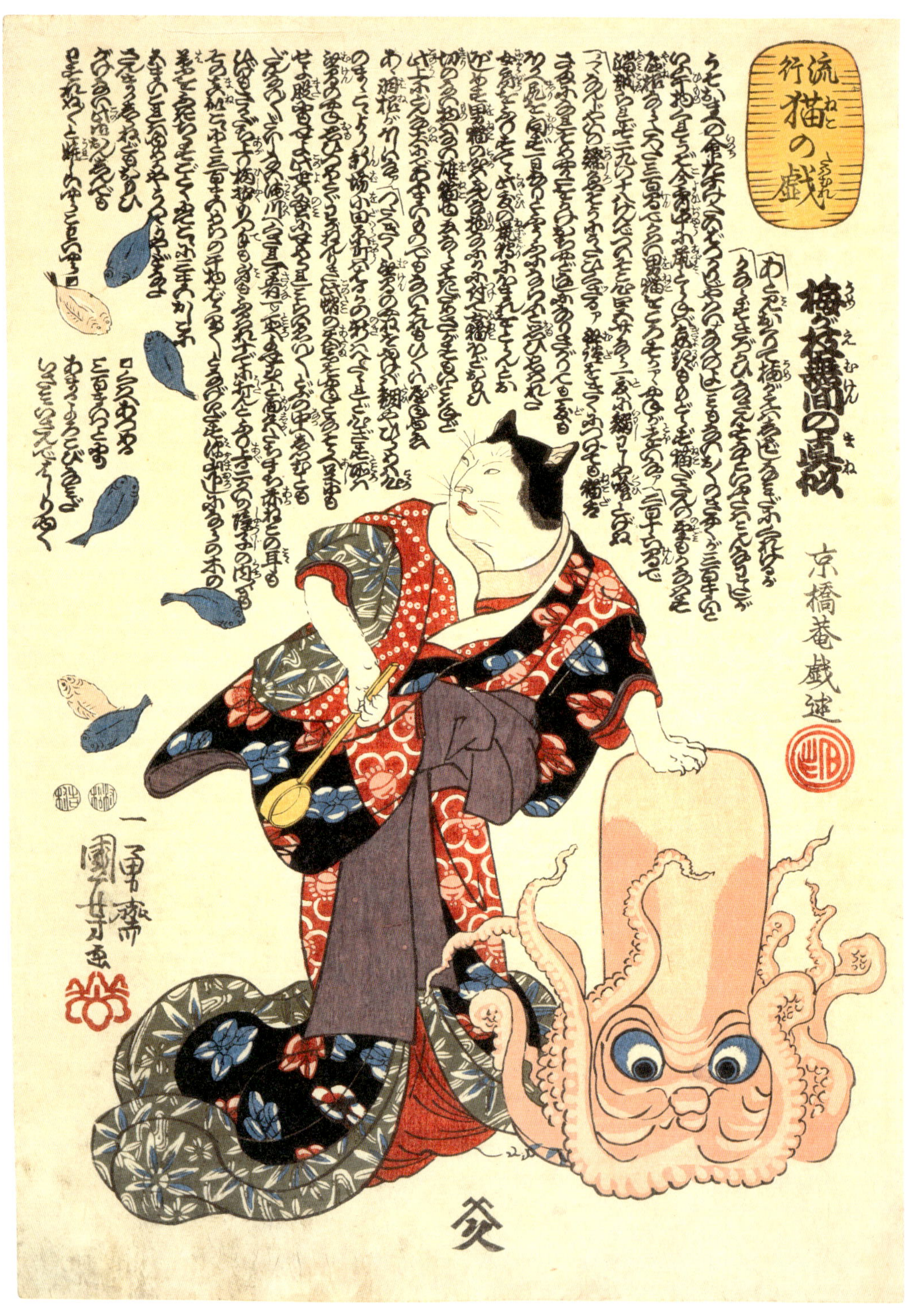

56 流行猫の戯 梅が枝無間の真似

りゅうこうねこのたわむれ　うめがえむけんのまね

　有名な演目の見せ場を猫が演じるシリーズ「流行猫の戯」。この一枚は歌舞伎「ひらがな盛衰記」から。勘当された夫を養うため、遊女梅が枝となった千鳥。夫が出陣するには、質に入れた鎧を取り戻さなければならない。さて、遠州観音寺の「無間の鐘」は、つけば富を得られるが、来世は無間地獄に堕ちるという。困った梅が枝は必死の思いで、手水鉢を鐘に見立てて柄杓で打つ。すると三百両の小判が降ってくる……。

　という話なのだが、猫の世界では、「無間の屋根」を行けば鯛や平目は心のままだという。しかし遠いので、蛸の頭を屋根となぞらえ、柄杓で打ち鳴らしているというわけだ。降ってきたのは三百枚の魚の干物。「これは夢かやうつつかや」と、くわえ集めて、喜び勇んで走り行く梅が枝であった。

Fashionable Cat Games:
Parody of Umegae Striking the Bell of Limitless [Hell]

The *Fashionable Cat Games* series features cats performing highlights from famous plays; this print is from the kabuki *Hiragana Seisuiki* (The Battles of Genji and Heike). To support her disinherited husband, Chidori reinvents herself as the courtesan Umegae. She must retrieve her husband's pawned armor so he can depart for battle. Now it is said that striking the "limitless bell" (*muken no kane*) at the Kannonji temple in Enshu brings wealth, but at the price of limitless hell in the next life. In despair, the desperate Umegae substitutes a water jar for the bell and hits it with a ladle. The result is a shower of 300 gold coins...

So the tale goes, but in the feline world, it is said a cat can traverse the "*muken no yane* (roof)" and feast on all the sea bream, flounder and other treats its heart desires. Distance however has prompted this cat to substitute an octopus's head for the roof, and hit it with a ladle, making it cry out. The shower consists of 300 dried fish, and emboldened by joy and wondering if it is a real or all a dream, this Umegae snatches the fish up in her mouth and runs off.

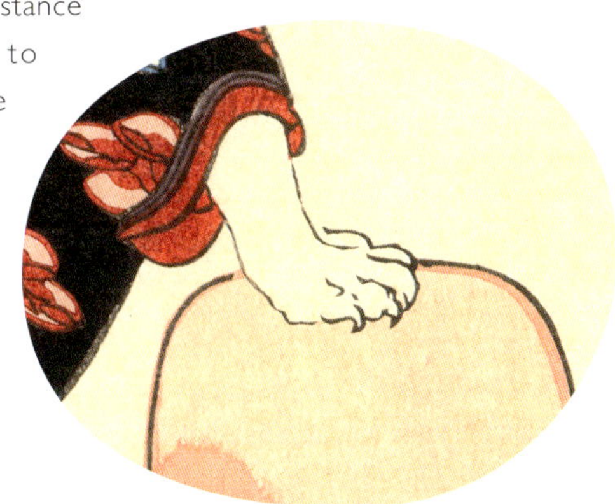

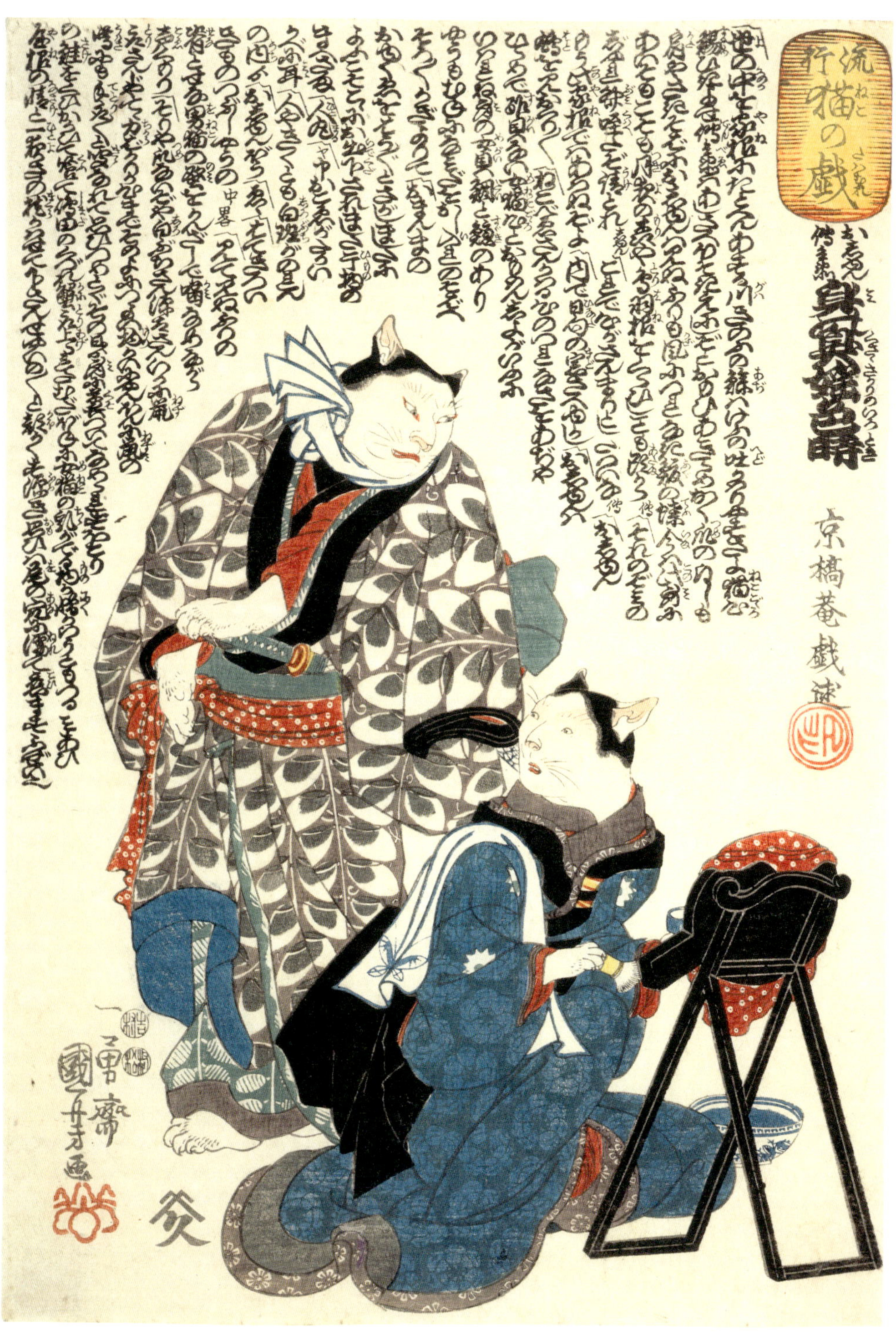

57 流行猫の戯 おしゆん伝兵衛 身の臭婬色時

りゅうこうねこのたわむれ おしゅんでんべえ みのくささ さかりのいろどき

前の図と同じシリーズで、歌舞伎「其噂桜色時（そのうわささくらのいろどき）」のパロディー。むっくりとしたオス猫の手（前足）に、ちんまりとしたメス猫の手を見ただけでもおかしい。

おしゅんは、屋根の上で逢瀬を重ねた伝兵衛と、理由あって別れることに。伝兵衛に縁切りの手紙を渡されて、おしゅん「これで心がさんまりとしたわいな（これで心がさっぱりとしたわいな）」。伝兵衛「おしゅん、もうこの屋根では会わぬぞよ（おしゅん、もうこの世では会わぬぞよ）」。

愛想尽かしをしたのはおしゅんだが、それは彼女の苦渋の決断。かつて仕えた主君を助けるためだった。おしゅんは、その後、源太という力士に討たれてしまう。左のオス猫は、その源太。しかし、彼も非情なわけではなく、主君の身替わりになろうというおしゅんの心を察したのである。

Fashionable Cat Games: Oshun and Denbei

A parody of the kabuki play Sono uwasa sakura no irodoki from the same series as the previous illustration. The sight of the male cat's fleshy front paw and the female's dainty mitt is funny enough, let alone the rest of it.

A clandestine rooftop rendezvous finishes in separation, Oshun being handed a letter by Denbei ending their affair, to which Oshun replies, "This eases my heart." Denbei then says, "Oshun, I'll never meet you on this roof (i.e. in this life) again."

It is Oshun who made the bitter decision to end their relationship, in order to save the lord she once served. Later on, she is killed by a samurai called Genta (the male cat on the left), not, however, because he too is cold-hearted, but rather, has read Oshun's mind, and her desire to sacrifice herself for the lord.

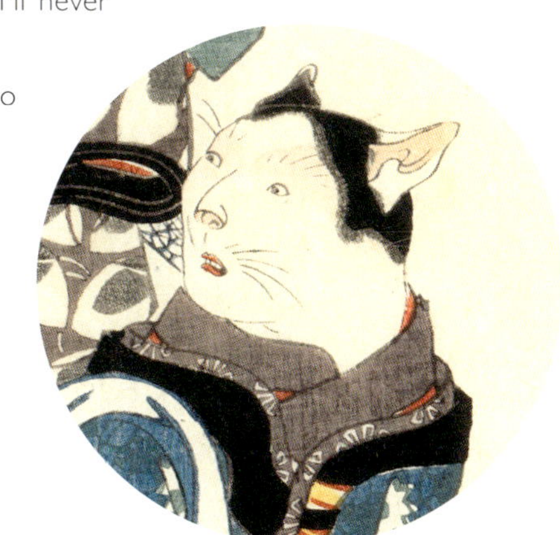

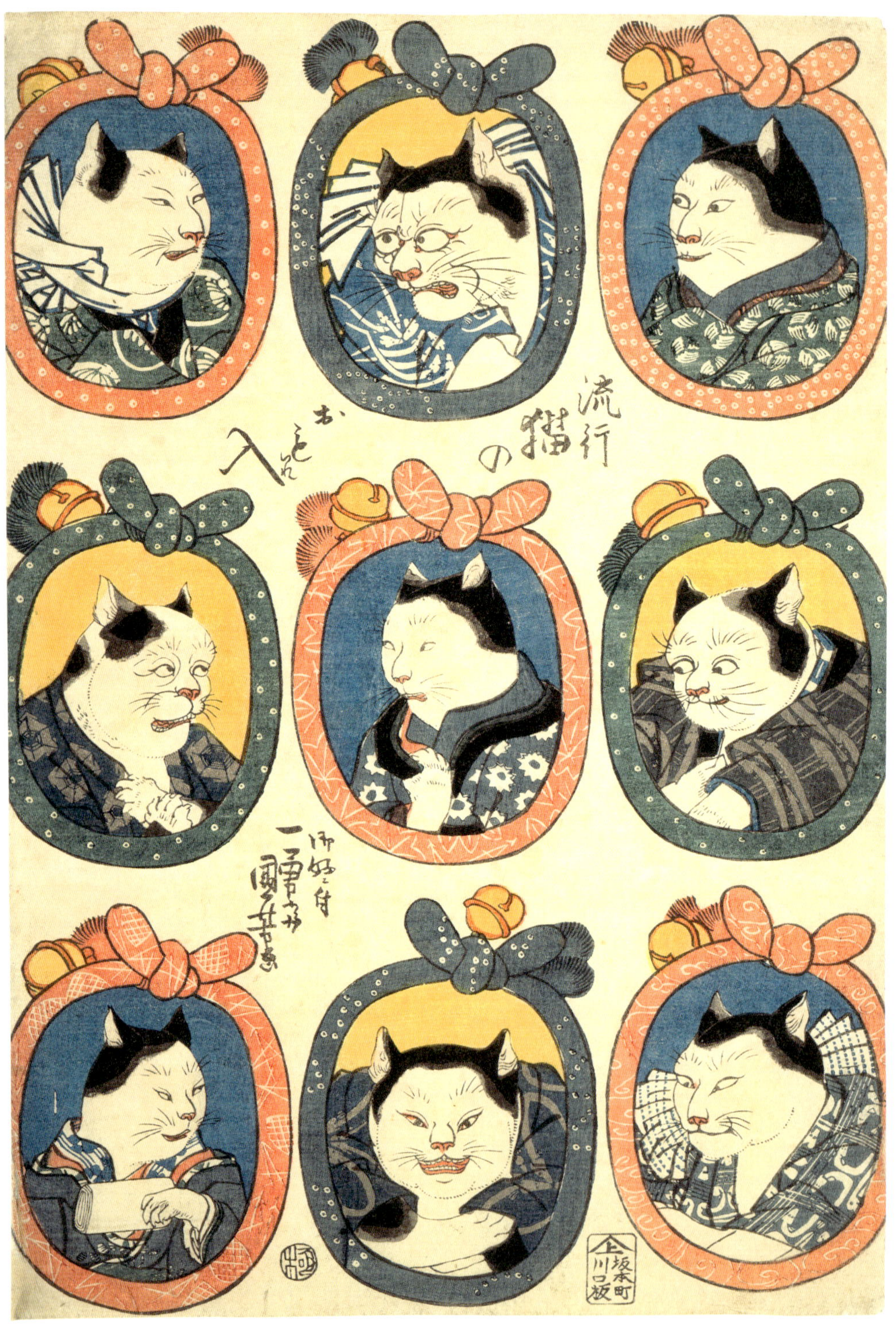

流行猫の
おもちゃ入れ
御好に付
一勇斎
国芳戯画
坂本町
川口板

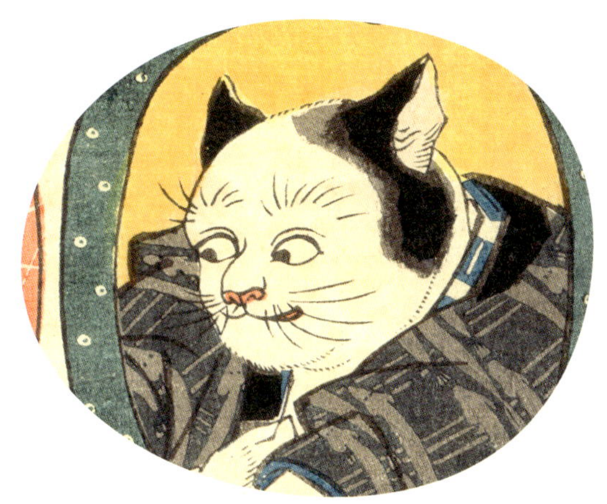

58 流行猫のおも入 <ruby>りゅうこうねこのおもいれ</ruby>

　鈴の付いた首輪の中に役者たちの似顔絵。素朴な色づかいだが、それがかえってほのかな愛らしさを醸し出す。タイトルにある「おも入」は芝居の言葉で、表情やポーズで心模様を表現すること。なるほど、それぞれの心の奥底まで滲み出ているようだ。

　もちろん、実在の歌舞伎役者の猫版で、それぞれが誰なのかも推定されている。国芳の猫には、本物の猫を写したリアル系と、この作品のように人間の姿かたちを合成した人間系があるが、ここまで違和感なく感情豊かに、そして猫としての性格も失わずに表現されていると、ふと、人と猫の顔かたちの違いとは何なのかと考えさせられる。

Fashionable Cats Doing Mime Performances
(Ryuko neko no omoire)

The subdued tones in these actor caricatures in collar and bell frames conversely adds to their charm. *Omoire* is a theatrical term meaning to show one's state of mind through facial expressions and poses, and indeed each cat seems to have truly taken its role to heart.

These are of course feline versions of actual kabuki actors, and there would have been much speculation about the identity of each. Kuniyoshi produced cats resembling the genuine article, and human-cat syntheses of the type shown here, but when they are rendered with so much feeling, in a manner not at all jarring and without losing their feline character, one does begin to wonder what the difference between the faces of men and cats might actually be.

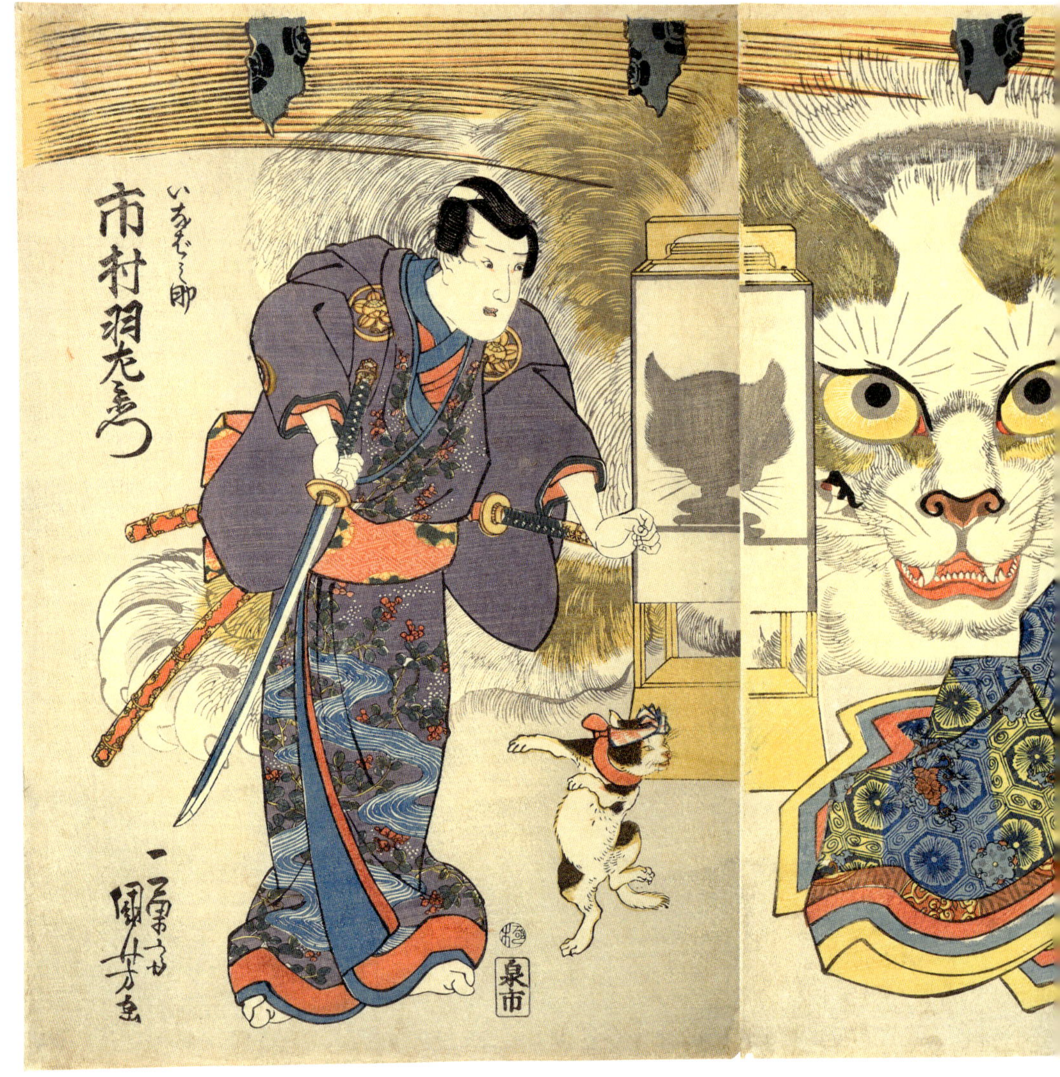

59 五拾三次之内　岡崎の場　ごじゅうさんつぎのうち　おかざきのば
60 古幸猫のよふくハい　ふるねこのようかい

　擬人化された猫が役者を演じるのではなく、実際にストーリーに猫が登場する演目がある。この《五拾三次之内　岡崎の場》と《古幸猫のよふくハい》は、「梅初春_{うめのはる}五十三駅_{ごじゅうさんつぎ}」など、複数の演目で上演された岡崎の場面を描いたもの。「梅初春五十三駅」は東海道を江戸へと向かう人々の話で、色々なエピソードがちりばめられた長い物語だが、猫が出てくるこの場面は、実はかなり恐ろしい話である。

　舞台は、岡崎の古寺。そこへ一夜の宿を求めた旅の一行だが、一人は猫の精霊に食

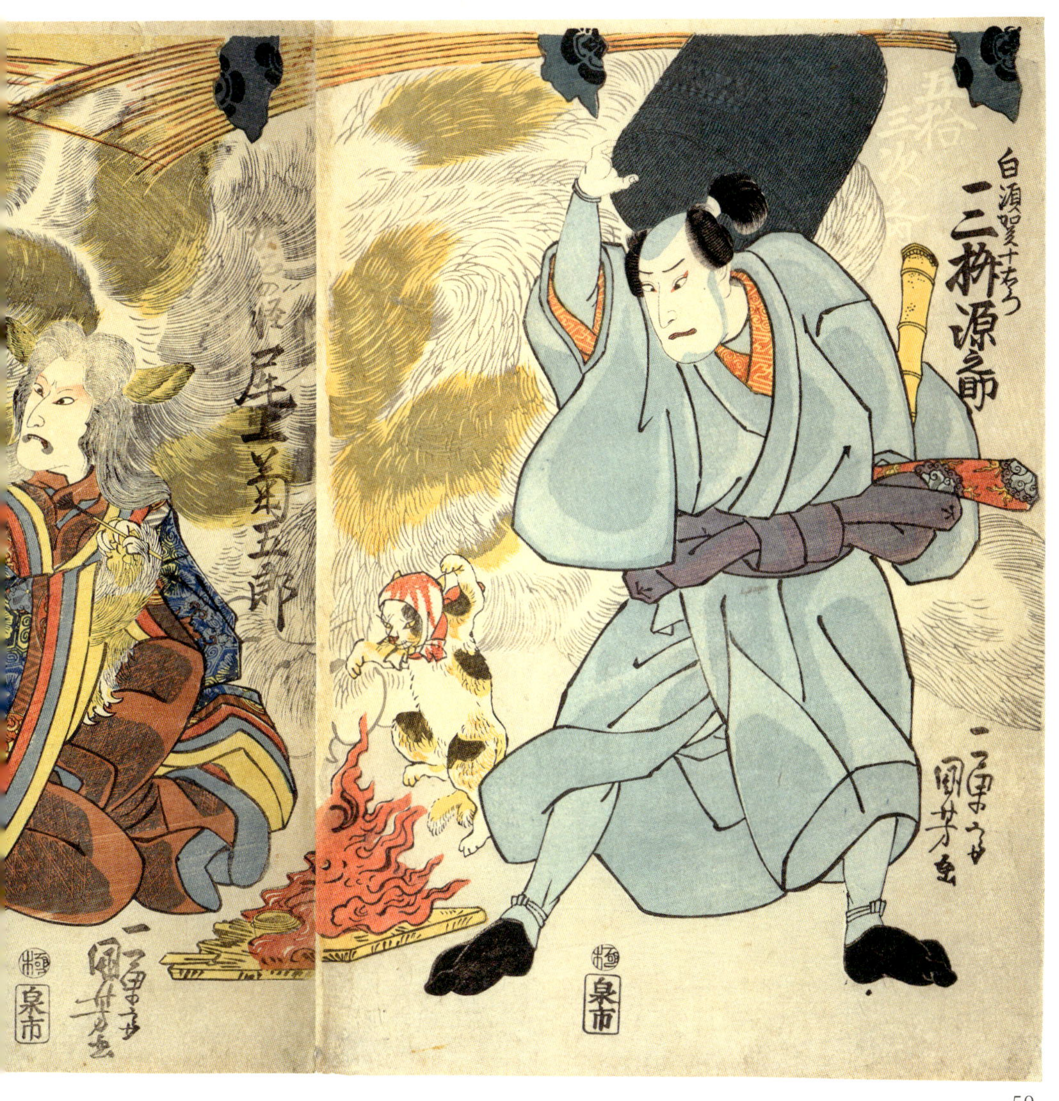

　い殺され、一人は猫の精霊と合体した死霊の怨念により命を落としてしまうという話である。描かれているのは、老婆に化けた猫の精霊が歌うと、飼い猫たち、すなわち化け猫たちが怪しく踊り出すという場面。

　踊る猫は、舞台では人形が使われたりもしたが、国芳の絵の中で演じているのは、どう見ても本物の猫たちである。懸命に踊る姿は、当時この絵を手にした人たちにも、破格の感動を与えたにちがいない。たとえ尾が二つに裂けた妖怪猫でも、その姿はあまりに愛らしい。

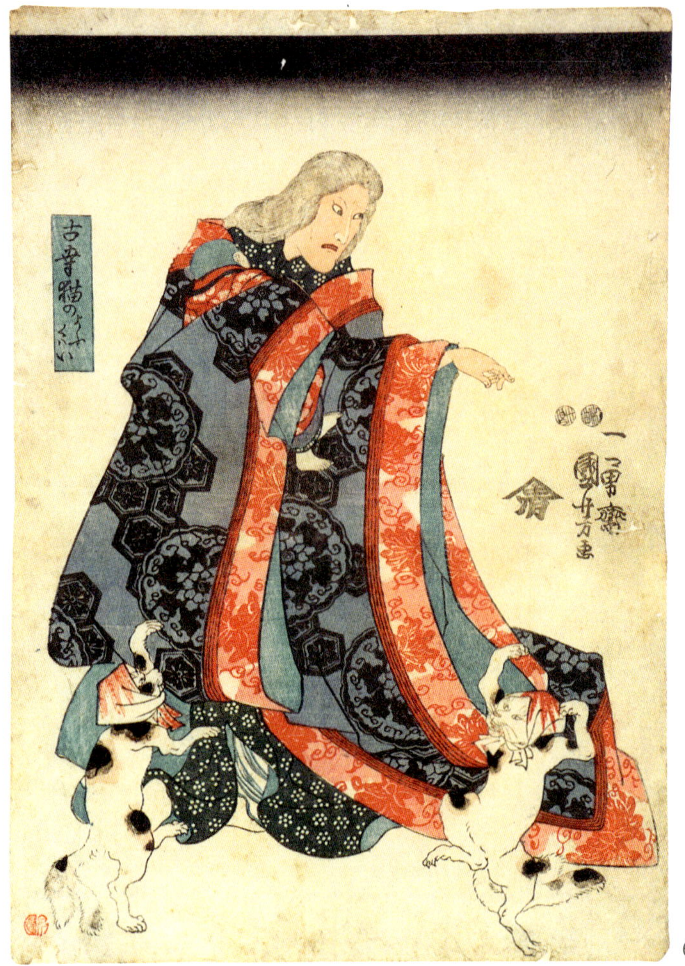

60

59 Scene from the 53 Stations of the Tokaido: Okazaki
60 *Furu neko no youkai*

There are plays in which cats actually feature in the plot, as opposed to anthropomorphized cats playing actors. These prints portray Okazaki scenes of the sort found in several plays such as *The Fifty-three Stations,* an epic and eventful tale of travelers on the Tokaido to Edo. This cat scene is actually a rather nasty example. The setting is an old temple in Okazaki. The story concerns a traveling party seeking accommodation for the night, only for one person to be devoured by a cat spirit, and another to lose their life as the result of a grudge held by a ghost whose form has joined with that of the cat spirit. The print depicts domestic cats, or rather, demonic cats, starting to dance in a suspect manner with the singing of the cat spirit taking the shape of an old woman.

On stage puppets were also used for the dancing cats, but in Kuniyoshi's painting the roles do actually seem to be filled by real cats. The sight of their determined dancing would no doubt have struck those who saw this picture as highly unusual. Even the phantom cat with the torn tail looks quite adorable.

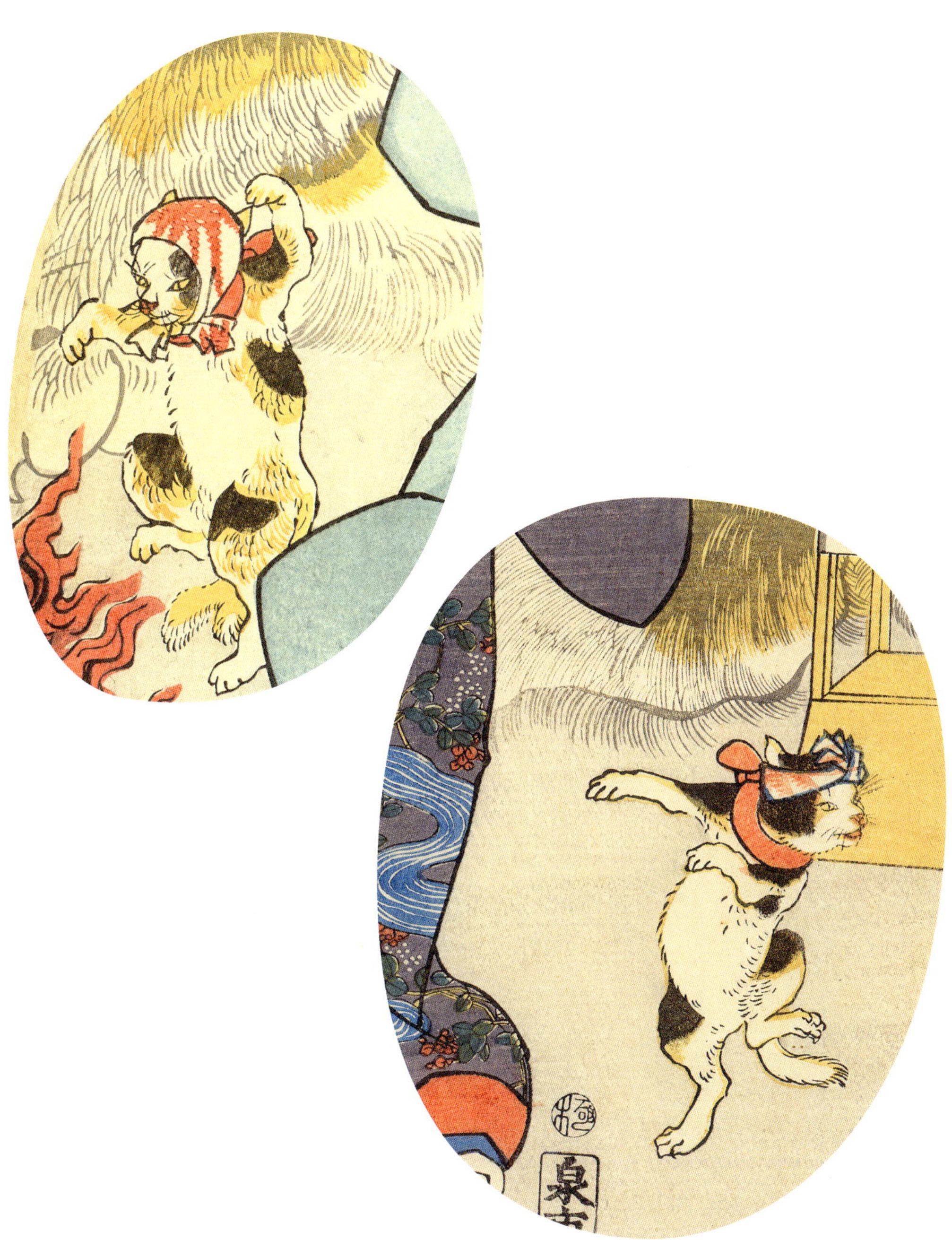

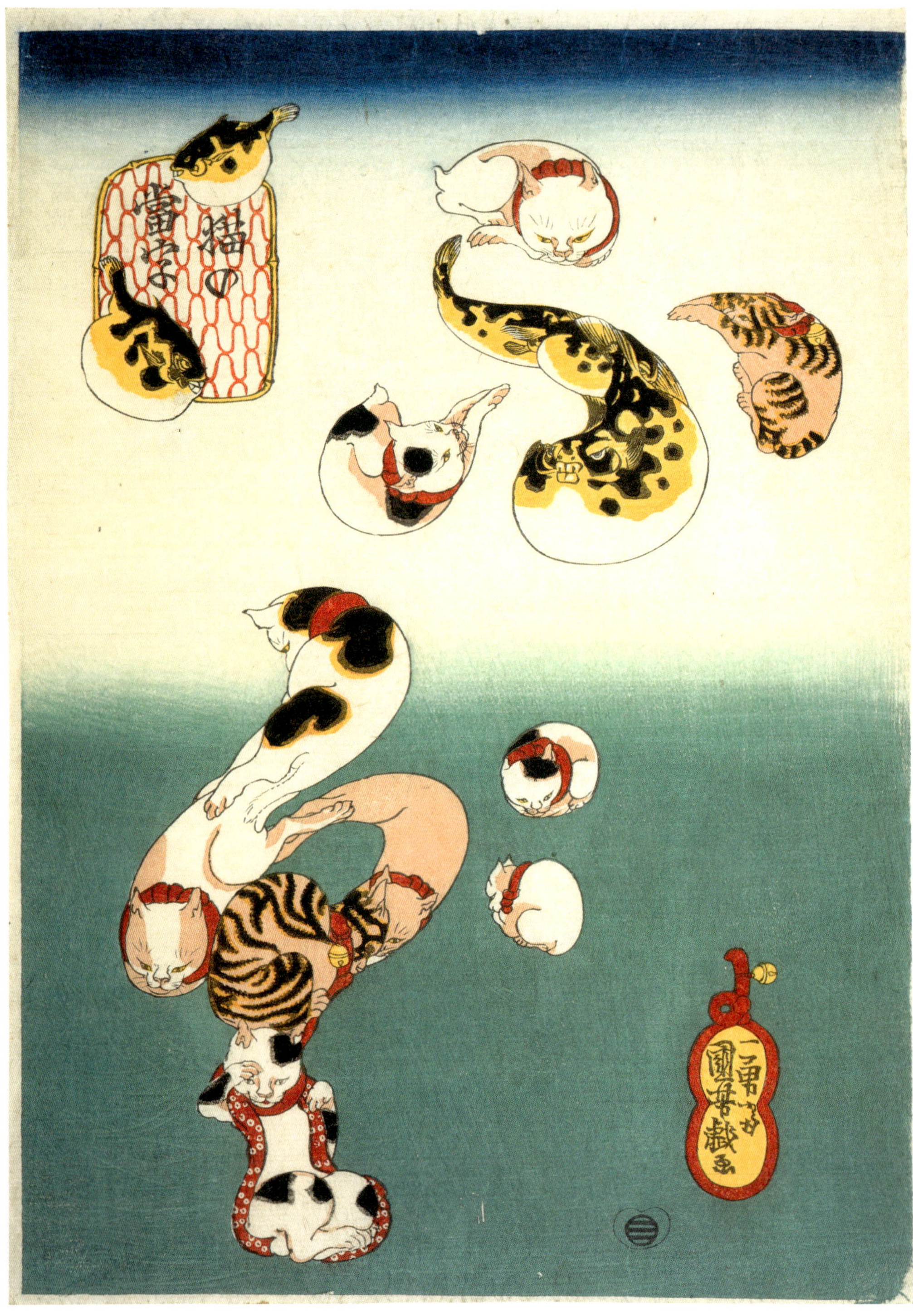

猫の當字
なまづ
一勇斎
國芳戯画

61 猫の当字 ふぐ　ねこのあてじ ふぐ

「猫の当字」というシリーズは、全部で5種類知られている。本書では、そのうちの4種類をご覧いただこう。そのおかしさは説明不要だが、それでもいくつか見逃せないところを紹介しようと思う。

　まずは「ふぐ」。すべてが猫の集団演技かと思いきや、「ふ」の真ん中の部分をなしているのは当のふぐ自身で、思いっきりふくれっ面。ふぐの左で前足をぴたりとくっつけて伸ばしている1匹や、「く（具）」の濁点のころっと身を丸めた2匹はもちろん、「く」の一番上を担当する1匹の、ひねり加減の後ろ姿もなかなか悩ましくて魅力的である。

Cat Letters: Pufferfish *(Neko no ateji: Fugu)*

There are five known prints in the Cat Letters series, of which four are included here. Their odd humor needs no explanation, but let us highlight a few unmissable points.

First, *Pufferfish.* An ensemble that appears to consist entirely of cats on closer inspection includes, forming the very middle of the *fu* of *fugu*, an actual fugu in all its puffy glory. The contorted rear view of the cat forming the top of the *ku (gu)*, not to mention of course the cat forming the left of the *fu* with its front paws stretched out tightly together, and the pair curled into the dots on the *ku* are enchanting, and appealing.

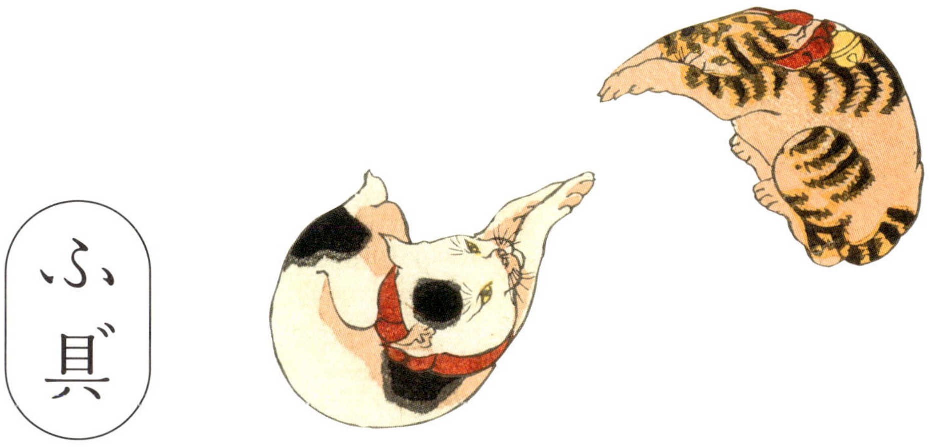

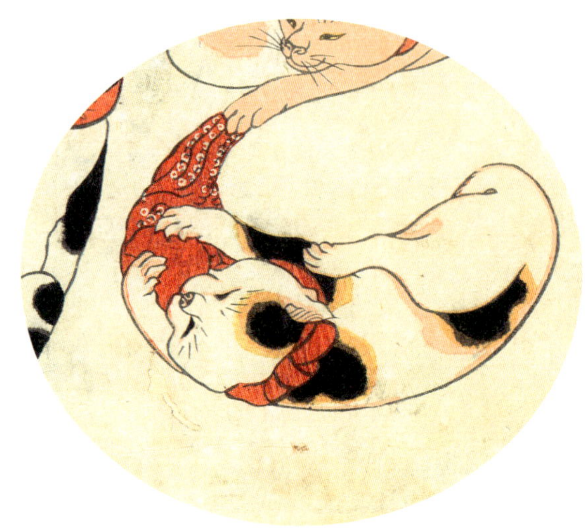

62 猫の当字 たこ ねこのあてじ たこ

　次に「たこ」。「た」の黒ぶち猫の内側に向いた後ろ足にも胸がきゅんとするが、随所で猫たちが蛸にむしゃぶりついているところがポイント。

Cat Letters: Octopus *(Neko no ateji: Tako)*

Next, *Octopus.* The inward-turning back legs of the black and white cat in the *ta* may tug at the heartstrings, but the main point here is the way the cats are entwined with octopuses.

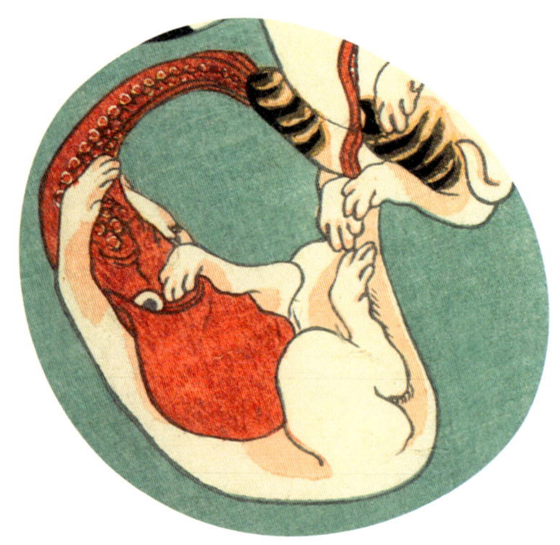

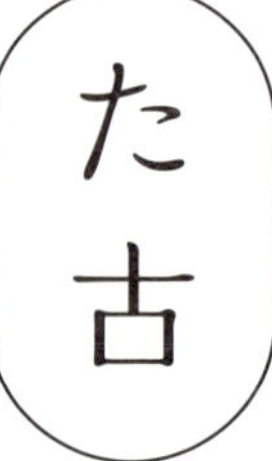

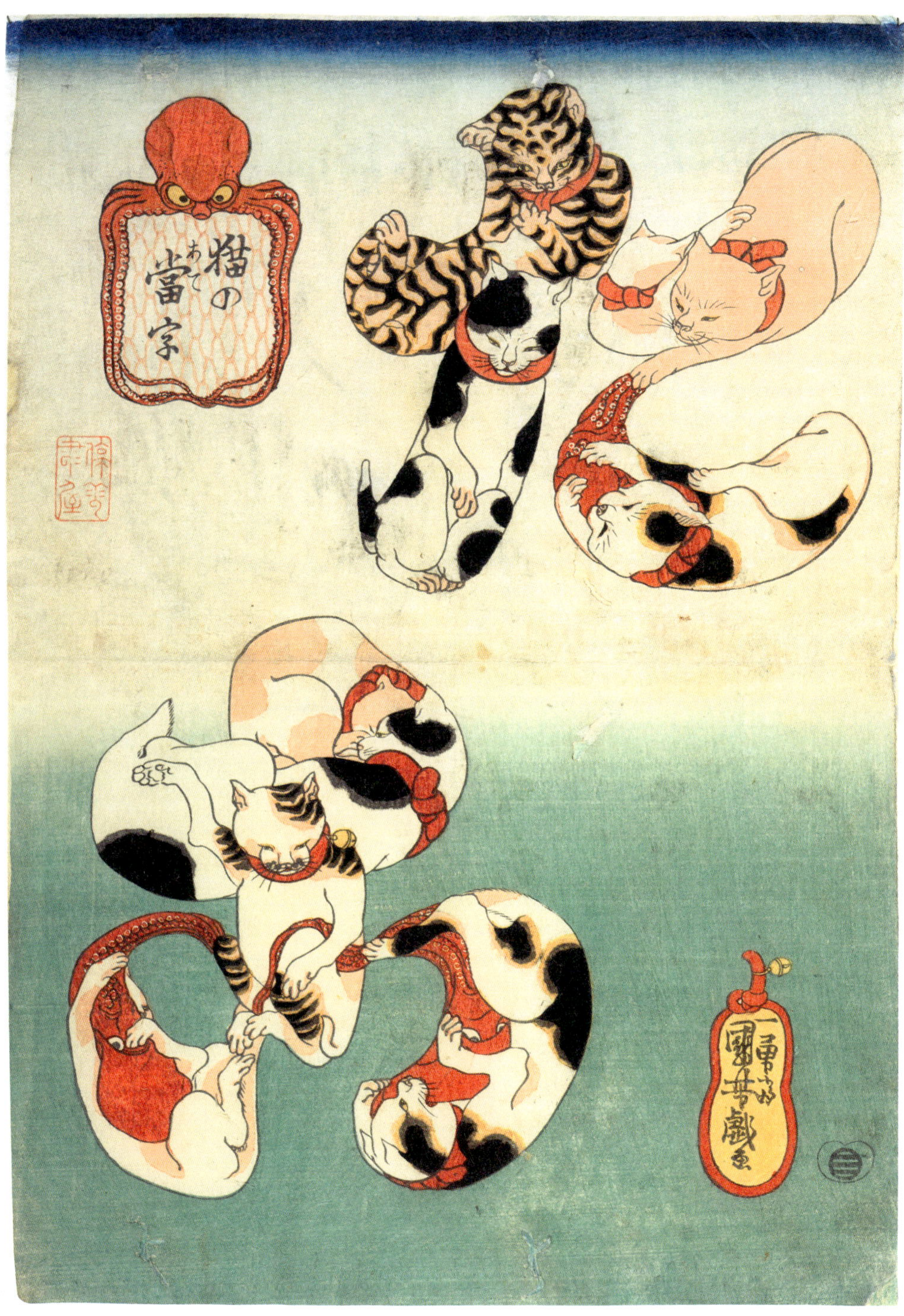

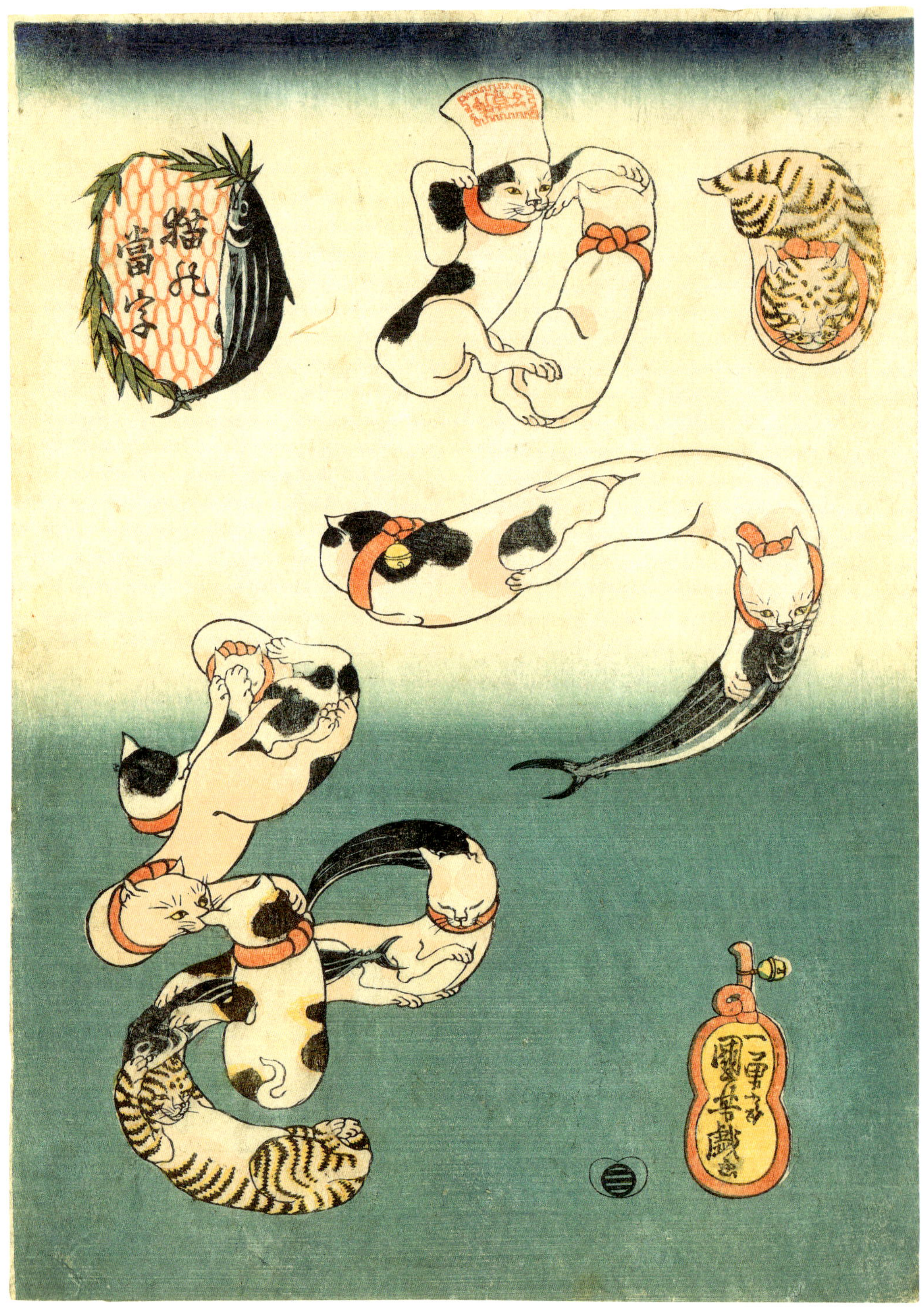
猫の当字
一勇斎國芳戯画

63　猫の当字 かつを ねこのあてじ かつお

　獲物に食いつく様子は「かつを」にも見られる。「つ」の字の先は、鰹で表されているからシャープである。また、この図で最も笑いを誘うのは、「か」を形づくる、かぶりものをした１匹。かぶっているのは「御菓子」と書かれた袋である。現代人にはコックさんのようにも見えて、それがまたかわいい。「猫に紙袋」という言葉もあるが、国芳は、猫にお菓子の袋をかぶせるのがよほど好きだったのだろう。26の作品からもそれがうかがえる。

Cat Letters: Bonito *(Neko no ateji: Katsuo)*

This grasping of prey can also be seen in *Bonito*. The tip of the character *tsu* is sharp because it is formed by a fish. Most certain to raise a smile here is the cat with the headgear helping to form the *ka*. That headgear consists of a bag with the word "sweets" written on it. To modern eyes the moggy resembles a chef, again very appealing. The Japanese use the idiom "A cat with a paper bag" [editor's note: meaning "to back away," like a cat with its head covered by a paper bag], but Kuniyoshi seems to have rather liked placing sweet packets on his cats' heads, as print number 26 also attests to.

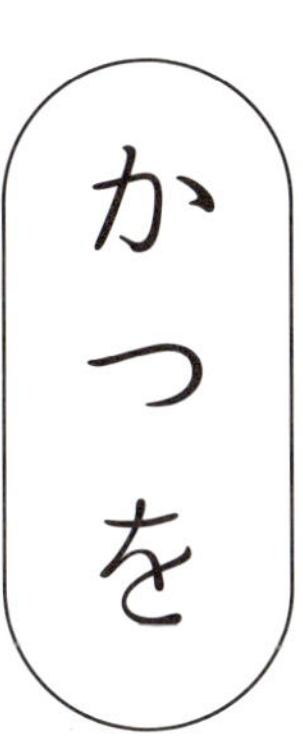

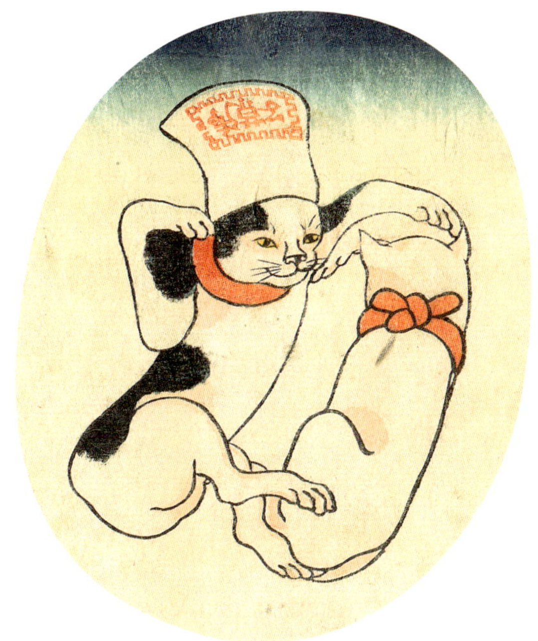

64 猫の当字 なまづ ねこのあてじ なまず

　そして「なまづ」。ここでも猫だけでなく鯰が参加しているが、「つ（川）」の３本の縦の線となっている猫たち、ことに真ん中の猫の棒状に押し込められた様子に気づいた時には、もう言葉を失うか大爆笑か、どちらかである。

　あえていくつかの見どころを述べたが、くまなく見ていただきたい。登場するのは役者と合成された人間系猫ではなく、すべてがリアル系猫。そんな彼らがありのままの猫の肢体を目一杯使って演技しているのである。ときに無理なポーズをとらされ、ときに自然なやんちゃぶりを見せる猫たち。リアル系猫の最高傑作と言いたい。

Cat Letters: Catfish *(Neko no ateji: Namazu)*

Finally, *Catfish*. Here too we have not just cats but catfish, and the sight of cats forming the three vertical strokes of the *tsu (kawa)*, and in particular the middle one forced into a stick shape, will render the viewer either speechless, or hysterical.

Here then are some highlights, but do have a thorough study yourself. All the cats are real cats, not cats with actor faces, utilizing their nimble feline limbs to wonderful effect to perform for our benefit, sometimes in tricky poses, and sometimes displaying their natural mischievousness. This could be described as Kuniyoshi's finest work using real cats.

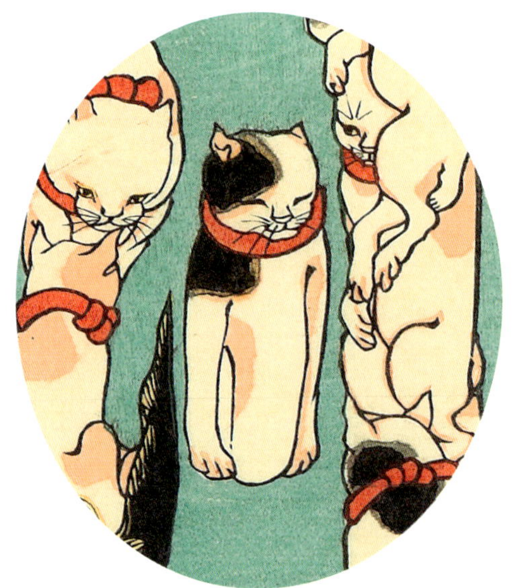

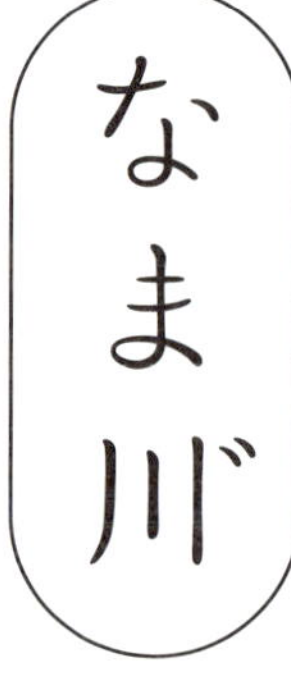

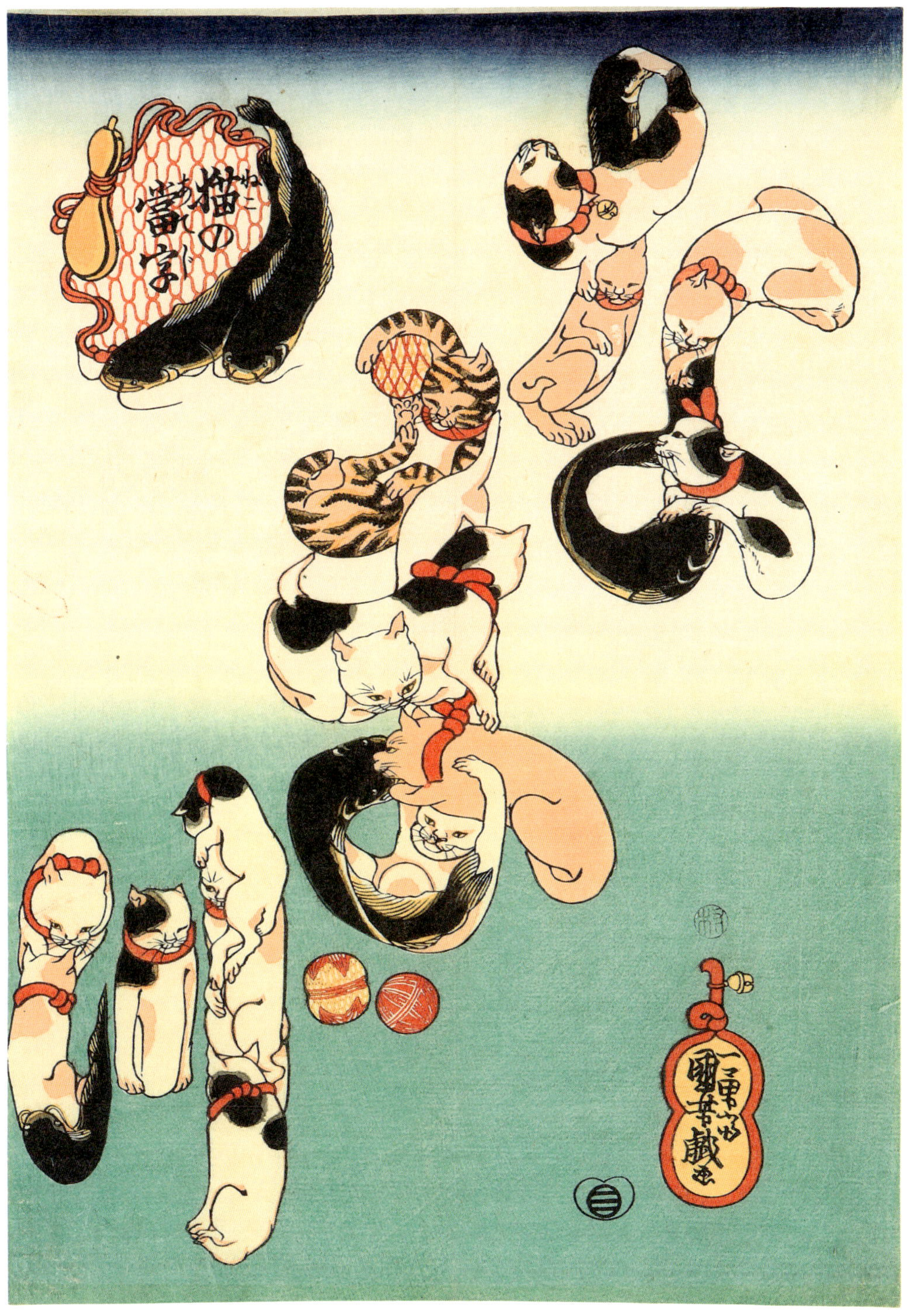

猫の當字
なまづ

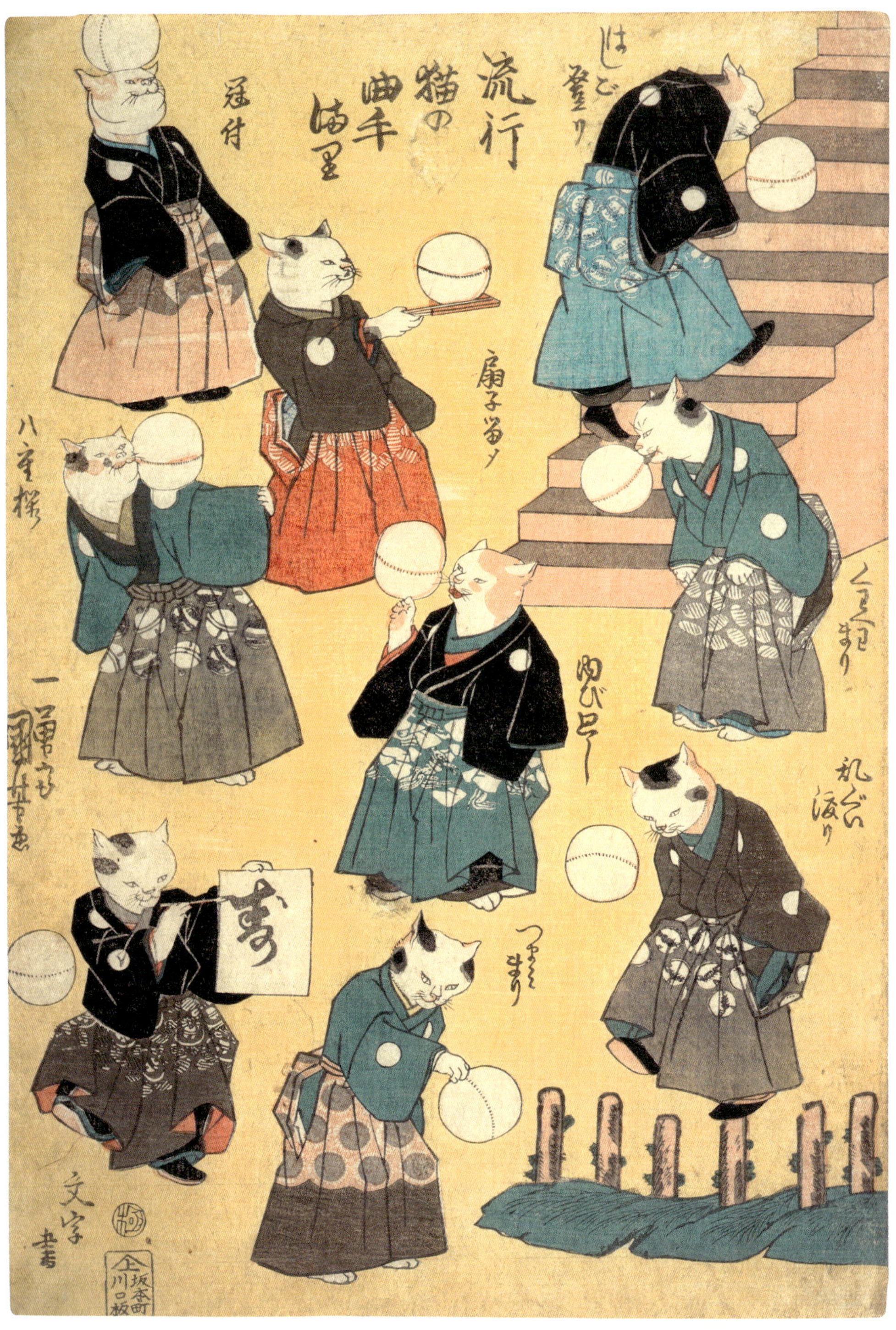

はご登り
流行
猫の
曲手毬
冠付
扇子当ノ
八重櫻
一勇斎
國芳画
くるくるまり
ゆびつり
丸ぐせ
返り
つづくまり
文字
坂本町
金川口板

65 流行猫の曲手まり りゅうこうねこのきょくてまり

　国芳の猫が演じたのは芝居だけではない。天保 12 年 (1841)、菊川国丸という芸人が江戸の浅草で興行して話題となった「曲鞠」。国芳は、当の国丸が演じているところも描いているが、ここはひとつ猫にもやらせてみようと思ったのだろう。その気持ちはよくわかる。そもそもが、魅力的な曲芸なのである。

　手に持った扇子の先に鞠をのせる「扇子留め」や、額にのせる「冠付」。跳ね上がった鞠を指でつまんでキャッチする技と思われる「つまみまり」や、鞠を蹴り上げながら、立ち並ぶ木の杭を渡るむずかしい技「乱ぐい渡り」。人間の国丸を描いたものよりも、猫バージョンの方が、演技者の緊張感や誇らしげな様子が伝わってくるから不思議である。

Fashionable Cat Juggler with a Ball

Kuniyoshi's cats did not only act in plays. In 1841 the entertainer Kikukawa Kunimaru and his juggling act were the talk of Edo's Asakusa district. Kuniyoshi also depicts Kunimaru himself performing, but here no doubt thought it might be fun to have a cat do it, a temptation one can readily understand. In any case, it's an appealing show of acrobatics.

Balancing the ball on a fan and on its forehead, catching a high-flying ball in its fingers, kicking the ball while walking over a row of wooden poles: the feline version of Kunimaru is amazing in that it conveys the tension and bravado of the performer more accurately than Kuniyoshi's portrayal of the human Kunimaru.

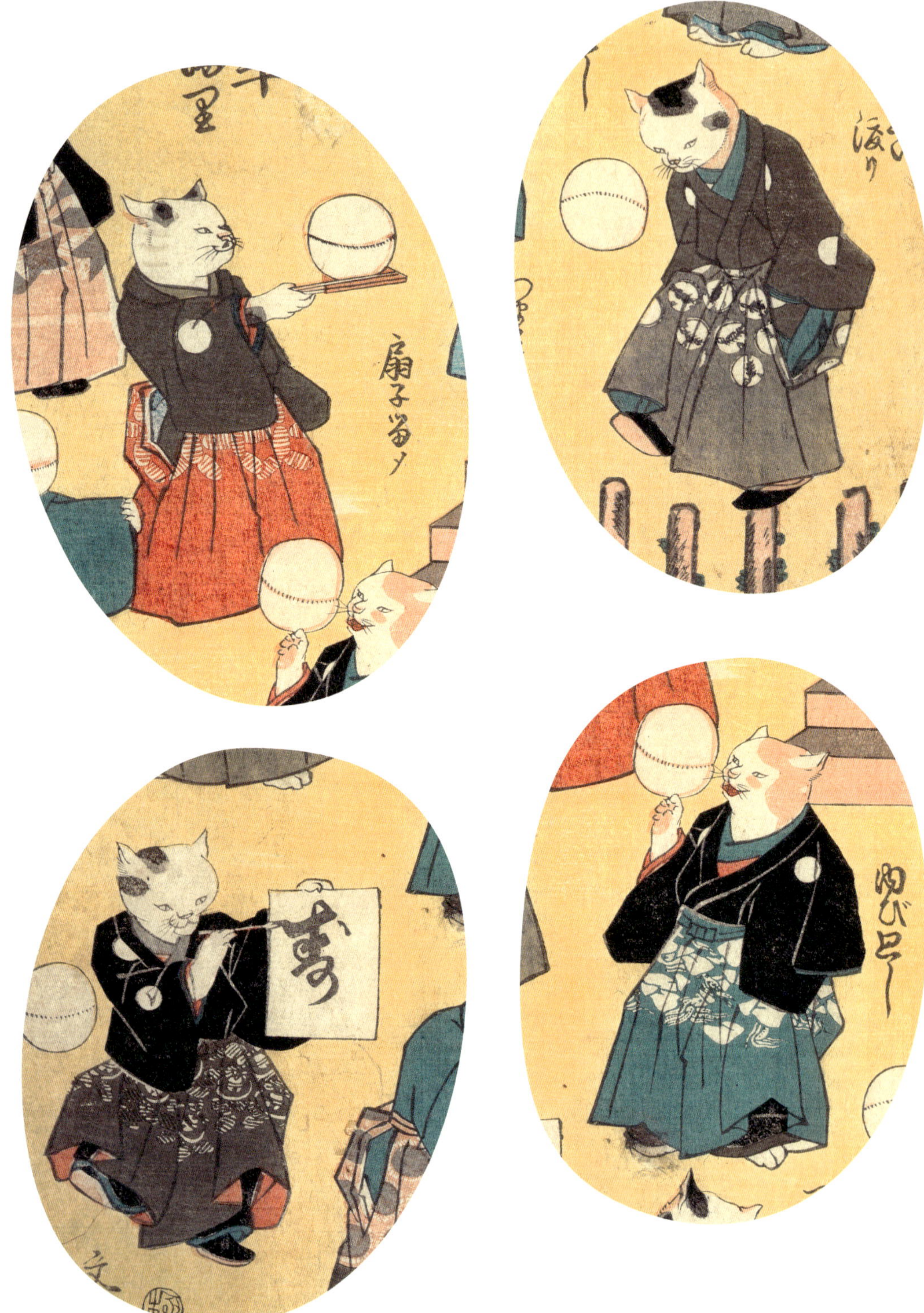
扇子當ノ
こゝ渡り
ゆびとゝ

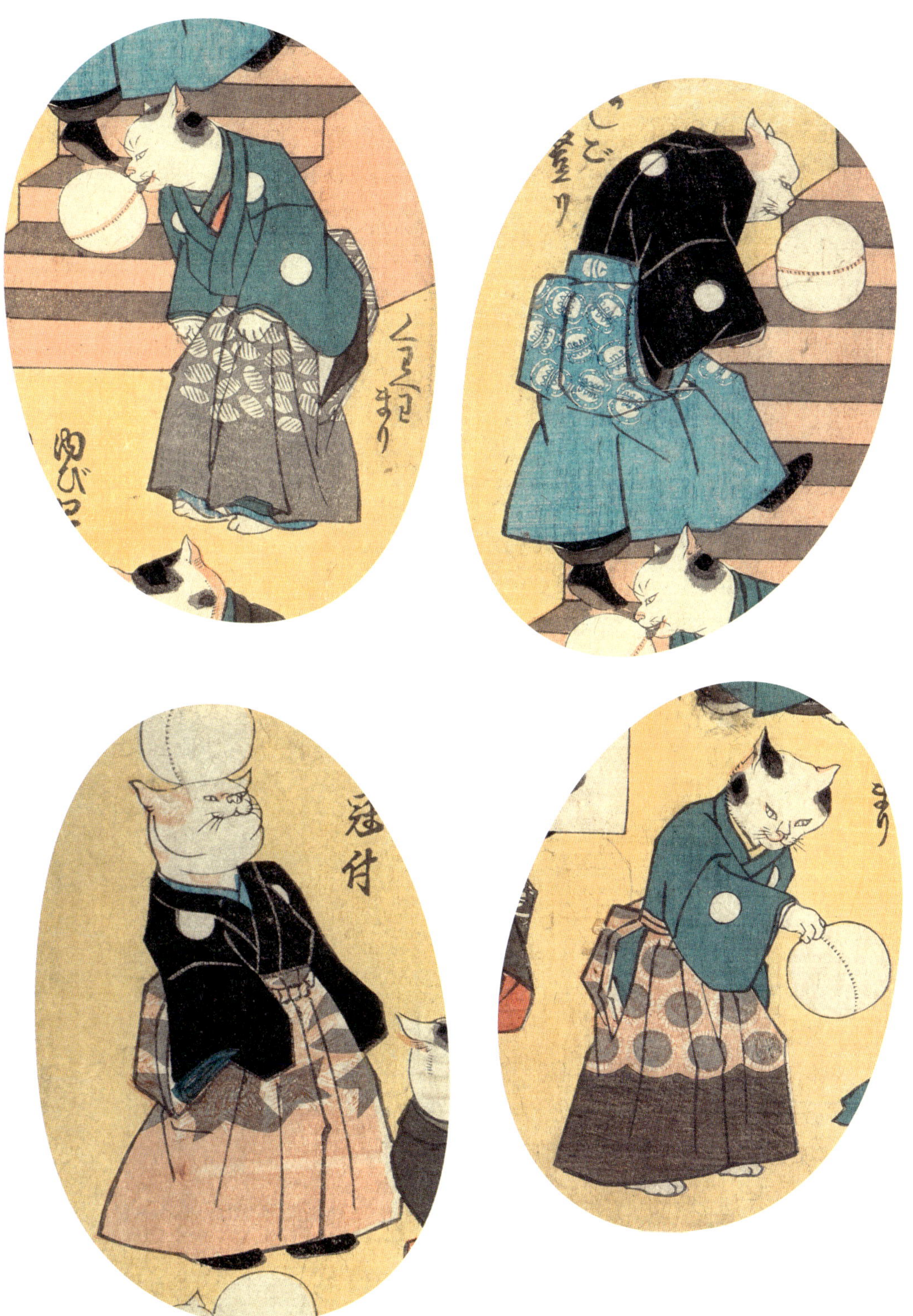

くつぬぎまり
ゆびつ
ごと
名ごり
冠付
まり

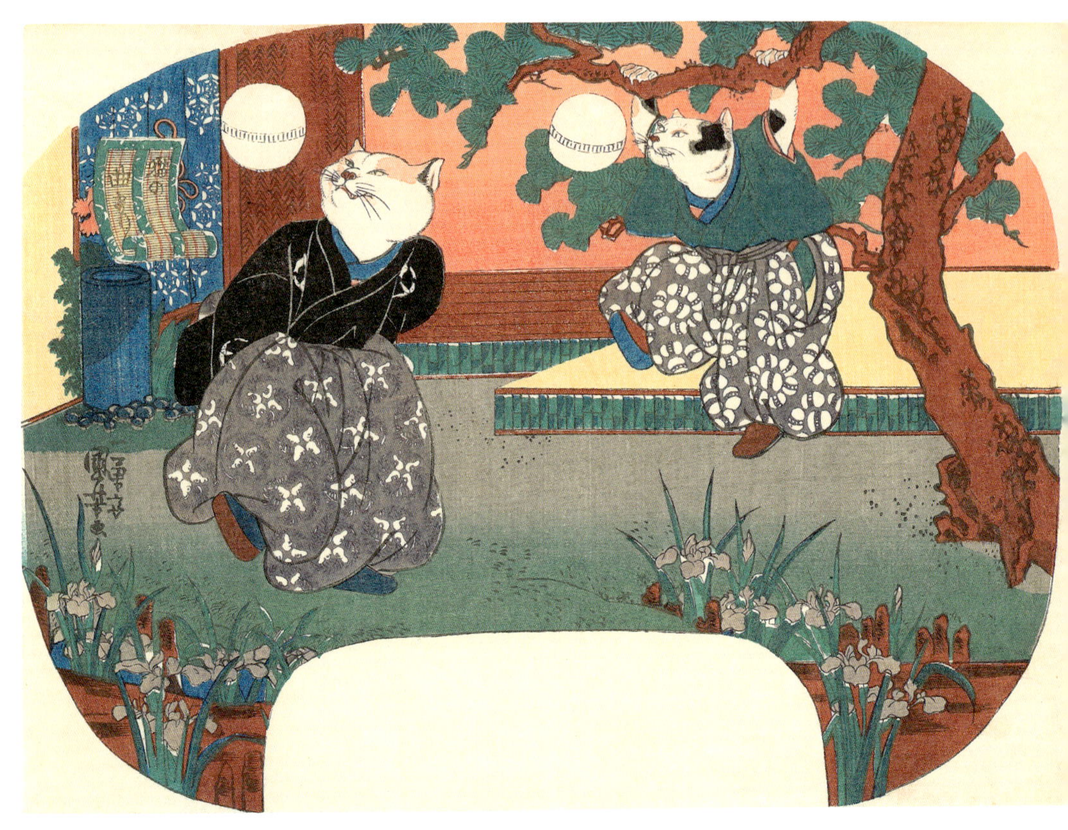

66 猫の曲まり　ねこのきょくまり

　前の一枚は、いわば曲鞠の演目一覧のようなものだが、こちらは団扇絵。猫が大きくなった分、姿や表情が一層細やかだ。燕子花の咲く美しい庭で、猫が曲鞠を演じている。一つは、膝で鞠を蹴りつづける「ひざまり」。これは基本技だろう。もう一つは、松の木にぶら下がり鞠を蹴り上げる、その名も美しい「さがり藤」。

　なぜ演目の名前がわかるかというと、本家本元の菊川国丸の絵や、先の一枚とは別の猫の曲鞠の図に、同じ技が説明付きで紹介されているからである。国芳は、ただおかしなものを描いたわけではなく、国丸の妙技一つ一つに敬意を払い、猫たちにも真剣に演じさせたのだろう。

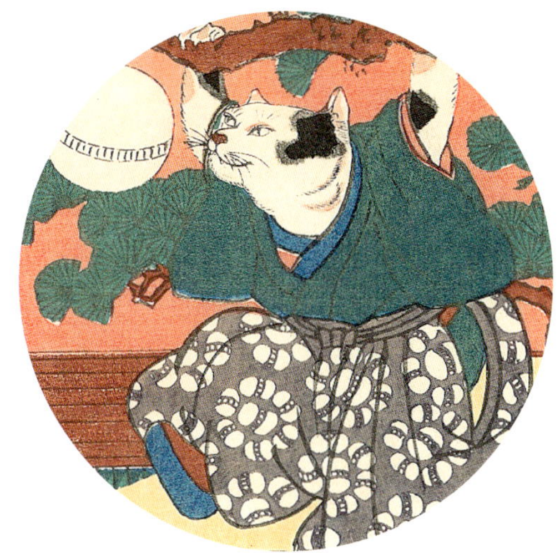

Cats Juggling Balls

While the previous print resembles a catalog of juggling acts, this is a fan design. Larger cats means more detailed forms and facial expressions. Here the dexterous felines perform juggling tricks in a beautiful iris garden. One is bouncing the ball repeatedly on its knee, a basic skill, while the other is kicking the ball while hanging from a pine tree.

The same tricks feature with explanations in pictures of their originator Kikukawa Kunimaru, and cat acrobatic prints other than the previous one. Here Kuniyoshi did not simply paint something that struck him as funny; out of respect for all Kunimaru's rare skills, he made his cats tackle them with earnest dedication.

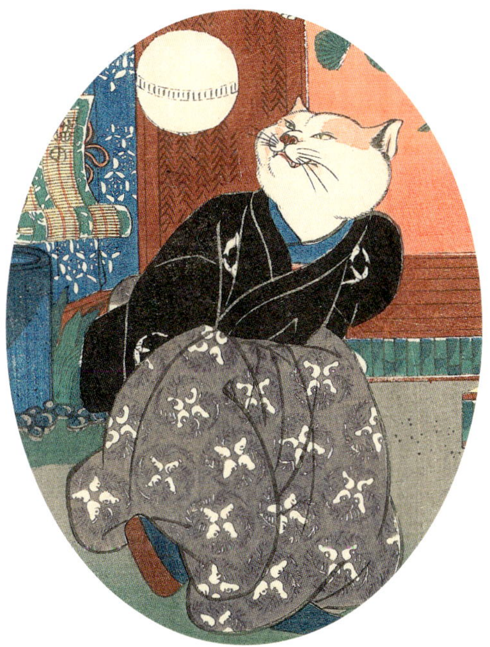

67 猫の歌舞伎 出語り図

ねこのかぶき でがたりず

　国芳の猫には団扇絵の傑作が多い。踊る猫と、左の後見役の猫。加えて、浄瑠璃を演奏する太夫や三味線弾きも猫。ふだんは姿を見せない彼らが舞台上にずらりと並ぶ、「出語り」の光景である。

　国芳のお気に入りの設定だったとみえて、次章の『朧月猫の草紙』でも、あるひと幕がこれとよく似た絵で始まる。そこでは本編の物語とリンクするように、恋仲の主人公二人が、舞台で道行、つまり悲しい恋の物語を演じている。一方、この団扇絵の猫が演じているのは、飴売り。天保年間に江戸で大評判となった実際の飴売りをまねた、歌舞伎舞踊である。

　国芳の演出はとても細かく、籠には小判、奏者の前には白湯の入った器を描き込む。踊る猫の小気味よい動き、しっかりと踏みしめた足先も見どころだが、やはりおかしいのは居並ぶ猫たち。一番左の1匹が画面から切れているところも、舞台の光景をのぞき見るようで臨場感がある。

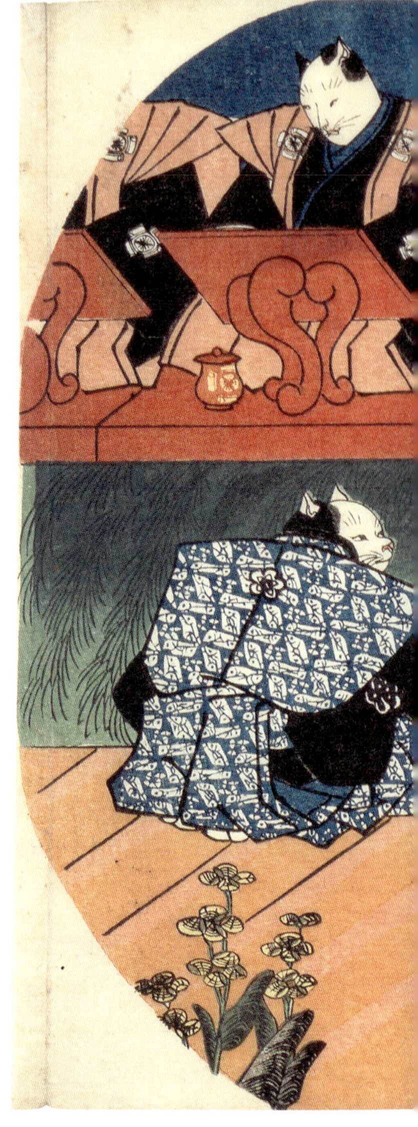

Cat Kabuki: Degatari

Many of Kuniyoshi's cats appear in brilliant fan designs. Here we have a dancing cat, and at left one in a mentor role. The accompanying storytellers and shamisen players are also cats, in the less usual *degatari* scenario in which the musicians all sit on stage, rather than staying out of sight.

In next chapter's *The Cat's Tale*, one act begins with a similar picture, one of Kuniyoshi's favorite settings. There, to form a link with the main story, the two lover leads elope on stage, i.e. act out a tragic love story. Meanwhile, the cat on this fan

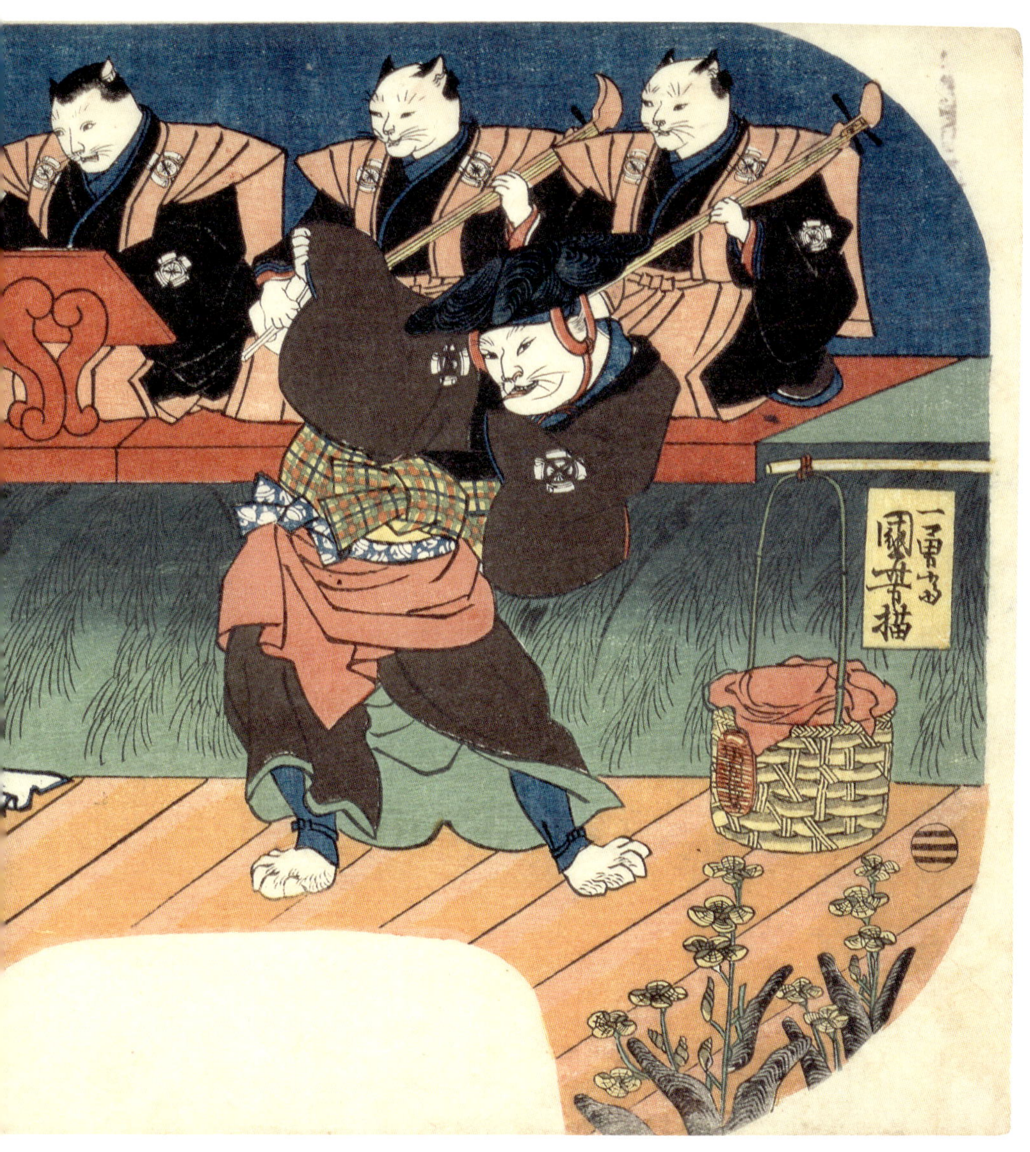

is playing a purveyor of boiled sweets, in a kabuki dance mimicking an actual sweet
seller of great renown in Tempo-era Edo.

Kuniyoshi's rendering is highly detailed, down to the coins in the basket and cups of
hot water in front of the instrumentalists. Highlights are the tidy movements of the
dancing cat, and its firmly planted feet. The humor however has to be in the lineup
of cats. Even the way the cat on the extreme left is cut off endows the illustration
with a theatrical immediacy.

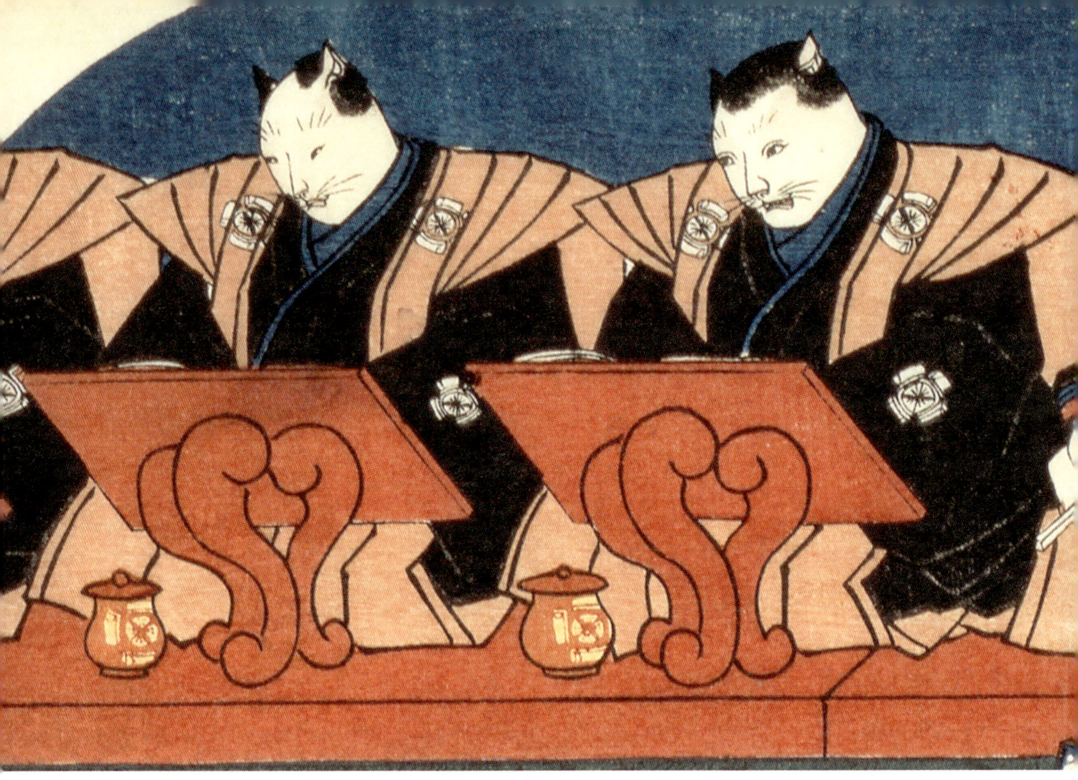

━━━ Column ━━━

屋根の上

　以前、電車から、毎朝のように何匹かの猫が屋根に集う家が見えた。高架線を電車が走る現代ならではの光景だが、猫にはこんな生活空間があるのだと感じ入った。人という動物は、道具を使わない限り地面を行き来するだけだが、猫は違う。彼らの行動範囲は三次元。そこを「ぴょん」と瞬時に移動する。

《流行猫の戯》のシリーズ（56, 57）の画中の文の作者は、実は国芳ではなく、6章でも取り上げる猫好き戯作者の山東京山。京山が語る猫の世界では、有名な「無間の鐘」は「無間の屋根」となり、「この世」も「この屋根」となる。人の手の届かない屋根の上こそ、彼らの舞台である。国芳の時代、屋根より高い建物は、せいぜい火の見櫓くらい。どこまでも屋根が連なり、富士山や筑波山まで見はるかす江戸の町。猫たちの目に映っていたのは、そんな風景なのである。

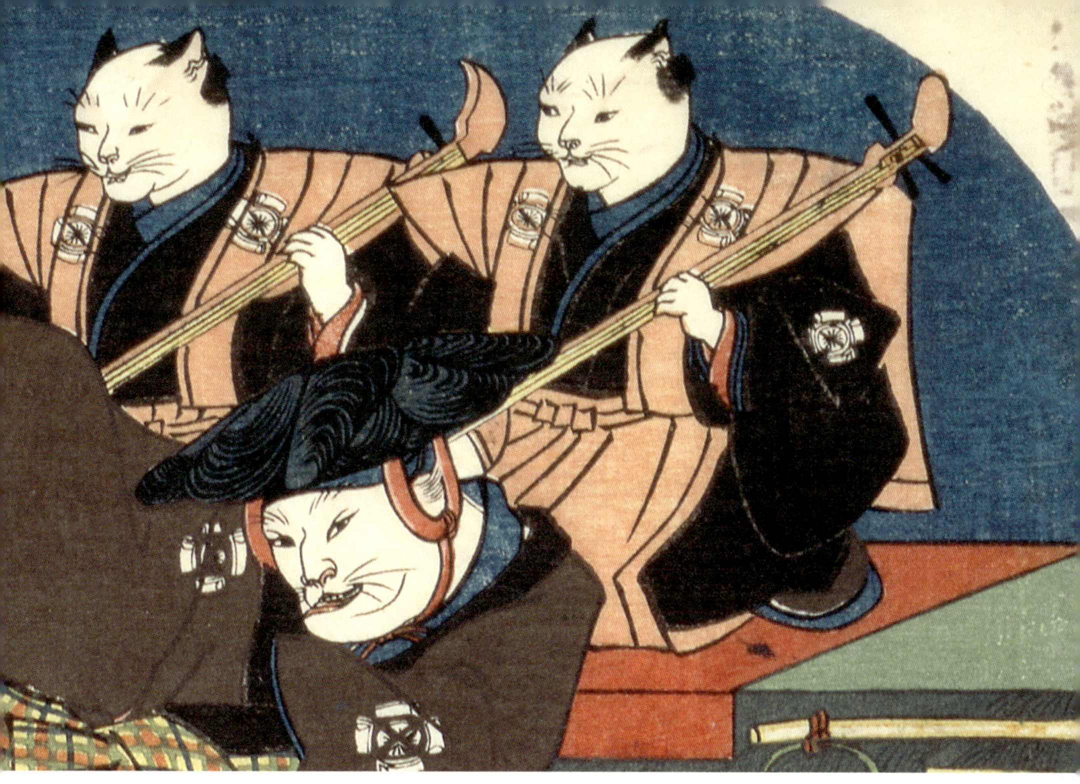

Up on the roof

From the train, pretty much every morning I used to see a house with cats assembled on the roof. A sight one could only see in these days of trains running on elevated lines, and impressed, I was reminded that for cats, rooftops are just another living space. Without the aid of tools, the human animal is confined to the ground, but cats have no such limits. They roam a habitat that is three-dimensional, and can move about it instantaneously, in a single bound.

The text for the *Fashionable Cat Games* series (56,57) was actually penned not by Kuniyoshi, but the cat-loving novelist Santo Kyozan mentioned in chapter six. In the feline realm Kyozan describes, the famous *Muken no kane* (Bell of limitless [hell]) becomes the *muken no yane* (*yane* meaning roof); *kono yo* or "this (temporal) world" becoming *kono yane* (this roof). It is on the rooftops, beyond human reach, that cats play out their various dramas. In Kuniyoshi's day, about the only structure higher than the roof would have been a fire observation tower. The Edo townscape was one of rows of roofs as far as the eye could see, with clear views as far as Mt. Fuji and Mt. Tsukuba. These were what cats saw from their lofty domains.

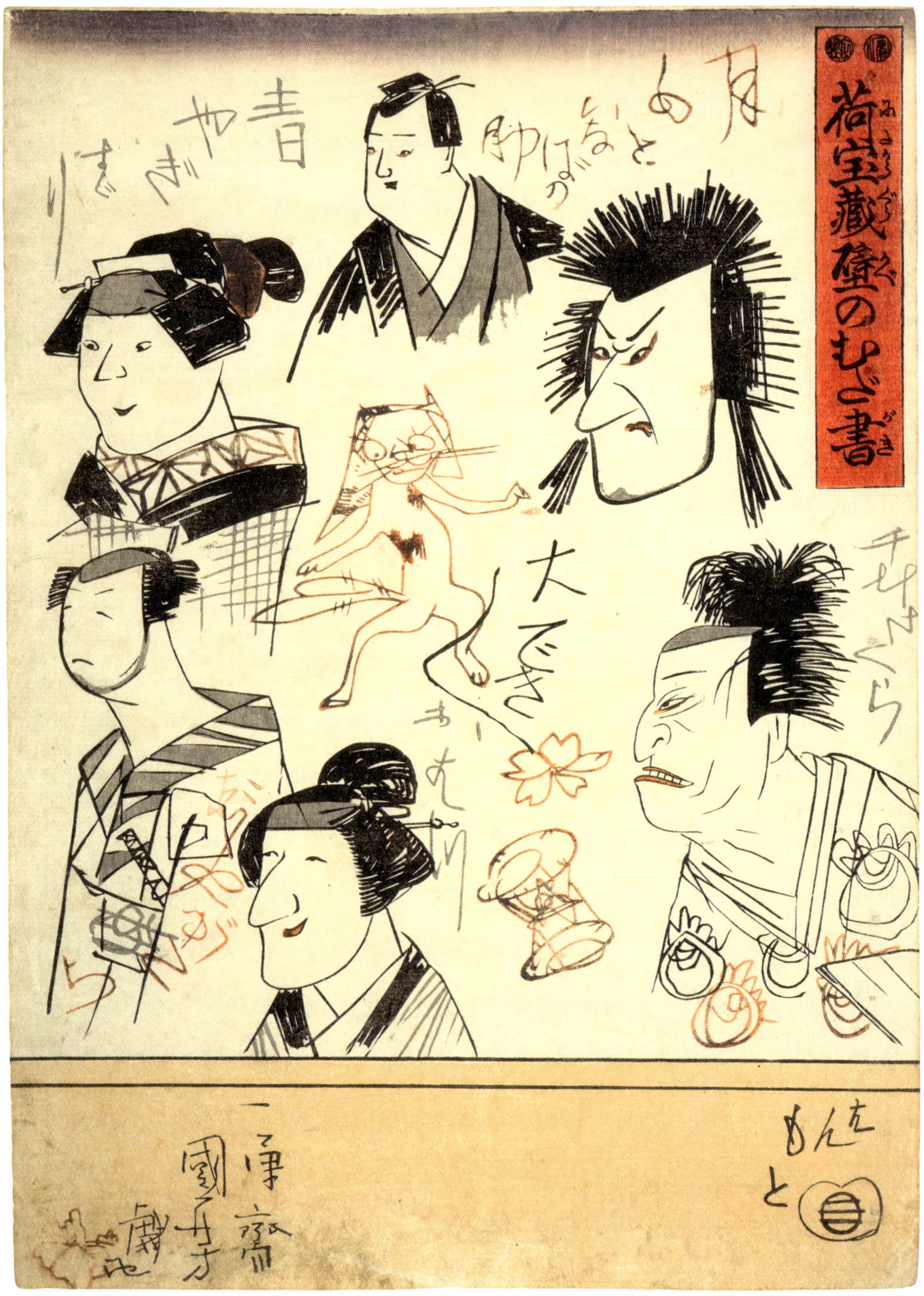

68 荷宝蔵壁のむだ書 にたからぐら かべのむだがき

　歌舞伎役者として大活躍の猫だが、これも異色の「役者絵」。国芳の全作品の中でも名高い《荷宝蔵壁のむだ書》である。天保の改革で役者の似顔絵が禁止されたことへの反発からか、こんな商品を考え出したのである。タイトル通り、そして見ての通り「壁の落書き」で、形から描線まで、すべてが本物の落書きを思わせる。アイディアもすばらしいが、こんな表現を木版画で成し遂げてしまうのだから、当時の浮世絵づくりの技術と表現へのこだわりは大変なものだ。

　さて、猫は真ん中にいるが、その上の人物に「月もといなばの助」との書き込みがある。つまり《五拾三次之内　岡崎の場》（59）にも登場する因幡之助。ということは、この猫は、岡崎の夜、怪しい踊りを見せた、あの化け猫である。なるほど、しっぽも二つに分かれている。

Scribbles on a Storehouse Wall

Cats as kabuki actors feature prominently in Kuniyoshi's prints, but this, one of his most renowned, is an actor picture of a different stripe. One surmises it to be a product Kuniyoshi developed in protest at the Tempo ban on actor caricatures. As both title and picture suggest, this is graffiti on a wall, and everything from shapes to lines resembles genuine graffiti. A splendid idea, but to persevere with it through to the woodblock print stage speaks of serious dedication to the ukiyo-e techniques and expression of the time.

The cat is at center, and on the figure above, the caption "Inabanosuke," a figure who also appears in *Scene from the 53 Stations of the Tokaido: Okazaki* (59). Making this cat the phantom moggy that danced that dubious dance one night in Okazaki. And yes, its tail is indeed split.

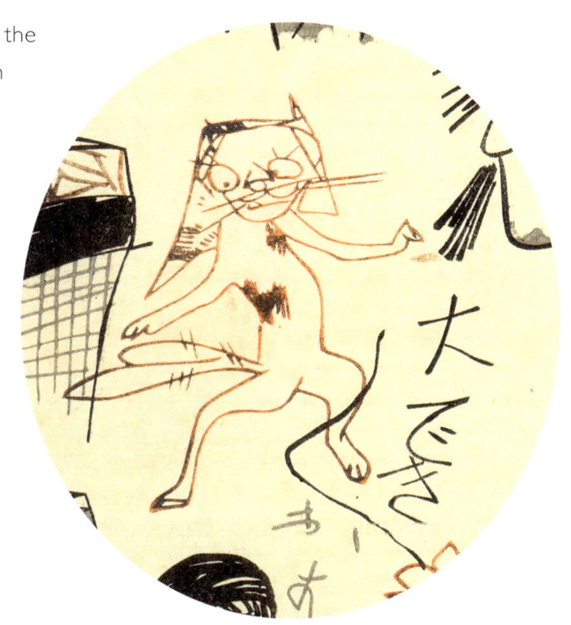

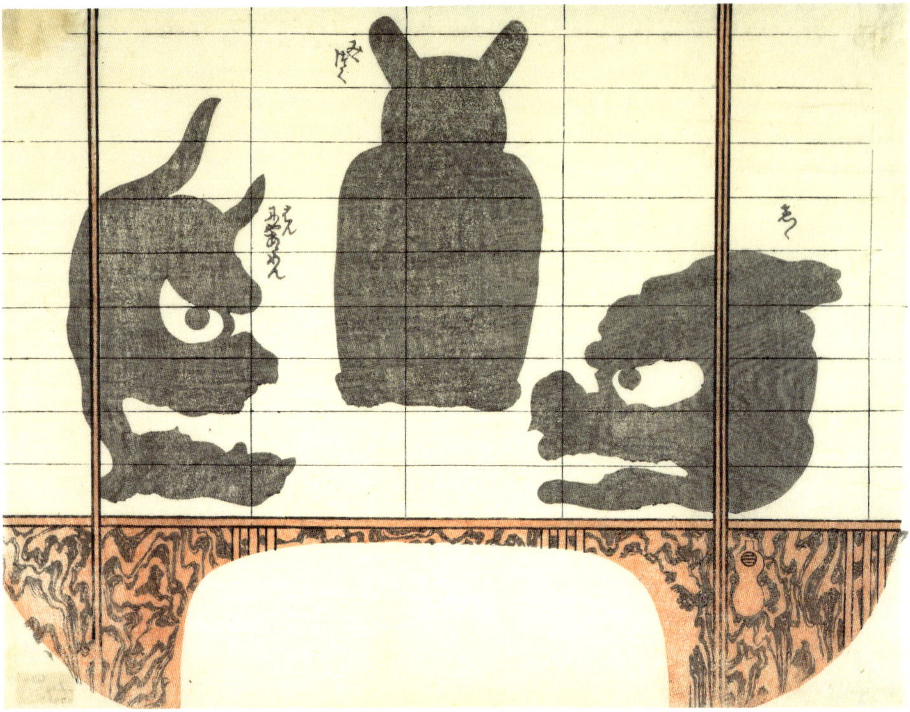

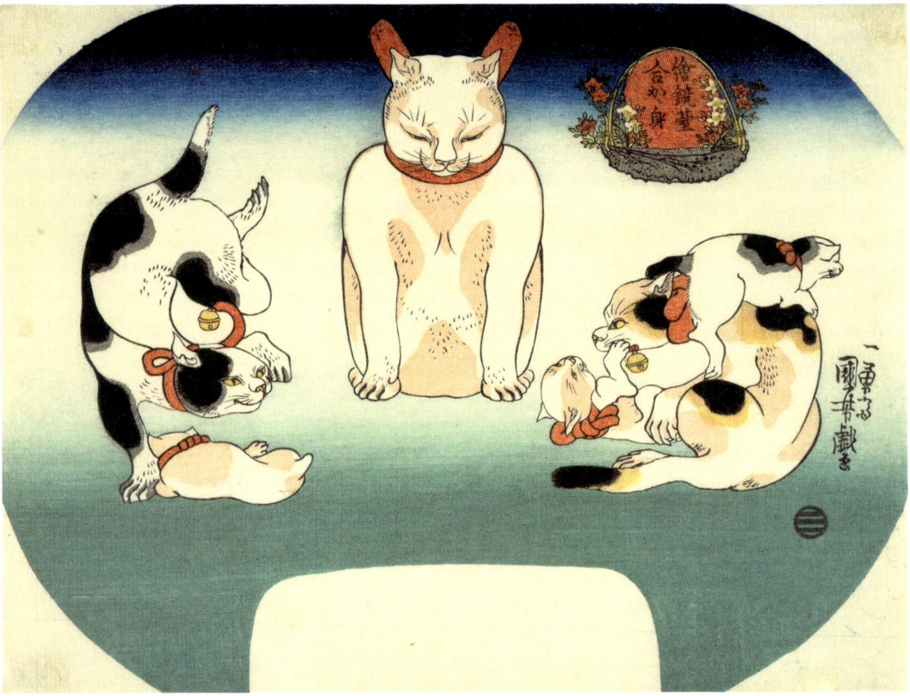

絵鏡台
人合か身
一勇斎國芳戯画

69 絵鏡台合かゞ身（みみずく・獅子・般若面）

　芝居、曲芸、集団演技と何でもござれの猫たちの、この章最後の演技は、影絵。団扇の表と裏に貼るように、2枚セットになっている。図柄が大きくて、どことなくまったりとした雰囲気もいい感じである。

　画中の文字は「しゝ（獅子）」「みゝづく」、そして「はんにゃあめん（般若面）」。「はんにゃ面」ではなく、あくまで「はんにゃあ面」。どの猫も生気に富むが、特に、みみずくを演じる猫のうつむき加減は、まるで猫が人間と目を合わせないようにしている時のようで、心に残る。

Mirror Images: Owl, Lion, and Female Demon

This chapter's final offering from those multi-talented felines capable of anything from drama to acrobatics to ensemble performances is the shadow picture, in this case a set of two prints for affixing to the front and back of a fan. The size of the design gives it an indefinably laid-back feel that is immensely appealing.

The text says "lion" "owl" and *hannyaamen* (a female demon mask) the elongated *nyaa* being a Japanese expression of "miaow." All the cats are full of zest, but that playing the owl is especially memorable for its downcast eyes, reminiscent of a cat doing its best to avoid a human gaze.

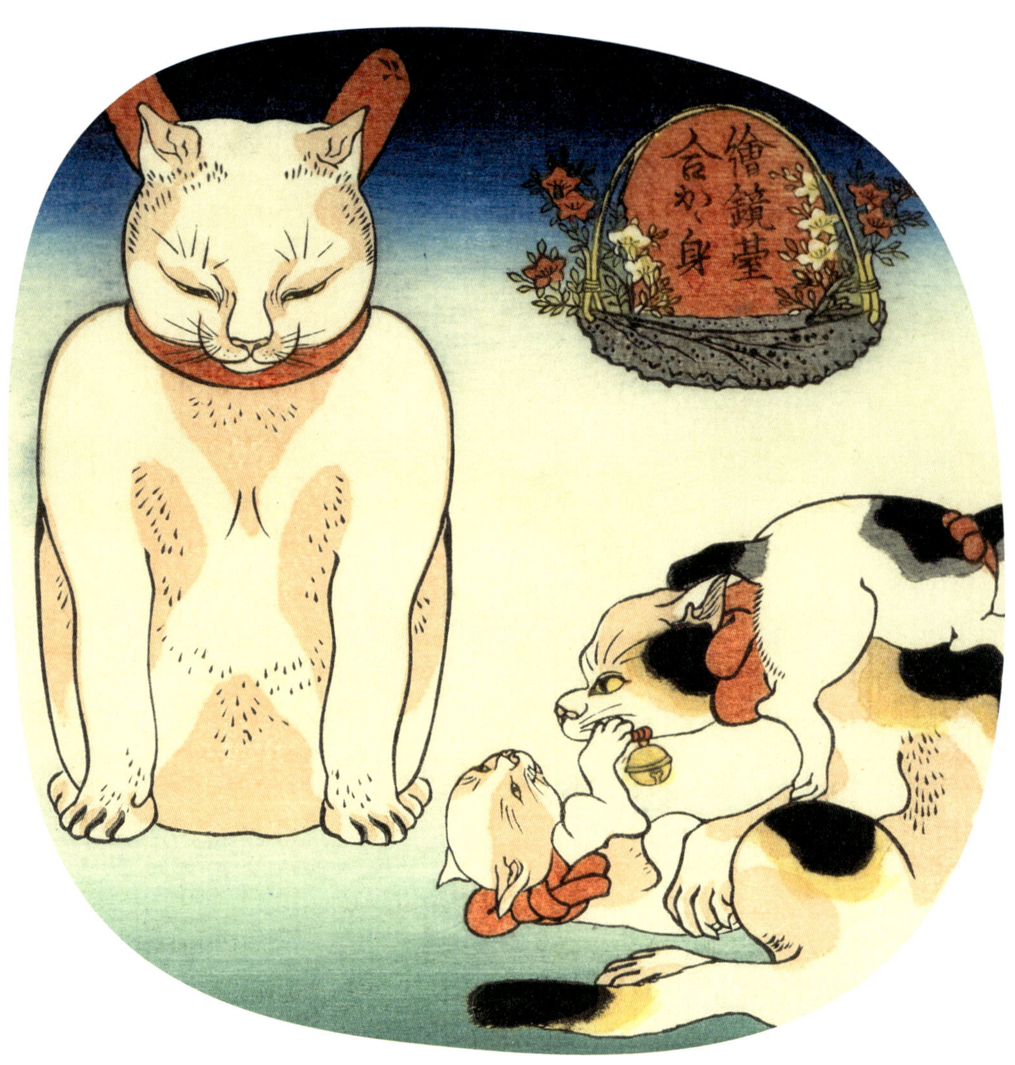
絵鏡臺合かゝ身

VI

おこまの大冒険

『朧月猫の草紙』から

Okoma's great adventure,
The Cat's Tale

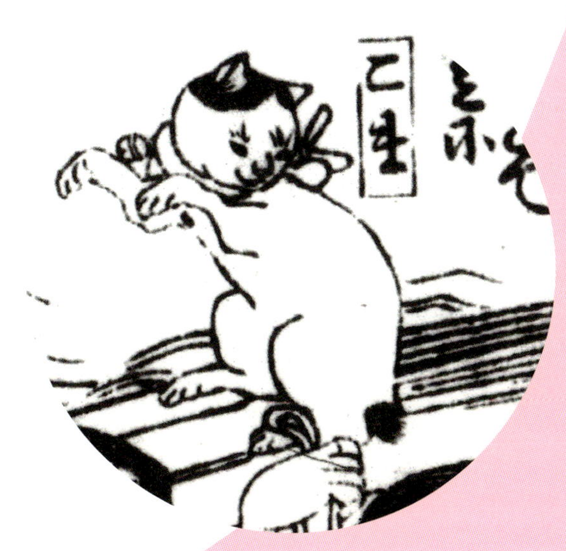

70 朧月猫の草紙　おぼろづきねこのそうし

　国芳の時代、もう一人の猫好きがいた。戯作者の山東京山である。『朧月猫の草紙』は、京山の文と国芳の挿絵が織りなす猫物語の傑作。メスの猫おこまの数奇な運命を描くこの物語は七編に及ぶが、全部を読まなくても、猫好きの心をとらえるエピソードに満ちている。ここでは第二編の中から、おこまの冒険の一部をご覧いただこう。

　まずは、ここまでのあらすじ。

　鰹節問屋、又たび屋こなえもんの家の飼い猫「こま」。隣家の恋猫「とら」と家を出て、ついに心中を決意する。「覚悟はよいか」「にゃんまみだぶつ」。そこへ「ぶち」が来て、2匹を思いとどまらせる。2匹はぶちから、今出川様の奥女中が住む長屋の縁の下が隠れ家によいと教えられるが、屋敷の犬に飛びかかられて、とらは行方知れずに。一方、おこまは勝手のわからない屋敷の廊下をうろついていたところを、女中の梅の井と下女のお竹に見つけられる。

The Cat's Tale

In Kuniyoshi's day there was another cat-lover: author of popular fiction, Santo Kyozan. *The Cat's Tale* is a feline epic combining Kyozan's text and Kuniyoshi's illustrations. This story portraying the checkered fortunes of Okoma, a female cat, runs to seven volumes, but even a partial reading offers much enchangting drama for cat fanciers. Let us join Okoma's adventures at the second volume.

In brief, the plot so far. Okoma is the pet of dried bonito wholesaler Matatabiya Konaemon. She absconds with her beloved Tora from next door, and at length the pair attempt double suicide. "Are you quite certain?" "Hail Ami(aow)tābha Buddha!" Then along comes Buchi, who stops them from carrying out the deed. Buchi informs them that under the eaves of the home of a certain Imadegawa-san's lady-in-waiting would make an excellent hideaway, but the pair are set upon by a dog from the big house, and Tora disappears. Meanwhile, a bewildered Okoma is found wandering the corridors of the main house by the maid Umenoi and serving girl Otake.

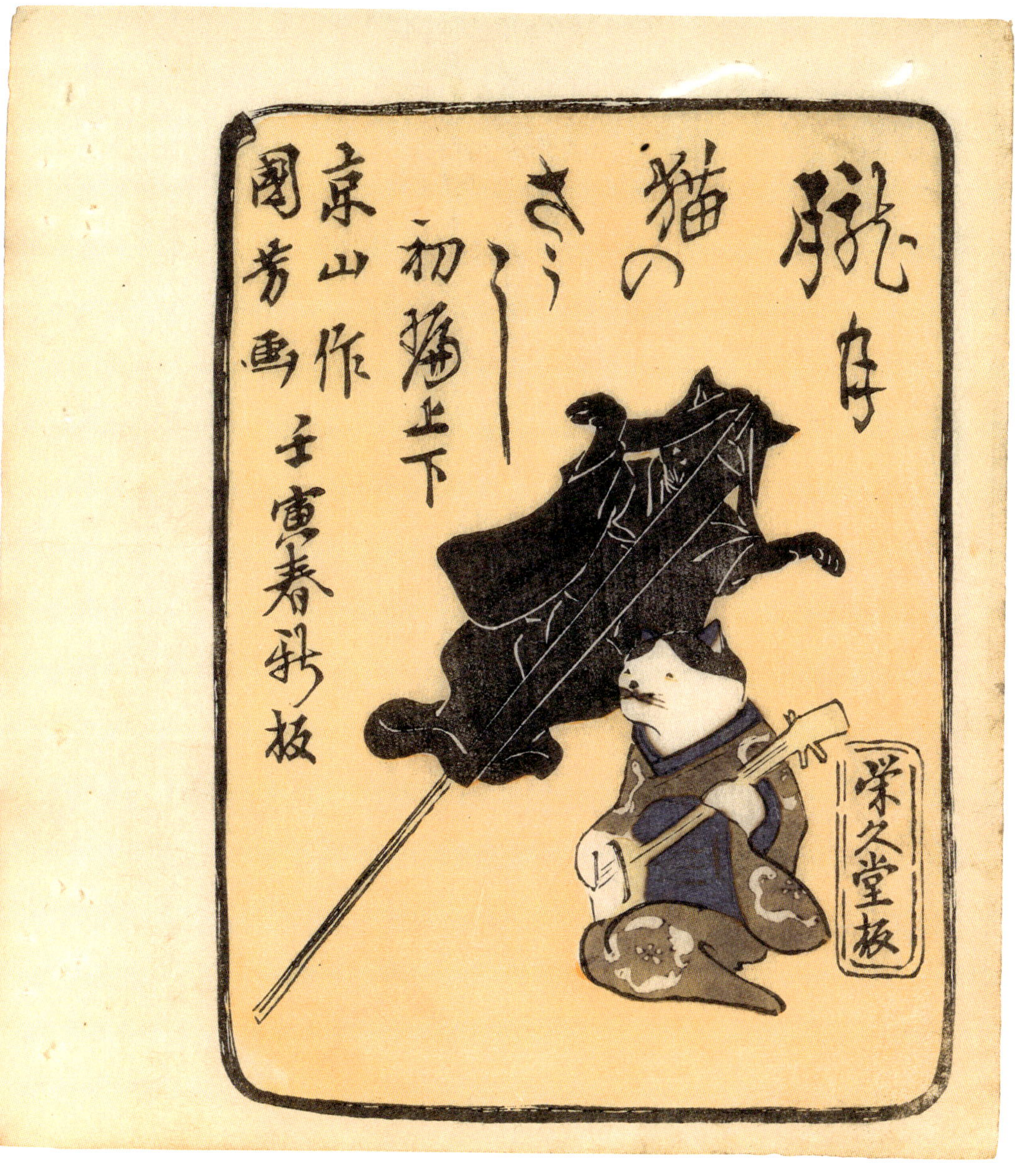

この本が発売された時の紙袋。手ぬぐいをかぶって踊る影絵人形と、お囃子の三味線を弾く猫の人形。

Paper bag from when the book was published, featuring a shadow puppet dancing with a towel on its head, and a cat puppet playing the accompanying shamisen.

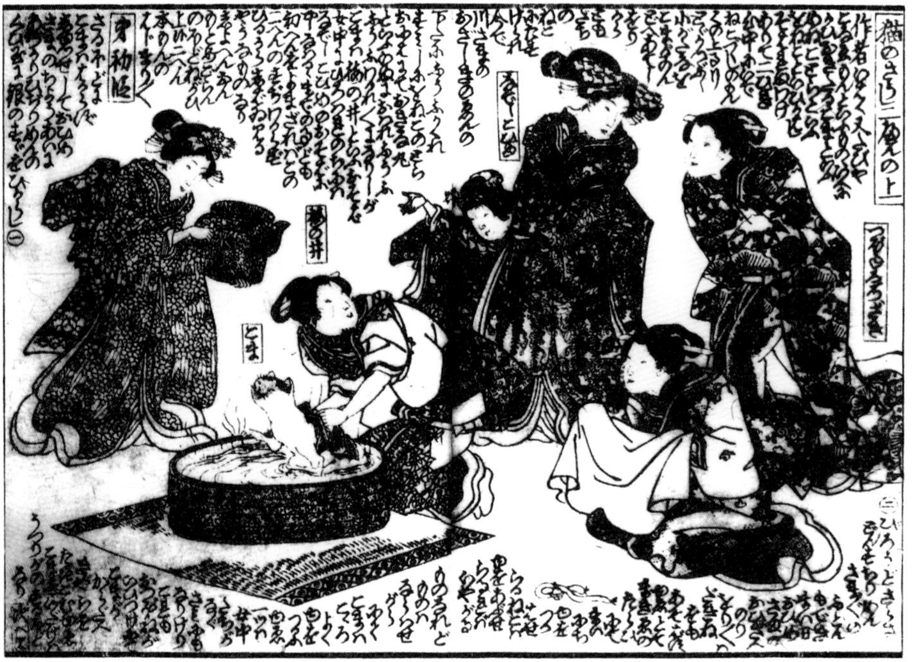

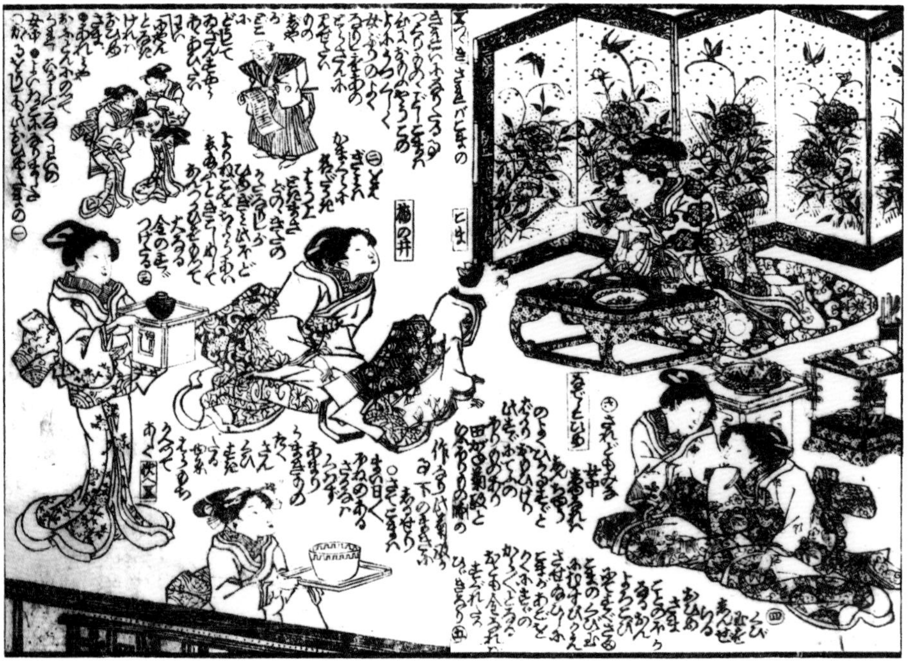

　折しもねずみに困っていたお竹は、「旦那さ
ま、よい猫がおりました」。梅の井に偶然にも、
以前と同じ名前を付けてもらい、屋敷のお姫さ
まにもかわいがられ、「おこま様や」と敬われ
る玉の輿の日々が始まった。

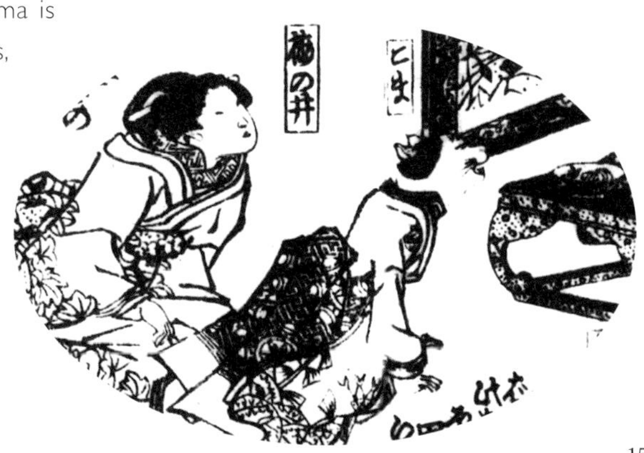

　お姫さまのお膝に乗り、ときに抱き寝もする
からと、風呂に入れてもらうおこま（上）。猫
は湯浴みを嫌がるものだが、おこまは快く湯を使うの
で女中たちの慰みにもなると文にある。体に伽羅まで焚きこむ念の入れよう。
「美しく女ぶりのよくなりしを、とらさんに見せたい」と鳴くおこま。お姫さまの伯
母君からは金の鈴が届けられ、毎日骨なしの魚を食べるという贅沢三昧である。
　下は、お姫さまの寵愛を受ける様子だが、場面ごとに普通の猫だったり、大きくなっ
て着物を着ていたりと臨機応変。それでも全く違和感がないところが面白い。

Just then, Otake, who had been having mouse trouble, tells her master that she's found a good cat. Having coincidentally been given the same name as before by Umenoi, Okoma becomes a revered favorite of the princess. So begins her gilded existence.

As she will be spending time on the princess's lap, and occasionally snuggling up in bed with her, the lucky puss is given a bath (top). Cats normally loathe bathing, but according to the text Okoma is only too happy to have a soak, providing some diversion for the maids. They even take care to burn fragrant aloeswood for the cat's wellbeing. "How I'd love to show Tora the beautiful female I've become," Okoma miaows happily. A gold bell arrives from the princess's aunt, and Okoma wallows in the lap of luxury, eating ready-boned fish every day.

In the bottom illustration, Okoma is enjoying the princess's attentions, but depending on the setting this extraordinarily adaptable creature may be an ordinary cat, or wearing a kimono. It is intriguing how none of this ever feels even slightly odd.

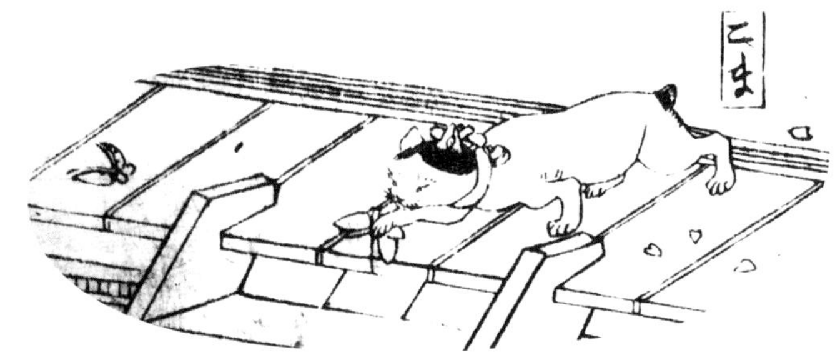

あまりごちそうばかりで、かえってお腹の調子が悪いおこまは、平目の刺身にも手をつけない。お姫さまがくださるものも食べられず、ご機嫌を損ねてしまう。「あなた様のくださるものならば毒薬でもいただきます」と、無理に鯛のかまぼこと鱚の身の部分を食べるおこま。その後、腹ごなしにとあちこち歩き、縁側の日の当たる場所で眠っていたが、桜の花盛りに舞い飛ぶ蝶々を食べてしまう（上）。

そして、とうとうお腹をこわしたおこまは、衝立の片隅に粗相をしてしまった（下）。

But Okoma's rich diet leads to stomachache, even putting her off her flounder sashimi. She is unable to sample tasty tidbits proffered by the princess, vexing the girl. Vowing to eat whatever her beloved princess offers, even poison, Okoma forces herself to consume sea bream fish cake and part of a whiting, then walks about to help them digest, before lying down to sleep in a sunny spot on the veranda. But then she chomps up a butterfly fluttering among the blaze of cherry blossoms nearby (top).

Now properly sick, she has an unfortunate accident by the corner of a screen (bottom).

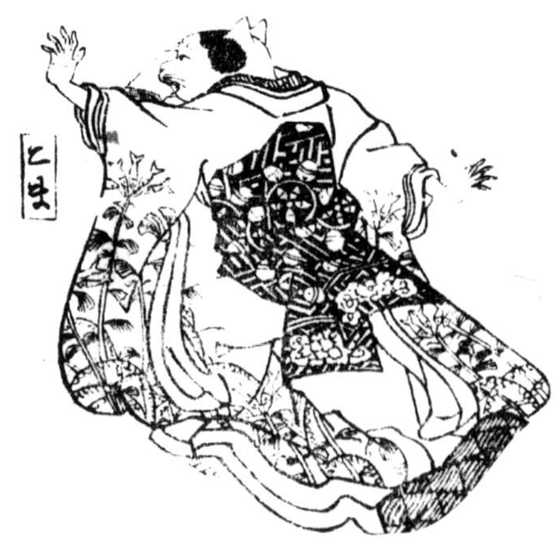

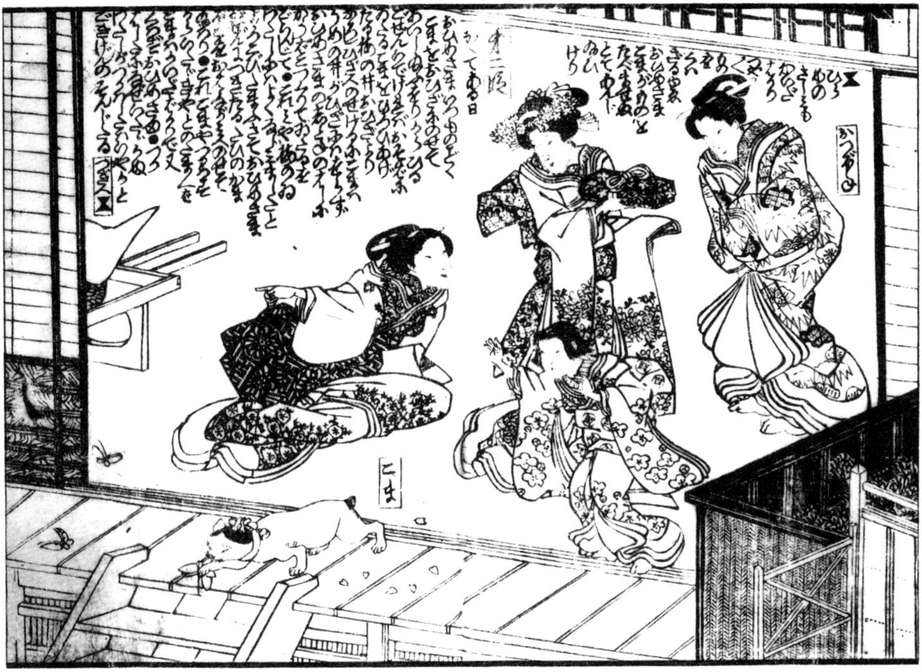

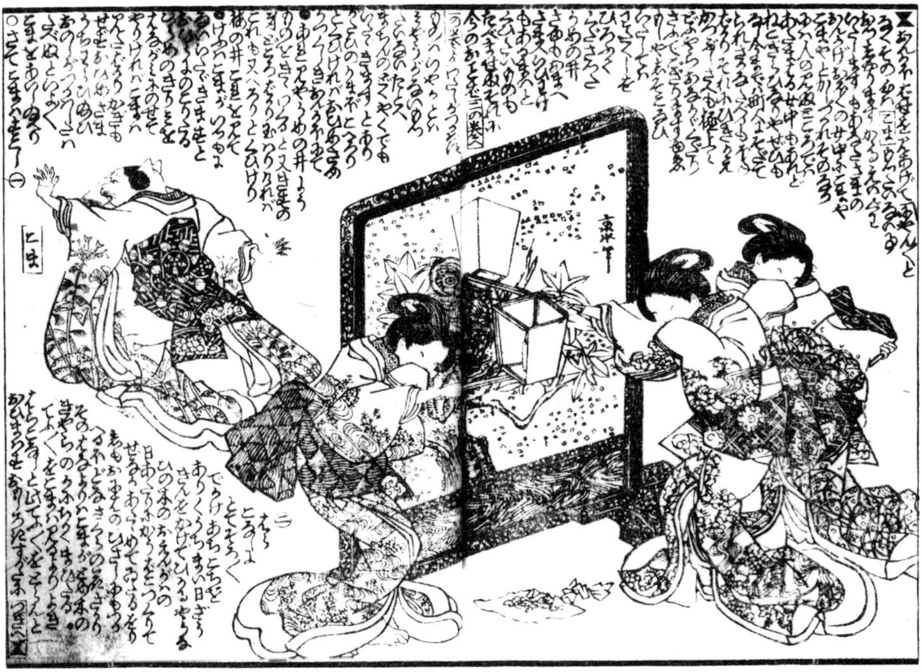

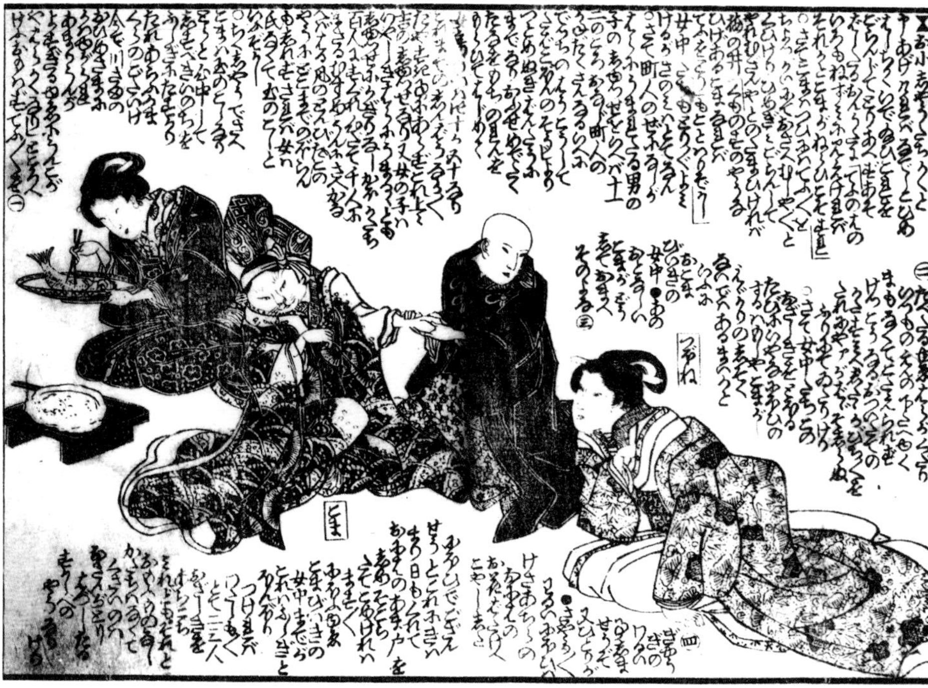

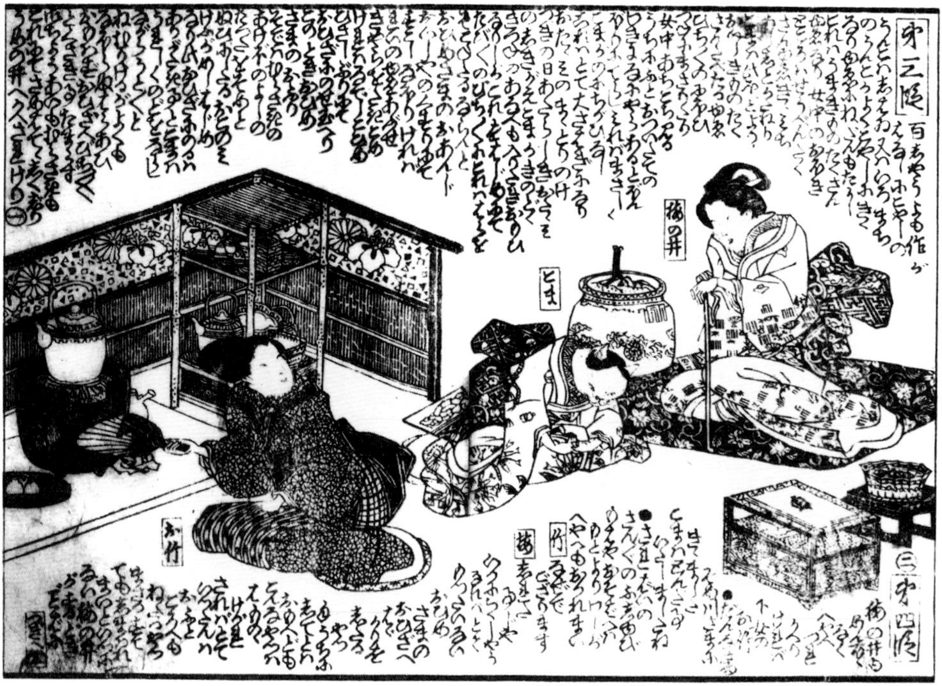

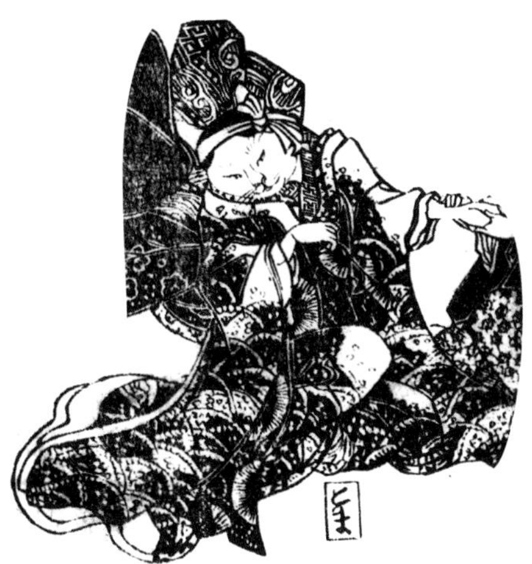

度々の粗相に医者にみてもらうおこま（上）。
薬で少し良くなったので、湯浴みをして久しぶり
にお姫さまのお膝へ。おこまは嬉しく喉を鳴らし
ながら、うとうと。ところが……よりにもよって
お姫さまのお膝へ粗相をしてしまう。

　ご籠愛も、もはやこれまで。梅の井も、お前を
拾い、良い暮らしをさせてやったのに、私の面目
までつぶしてくれたと悔しがる。首をうなだれて
聞くおこま。ついに、暇を出されてしまうのであっ
た（下）。

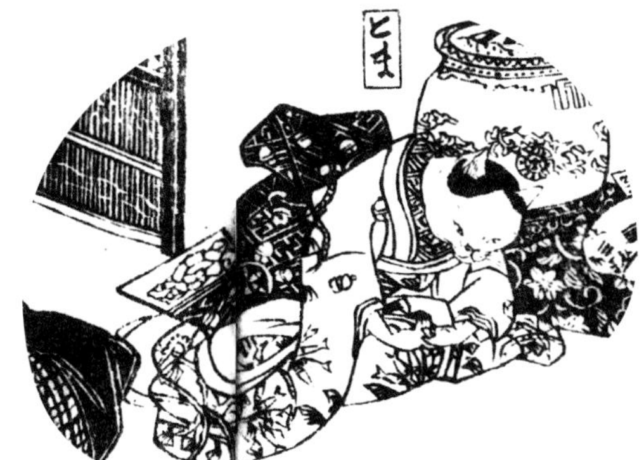

The doctor is called to investigate
Okoma's repeated vomiting (top).
Feeling somewhat better after some
medicine, she takes a bath and settles
down on the princess's lap for the first time
in a while, dozing and purring contentedly. Then, you guessed it, throws up again, this
time all over the princess's lap.
Love it seems, does have limits. Even Umenoi holds a grudge against the little cat,
complaining that Okoma has caused her to lose face even though she, Umenoi
rescued her and gave her a good life. Head bowed, Okoma listens to it all. Then it's
goodbye, puss (bottom).

恩を仇で返す自分の不調法を反省
し、嘆くおこま。にゃんにゃん鳴い
ても、お竹は「鳴くな、宿無しめ」。
そこに商売人のおかんが来合わせた。
おかんは、おこまの所持品である上等な
布団目当てに、おこまを引き取る。悲しそ
うに屋敷をあとにするおこま（上）。
　梅の井からある所へ手紙を届ける用も言いつかっ
たおかんは、手紙がちゃんとあるか確かめようと、途中、抱
いていたおこまを橋の欄干に乗せる。波を見て気味悪くなり、
鳴くおこま。すると、それを聞きつけた犬が飛びかかってき
た（下）。おこまは川に真っ逆さまに……。

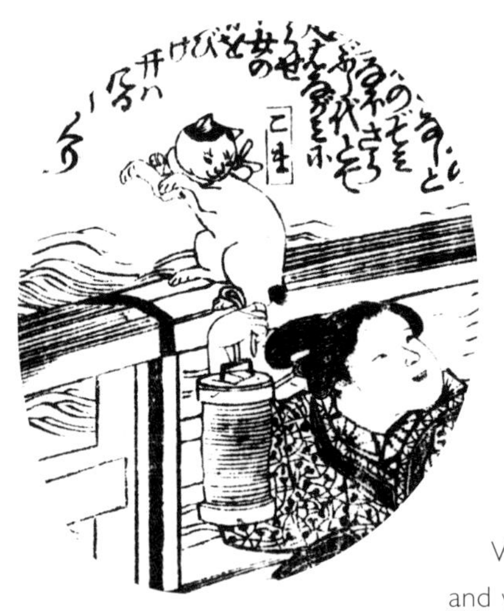

Regretting her careless repaying of kindness
with ingratitude, Okoma miaows unhappily
but is told by Otake, "Don't complain, stray."
Just then the merchant Okan comes along.
Spying the cat's luxurious quilt, she takes her.
Sadly, Okoma leaves the mansion behind
(top).

Also entrusted by Umenoi with a letter to
deliver, along the way Okan stops and places
Okoma on the handrail of a bridge while
she checks whether she actually has the letter.
Watching the current below Okoma grows afraid,
and wails unhappily. Hearing her cries a dogs jumps on
her (bottom), tipping Okoma into the river...

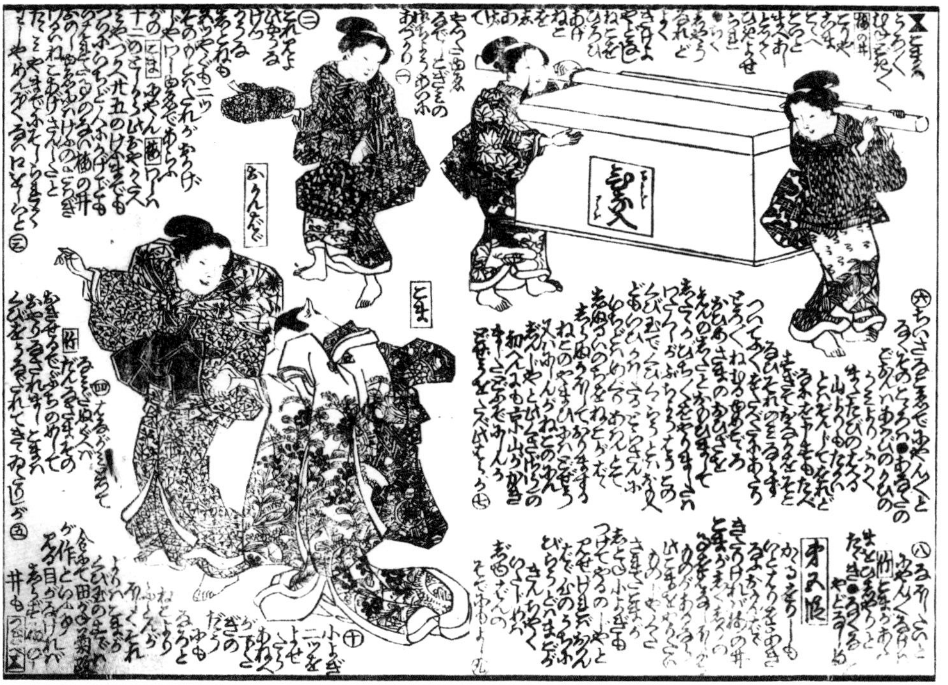

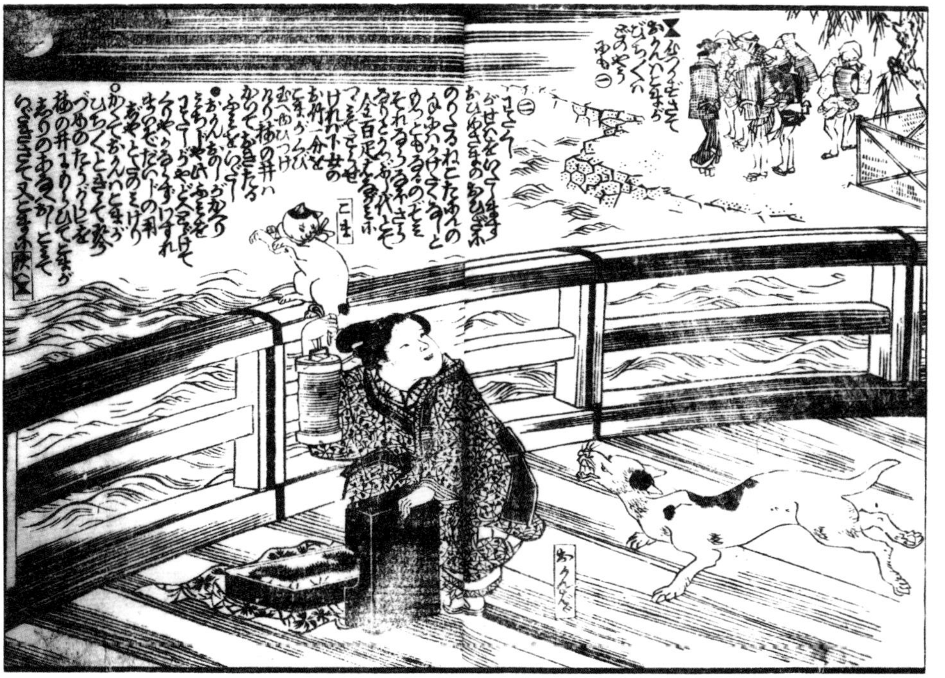

後日談

　おこまちゃんの冒険のほんの一部をご覧いただいたが、いかがだったろうか。京山による波瀾万丈のストーリー、そして、その世界をさらに豊かにして読者の前に映し出してくれる国芳の絵。普通の猫の姿からきれいな着物姿まで、主役おこまの表情は、どれをとっても見事というほかない。絵を見ていると、おかしさがこみ上げ、そして感情移入せずにはいられない。

　さて、川に落ちたおこまが心配でならない方のために、少しだけその後のお話を。川に落ちたおこまは漁師の網にかかり、その家に引き取られる。そこのオス猫にちょっかいを出されたりしながら暮らしていたが、おこまの金の鈴を作った彫物師にめぐり会い、今度はその家へ。そこで、恋しい「とらさん」との間にできた娘と再会を果たし、物語はさらに続くのである。

What happens next etc.

This then is just a small fraction of Okoma's adventures. How did you find Kyozan's story with its myriad twists and turns, and Kuniyoshi's illustrations adding another layer of richness to this narrative realm to present it visually to the reader? In every scene, whether as plain old moggy or feline in fantastic kimono finery, the main character Okoma can only be described as superb. Looking at the pictures one feels a chuckle welling up, and an irresistible empathy with the furry heroine. For those worried about her falling into the river, let us continue slightly further. In the river Okoma becomes caught in a fisherman's net, and is taken to his home. Teased by the resident tomcat she makes a life there before encountering the engraver who made her gold bell, and going to live with him. There she is reunited with the daughter she had with her beloved Tora. The story continues.

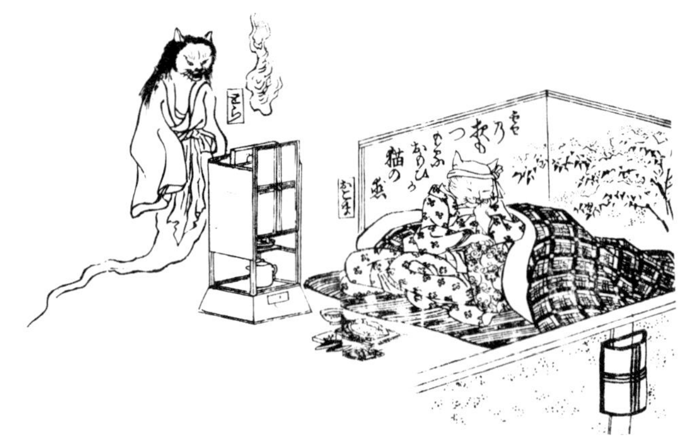

VII

国芳のねこ、もう止められない

The irresistible allure
of Kuniyoshi's cats

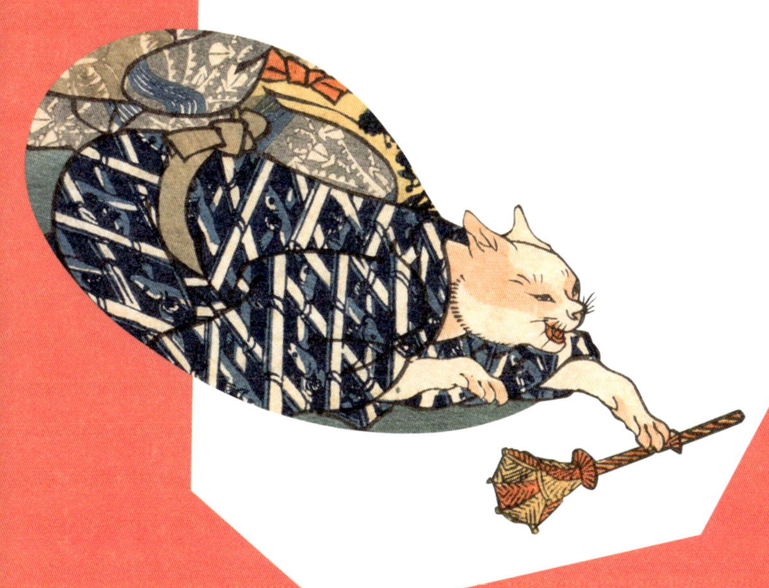

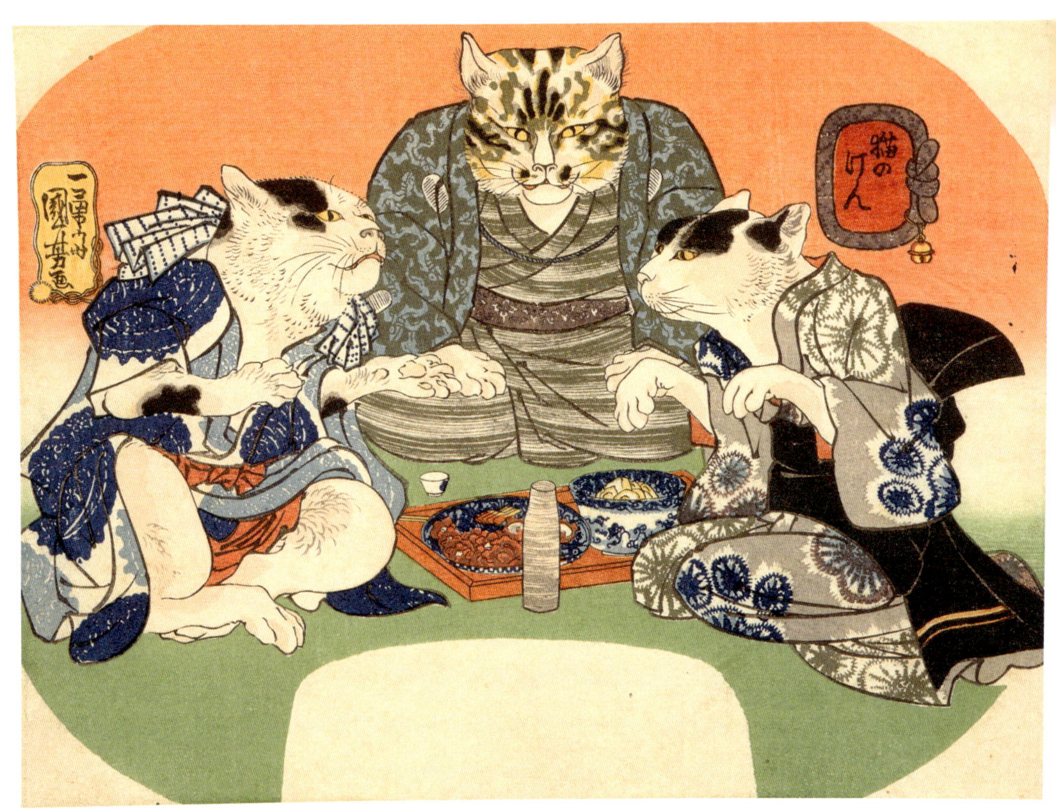

71

71 猫のけん　ねこのけん
72 猫のけいこ　ねこのけいこ

　身近な猫をリアルに捉えたかと思えば、猫たちに芝居や曲芸を演じさせたり、同じ猫好き仲間の戯作者と力を合わせて長大な物語の主人公にしたりと、国芳の目と想像力は、猫たちを多彩に描き出している。そしてもうひとつ、大活躍をみせるのが、何かを演じるのではなく、すっかり人間に取って代わってしまった猫。もはや人間など存在しない、猫の世界の主たちである。この最後の章ではそんな彼らを眺めるが、国芳の果てしない想像は、誰にも止められないところにまで到達してしまったという感がある。

　《猫のけん》は、拳遊びに興じる猫たち。「けん（拳）」は、じゃんけんのように、何かを表す仕草を出し合って勝ち負けを決める遊び。江戸時代には色々な拳が流行した。これは「狐拳」といい、右が狐、真ん中が庄屋、左が鉄砲打ち。真ん中の猫は他の2匹を見ているわけではなく、庄屋の仕草をしているところである。

　次は、色っぽい師匠のもとにせっせと通う弟子。《猫のけいこ》は、よこしまなオス猫たちの涙ぐましい光景である。必死な黒ぶちの横で、茶の1匹は順番待ちか。いつの時代も変わらない滑稽で普遍的な世界が、一枚の団扇絵に凝縮されている。

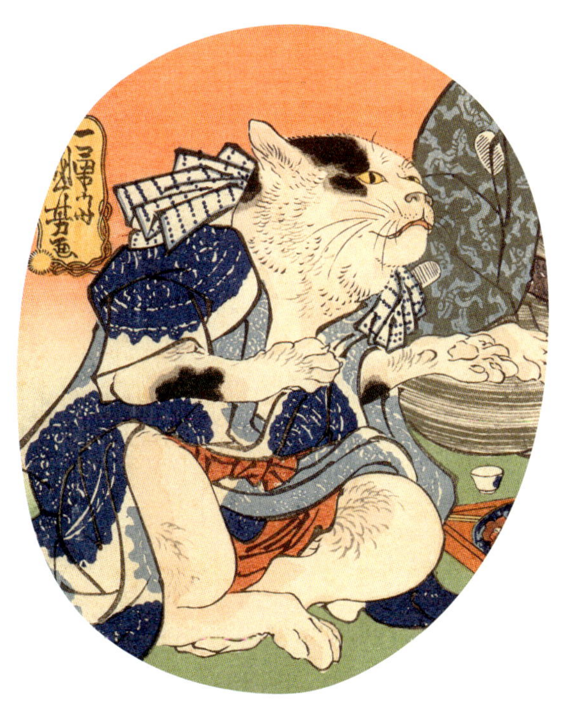

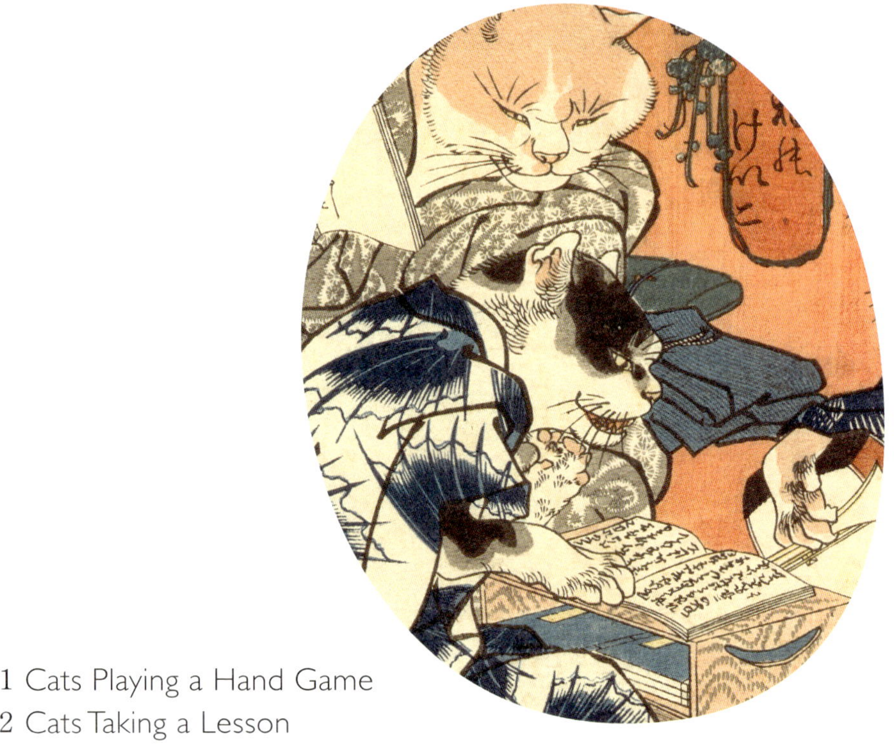

71 Cats Playing a Hand Game
72 Cats Taking a Lesson

Just when we think Kuniyoshi has captured our familiar feline friends with perfect realism, his perceptive eye and flights of imagination have him making cats perform plays and acrobatics, or joining forces with a writer and fellow cat-lover to make them the heroes of an epic story. Also featuring prominently in his oeuvre are cats that rather than performing or acting serve as straight substitutes for humans, lords of a feline fiefdom from which people are absent. This final chapter focuses on these cats, and one senses that by this point, Kuniyoshi's limitless imagination was unstoppable.

Cats Playing a Hand Game features cats amusing themselves with a game similar to paper-scissors-rock in which players simultaneously proffer gestures representing something to decide the winner. Many such games were fashionable in the Edo period, and this one features on the right a wolf, at center a village headman, and on the left, a man with a gun. The middle cat is not looking at the other two, but performing the gesture for headman.

Next are pupils studying assiduously under the watchful eye of a rather seductive teacher. *Cats Taking a Lesson* is a pathetic vision of two tomcats whose motives are, shall we say, not entirely pure. Next to the black pied cat trying desperately to impress, the brown cat is probably waiting his turn. A timelessly comical, universal scenario encapsulated on a single fan.

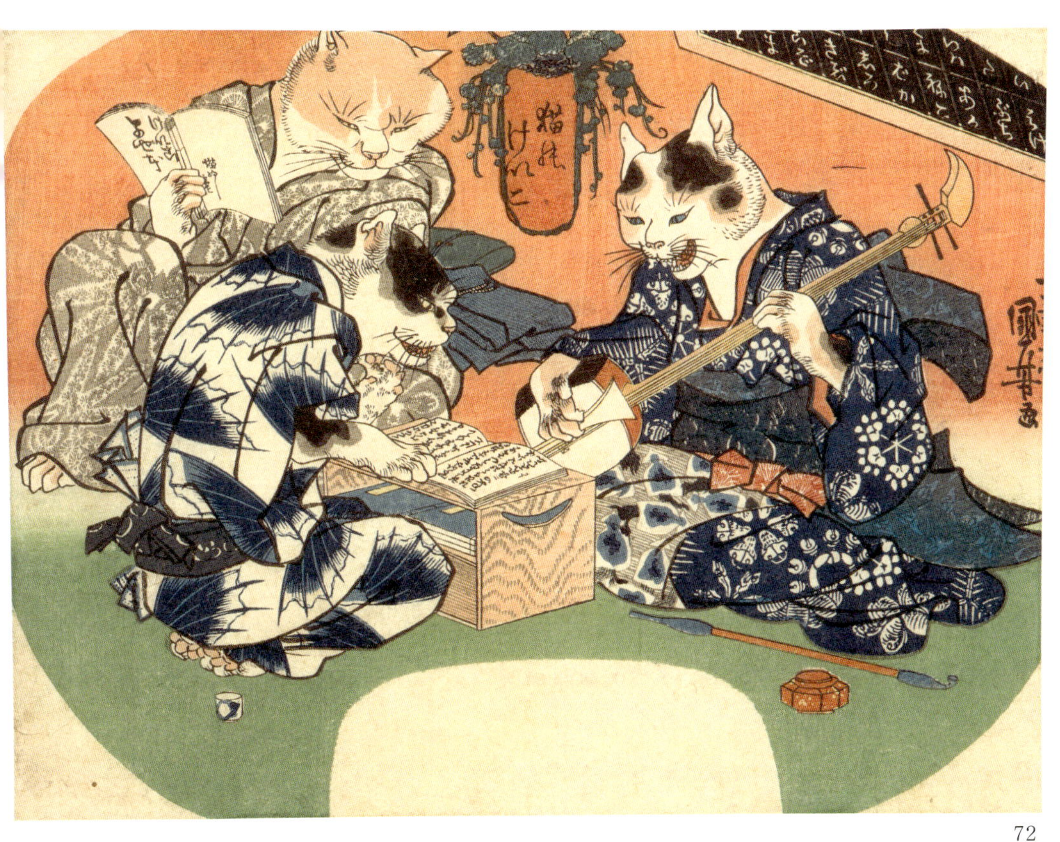

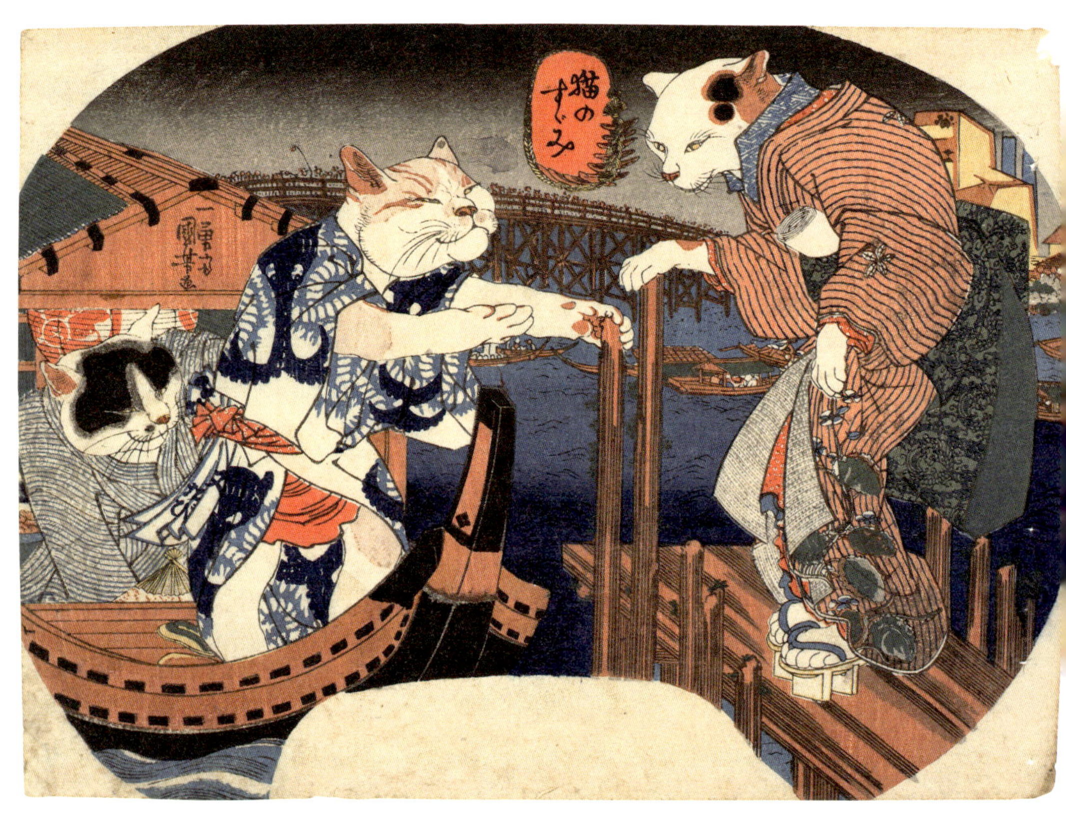

猫の
すゞみ
一勇斎
國芳画

73 猫のすゞみ　ねこのすずみ

　猫ワールドを描いた最高傑作はこれだろう。隅田川の川遊びといえば、江戸の夏の風物詩。川舟を出した羽振りのいい猫が、芸者を待っている。「さ、さ、足元、気をつけなすって」とばかりに、むっくりした手を出す船頭。正確には前足だが、舟を安定させながら桟橋に少しでも近づけるべく、左手はぐっと杭を握っている。右の掌が上を向いているところに、受け入れ態勢十分な気持ちが表れている。舟の中の１匹も、嬉しくて仕方ない様子。芸者を奥へ招き入れるため、場所をあけようとしているようにも見えてくる。

　花火の音、見物客の歓声、そして川音が聞こえてきそうな、江戸の情緒があふれた一枚。橋の上を埋めつくす群衆も、もちろん皆、猫のはずである。

Cats Enjoying the Cool of Evening

Probably Kuniyoshi's most masterful rendering of his cat world. Boating on the Sumida River was a staple of the Edo summer. The cat of means taking out his riverboat is waiting for a geisha, and the captain extends a plump hand to help her aboard. With what is strictly speaking his front paw, he grips the pole tightly in an attempt to move closer to the jetty while stabilizing the boat, his upturned right palm meanwhile signaling eagerness to take the woman on board. The cat on the boat can hardly contain his delight. He also seems to be making space for her alongside him.

In this classic Edo scene one can almost hear the fireworks, the cheers of the spectators, and sound of the water. The crowd on the bridge are also – presumably – cats.

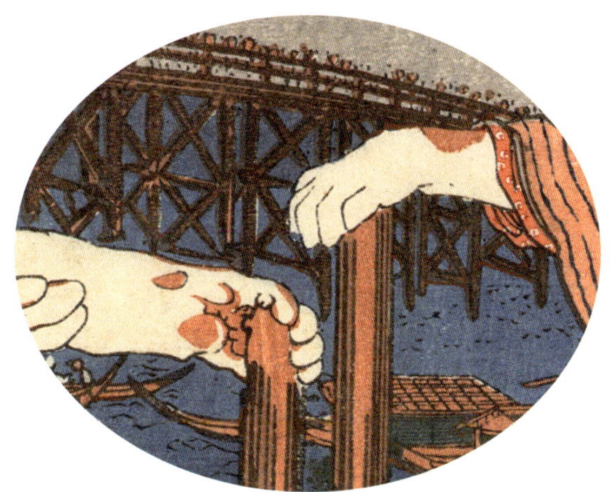

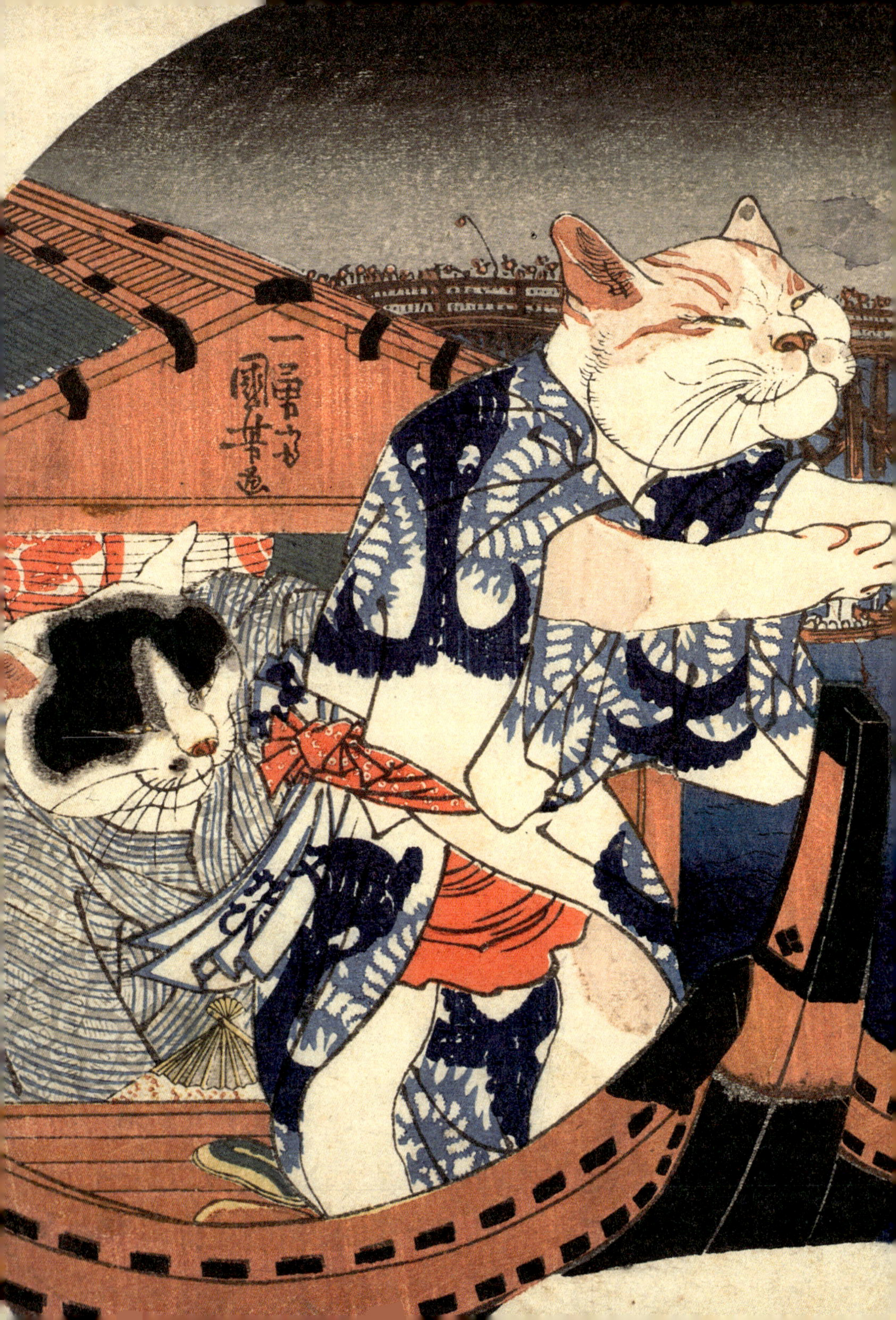

一勇斎
國芳画

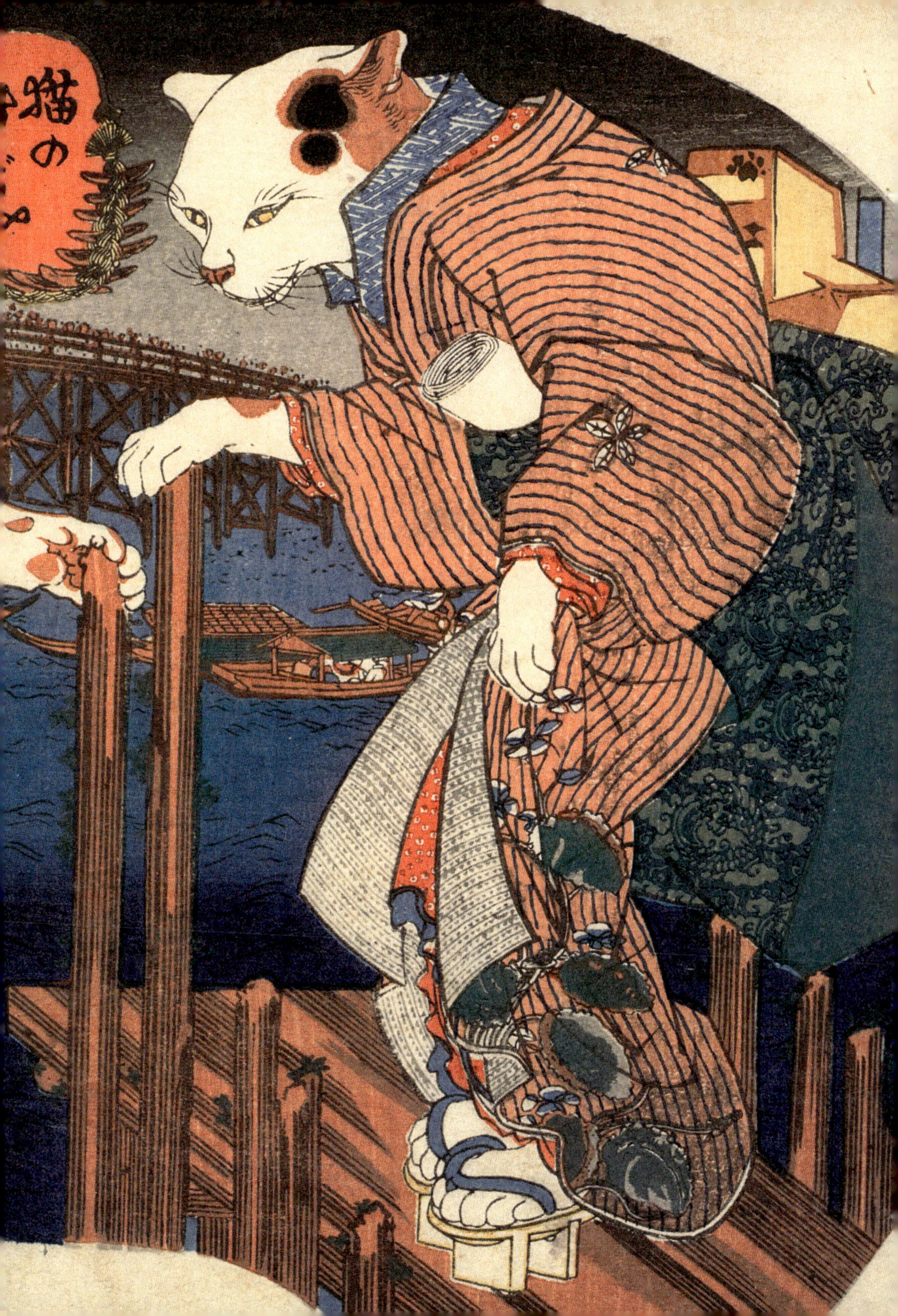

猫の

74 くつろぐ夏の猫美人たち　くつろぐなつのねこびじんたち

　画中にタイトルはないが、美しいメス猫たちの夏の日常である。いかにもプライベートな場面。夏の暑さにすっかりまいってしまったようだが、それがまた、やるせないムードを醸し出す。こんな絵柄の団扇が猫の世界で売られれば、オスの猫たちは競って買うことだろう。

　たらいの水をぺろぺろと飲んでしまう1匹。柱にもたれた1匹が弾く三味線のけだるい響き。色合いもさっぱりと、涼味豊かな雰囲気である。「魚」の字の団扇や蛸の柄の浴衣、飼われている金魚、そしてさりげなく吊り下げられた鰹節など、細かいところまで風情を味わいたい。

Cat Beauties Relaxing in Summer

Though bearing no title, this is obviously a slice of daily summer life for three sensuous feline females. In very much a private scene, the beauties appear to be suffering in the summer heat, this in turn giving the picture a languid, melancholy air. If fans of this design were sold in the cat world, every tomcat would be scrabbling to get his paws on one.

One cat is thirstily lapping water from a basin. Another lounging against a pillar is plucking listlessly at a shamisen. The clean coloration amplifies the cooling ambiance. An image to savor down to the finest details from the fan bearing the character for fish to the octopus-patterned robe, the pet goldfish, and the casually hung string of dried bonito.

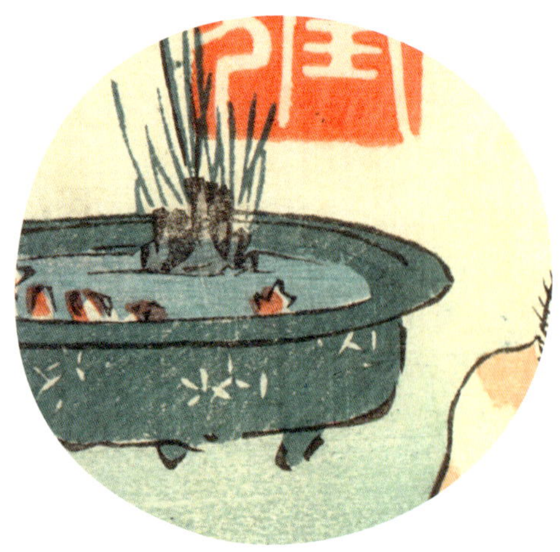

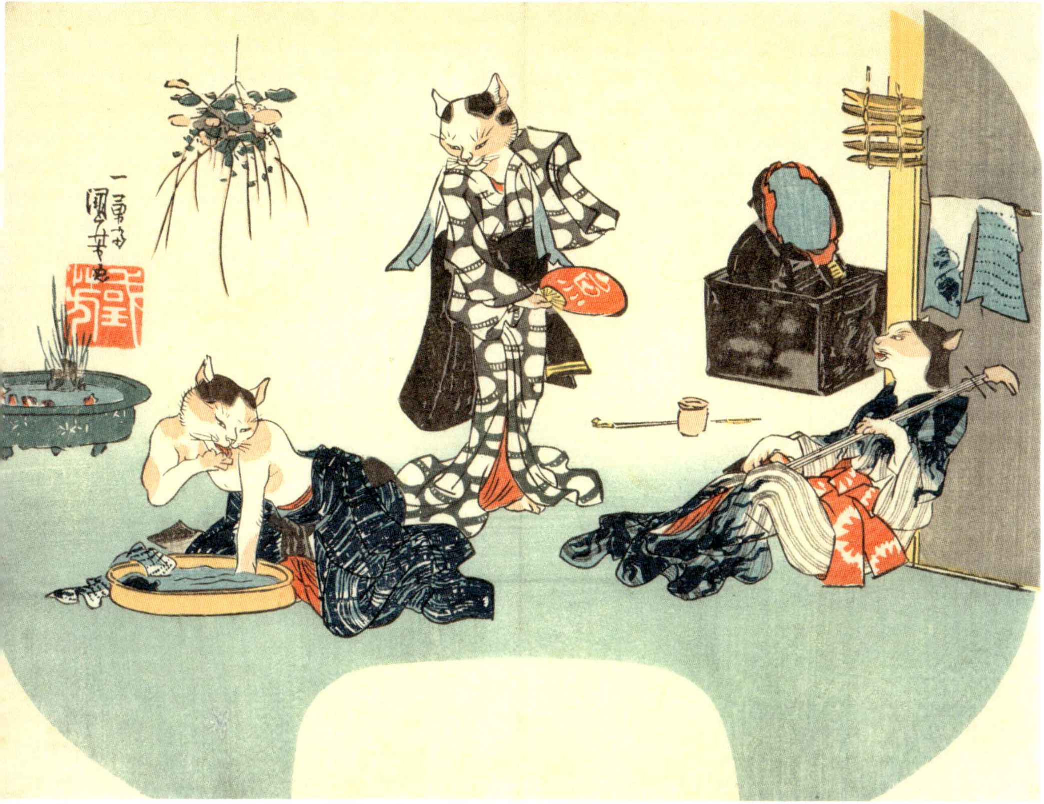

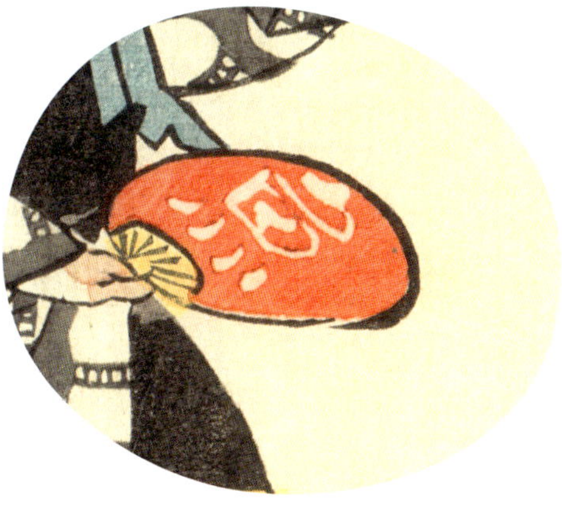

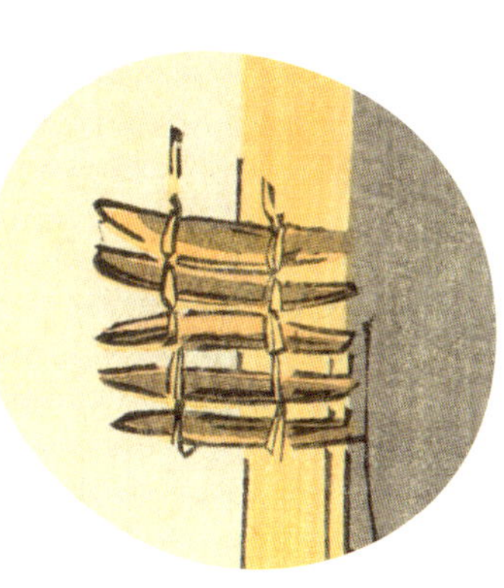

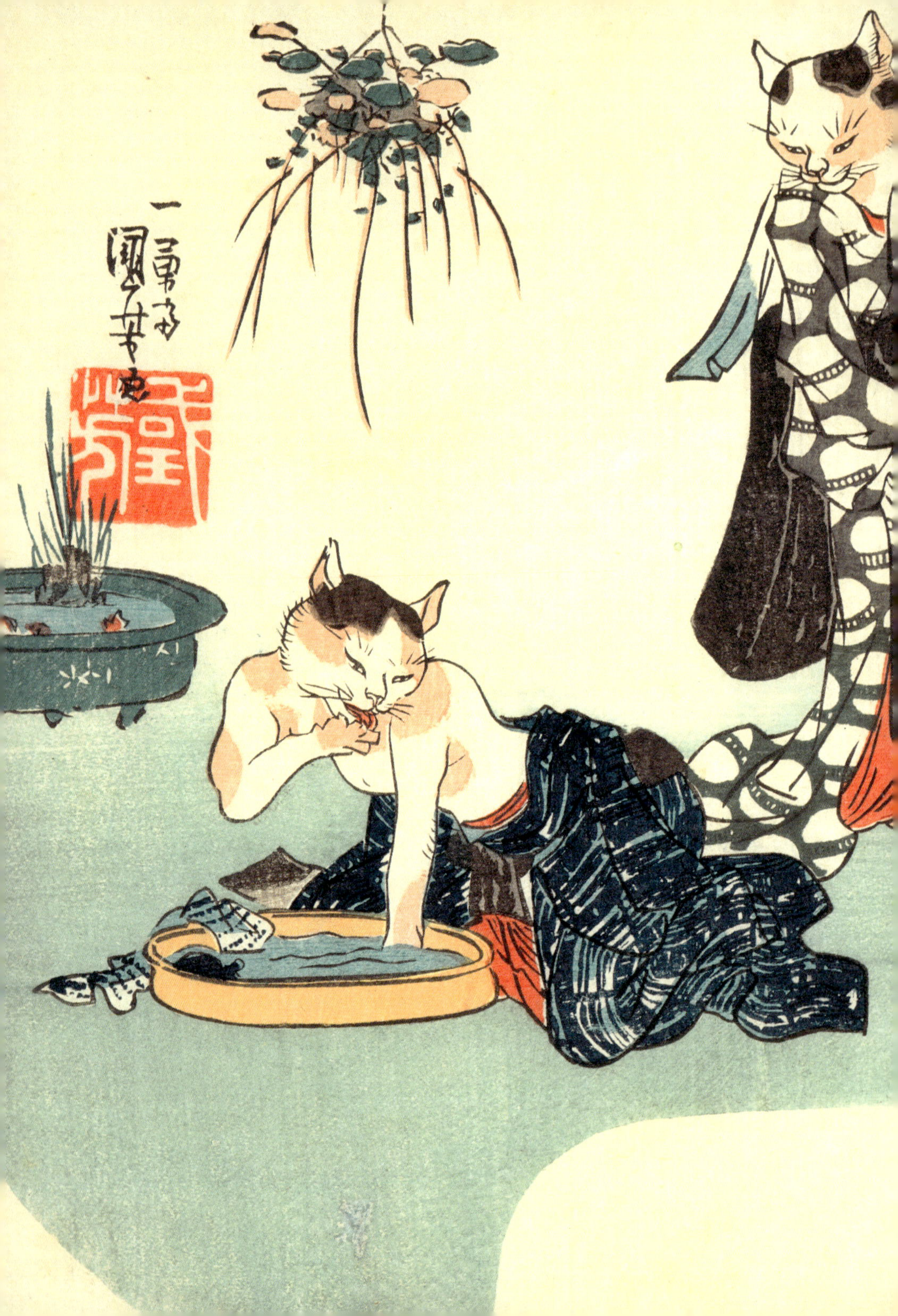

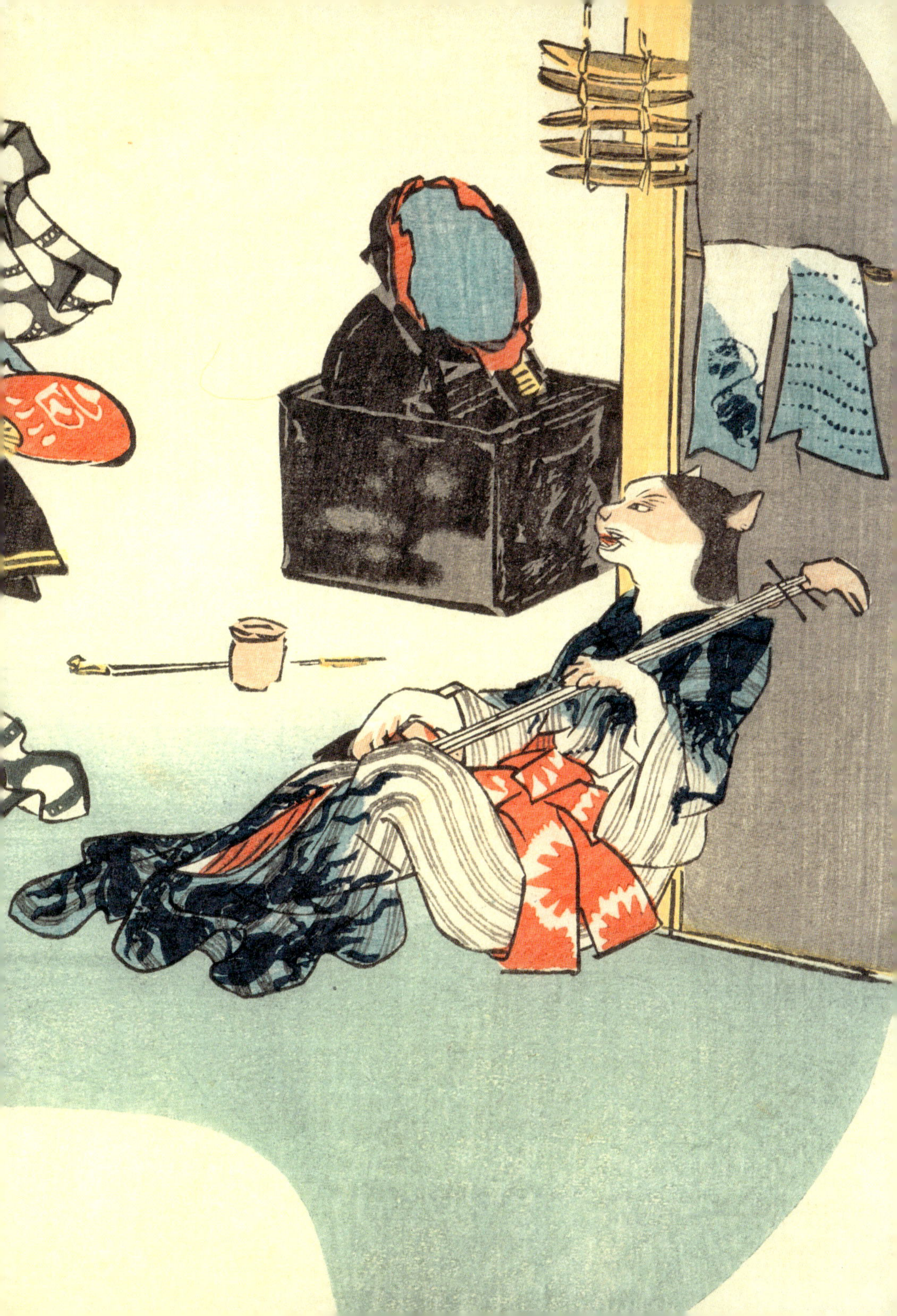

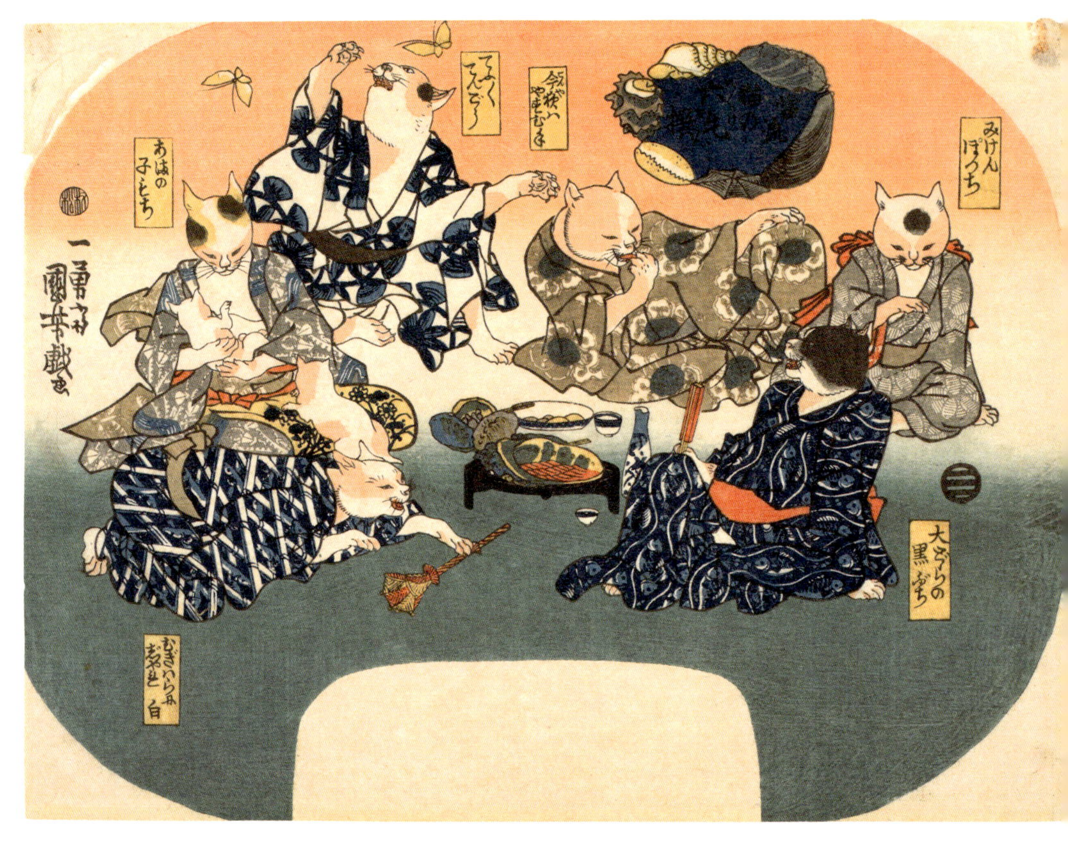

75 当流猫の六毛撰　とうりゅうねこのろくけせん

　猫たちのどんちゃん騒ぎの図のようだが、6匹は猫の六歌仙。そう思えば、一層、趣深いというものだ。

　右下の態度の大きい1匹は、大友黒主ならぬ「大どらの黒ぶち」。左で赤ん坊にお乳を飲ませる猫は、メスだから「あまの子もち」で小野小町。蝶々に戯れるのは僧正遍昭で、「てふてふてんごう（蝶々てんごう）」。てんごうは、いたずらの意味である。そして、右でぽつねんとしているのは喜撰法師。眉間にぽちりと丸い模様があって、「みけんぽっち」。

　さらに、かわいいネーミングは続く。左下で麦わらにじゃれる猫は在原業平で、「むぎはらにじゃれ白」。膝を立てて横になる1匹は、文屋康秀ならぬ「今夜はやすむね（あるいは「今夜はやすむ手」か）」。どうしたら、こんな名付け方を思いつくのだろうか。

Six Poetic Geniuses of the Heian Period

At first glance a study of feline revelry, in fact the six cats here represent the Six Immortal Poets of Chinese legend. Once one realizes this, the print takes on a whole new dimension of meaning.

The self-important fellow at lower right, "Odora no kurobuchi" i.e. the "black pied cat Odora" is Otomo no Kuronushi, while the cat on the left suckling a kitten, being female, must be Ono no Komachi, or here "Ama no Komochi" i.e. "nurse with child." Playing with the butterfly is Sojo Henjo or "Chocho (butterfly) Tengo," tengo meaning mischief. To the right looking a little lost and alone is Kisen Hoshi. With the round mark dabbed between his eyebrows, he is "Miken (between the brows) Potchi (spot)."

The delightful naming continues. The cat playing with the straw at bottom left is Ariwara no Narihira: "Mugiwara ni jareshira" i.e. "white playing with straw." The cat prone with its knees raised is "Konya wa yasumu ne" ("This evening I'll rest, OK?") [or perhaps "Konya wa yasumu te" ("This evening these hands will rest"], otherwise known as Funya no Yasuhide. One marvels at how Kuniyoshi came up with these names...

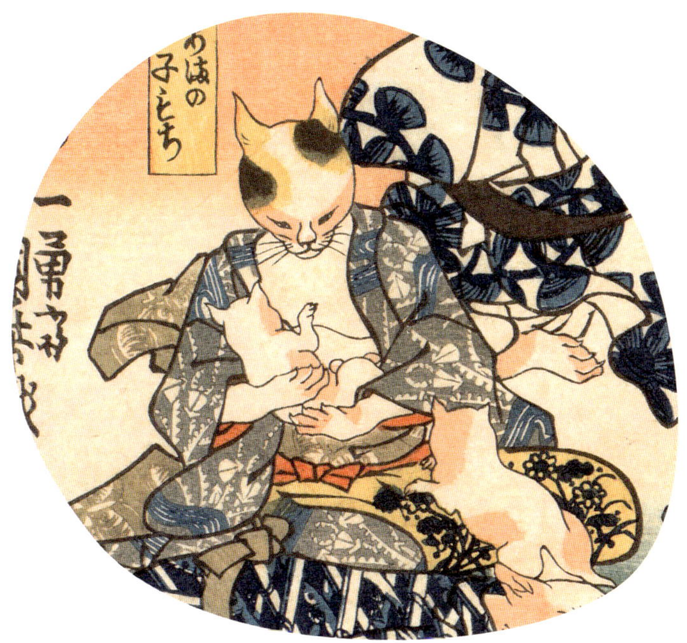

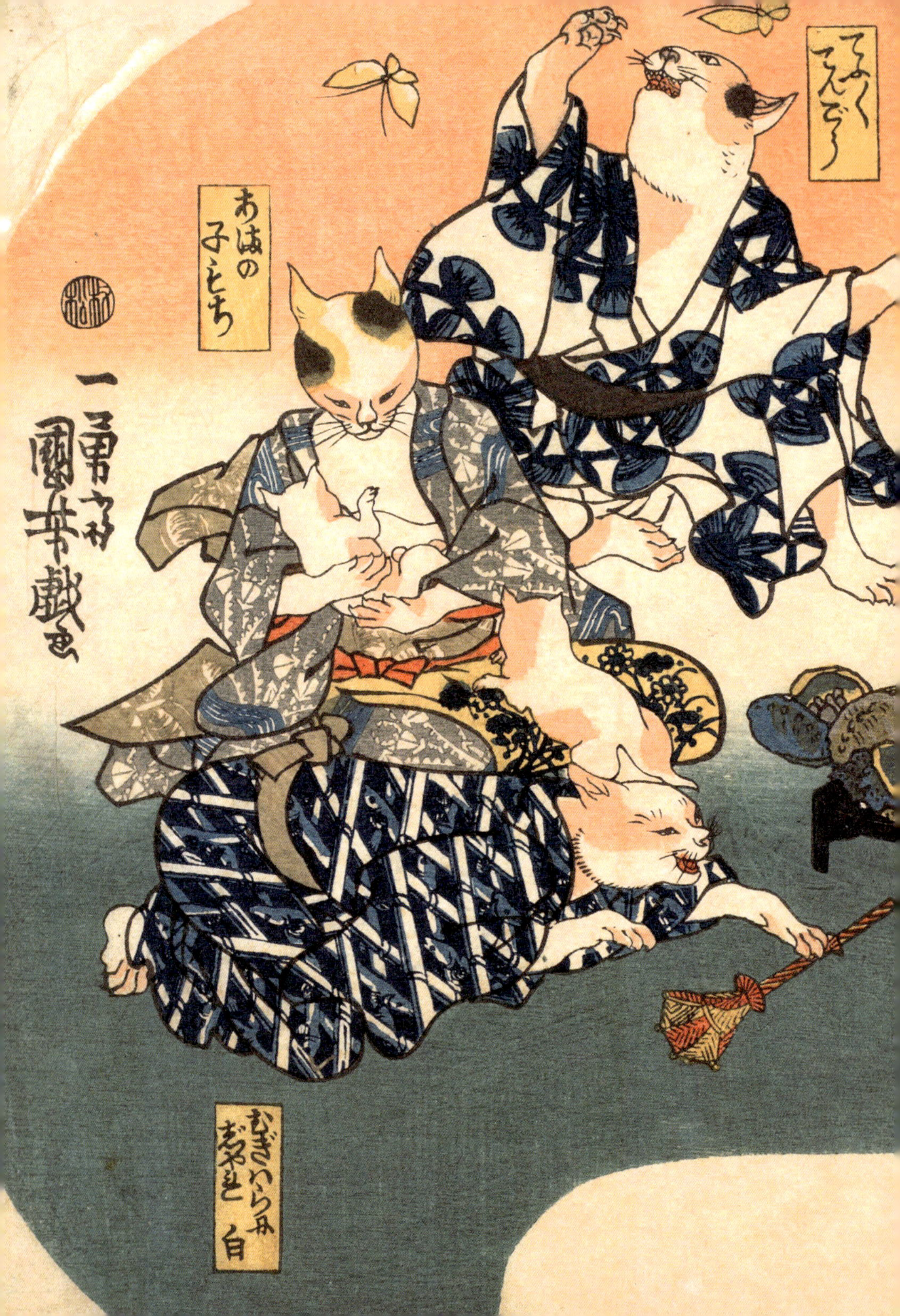

てふく　てんぐう
あはの　子とち
一勇斎　國芳戯画
むぎわら丹　おやを　白

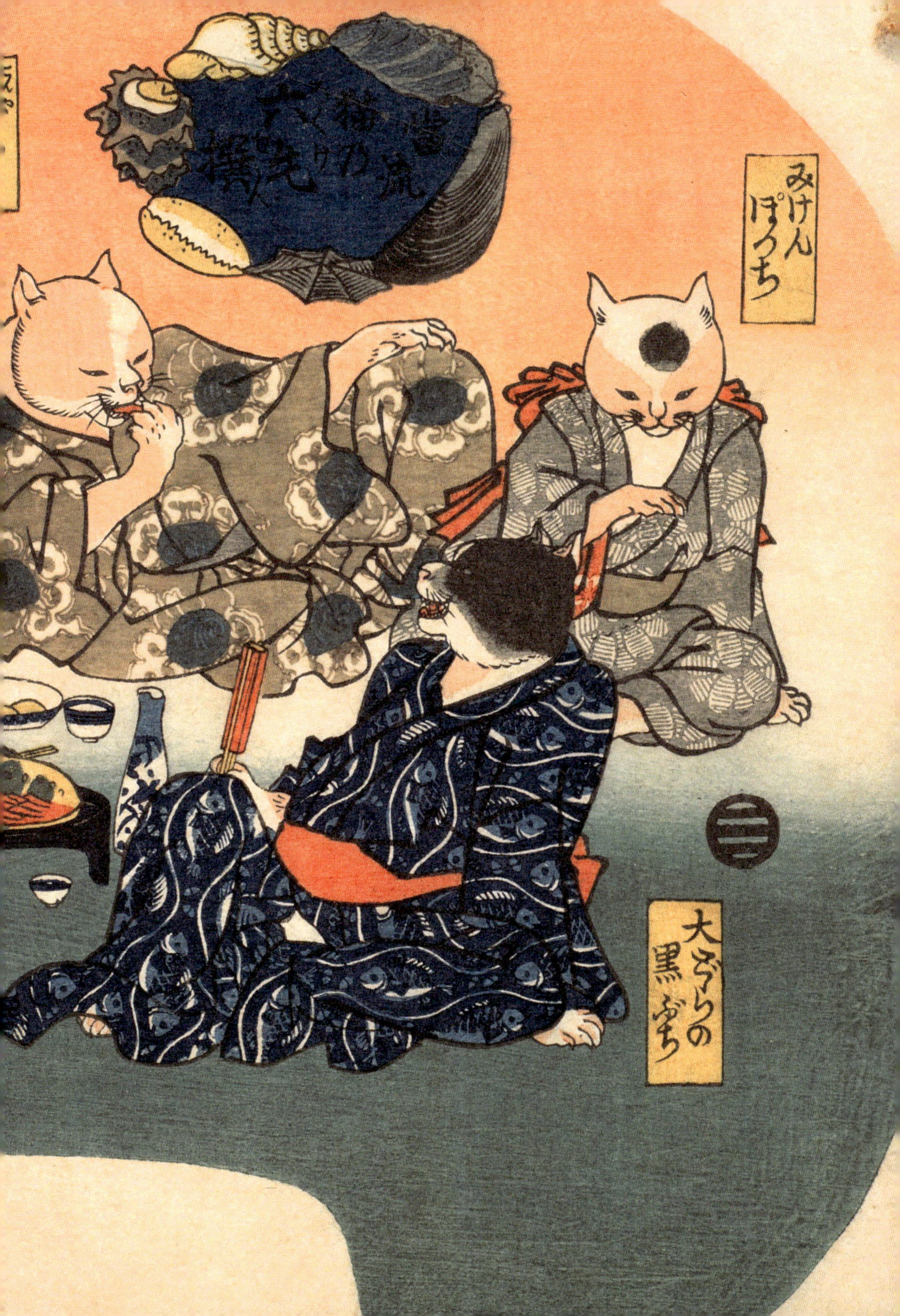
みけん
ぽつち

大ぐらの
黒ぶち

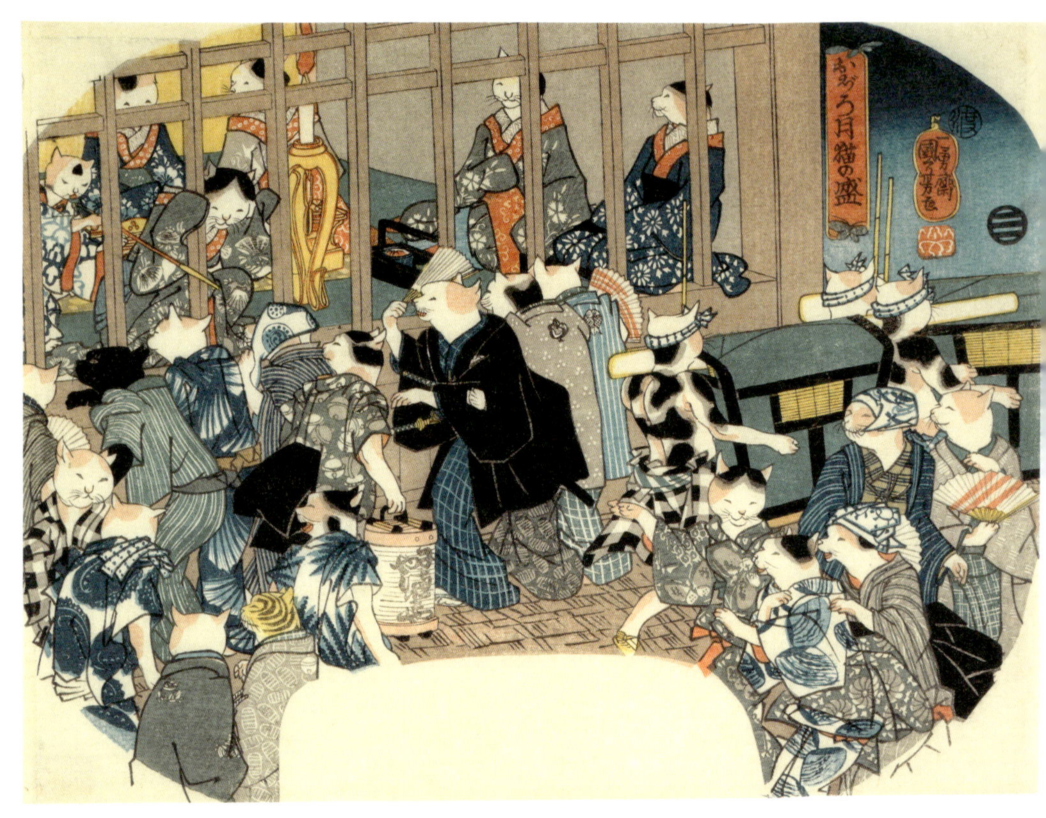

76 おぼろ月猫の盛　おぼろづきねこのさかり

　いよいよ本書の最後の作品である。《おぼろ月猫の盛》という、タイトルだけで笑ってしまう一枚。遊里である吉原が「悪所」と呼ばれたのは、現代人でも考えればわかる。かといって、そうした理解を超えた、独特の盛り場でもあったようだ。いかにもにぎやかで楽しそうな場所として、たくさんの浮世絵に描かれている。

　しかしこれは、猫の世界の吉原。描かれているのは、「盛」のついた輩ばかりではない。愉快そうな女性たちもいれば、せっせと働く駕籠かきもいる。彼らは上半身をはだけて、自慢の三毛模様を見せつけているが、3匹の同じような後頭部が並ぶさまには、思わずにんまりしてしまう。もちろん女性に見とれる輩も大勢いるが、国芳には珍しい黒猫がいるのも見逃せない。

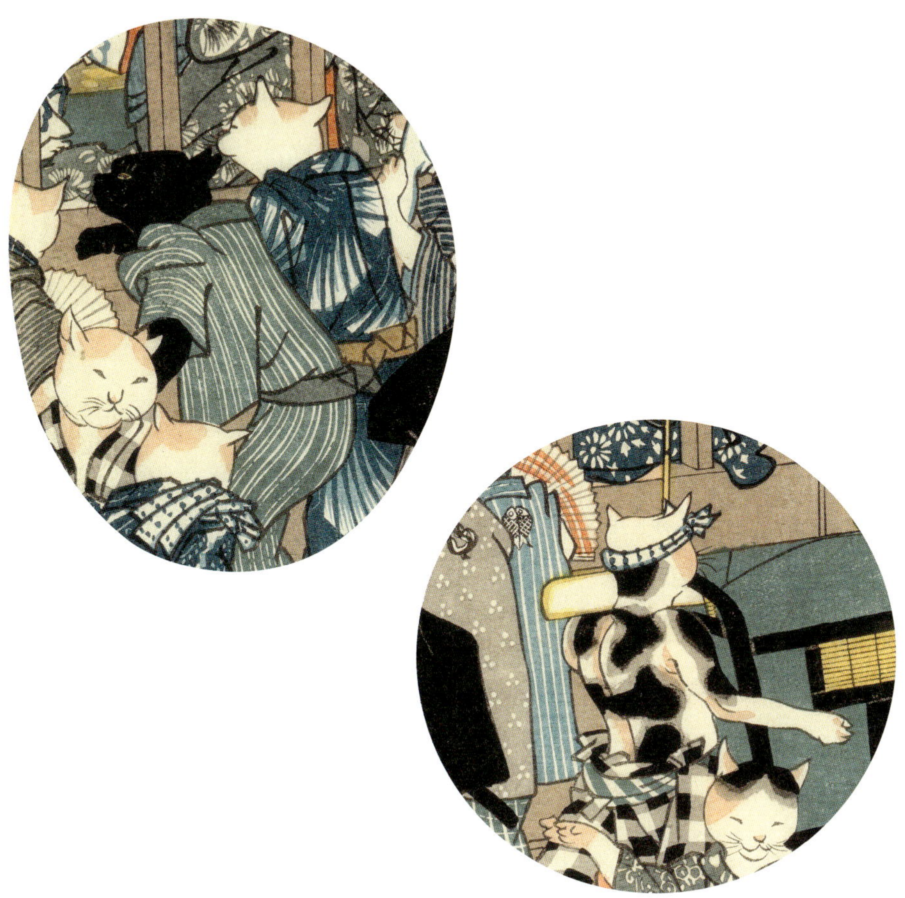

Pale Moon, Cats in Season

Finally, the last work in this book: *Pale Moon, Cats in Season*. The title itself is a hoot. Even today we understand why the red-light district of Yoshiwara was known as an "immoral place." Still, it appears to have been a unique sort of entertainment quarter that also managed to transcend this image. As such it features in many ukiyo-e as a bustling, fun place to be.

Except that this is the Yoshiwara of the cat world. But these are not only the gang "in season." Yes there are some very pleasant-looking women, but also litter-bearers speedily plying their trade. Topless, they proudly display their tortoiseshell pattern, but there is something about the alignment of their heads that raises an involuntary grin. Of course there are plenty of the sort of males with eyes only for the women, but one cannot overlook the presence of a black cat, unusual for Kuniyoshi.

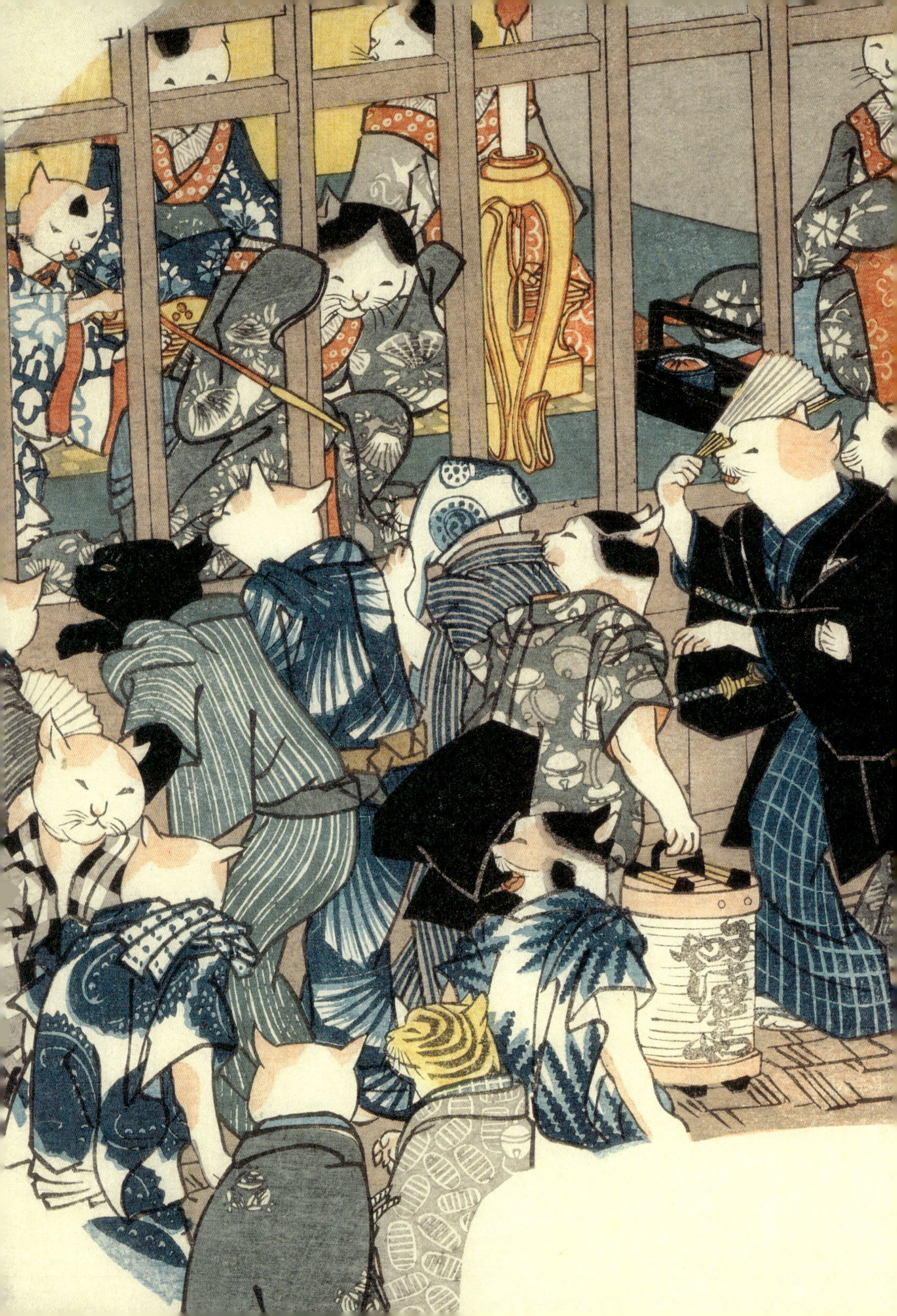

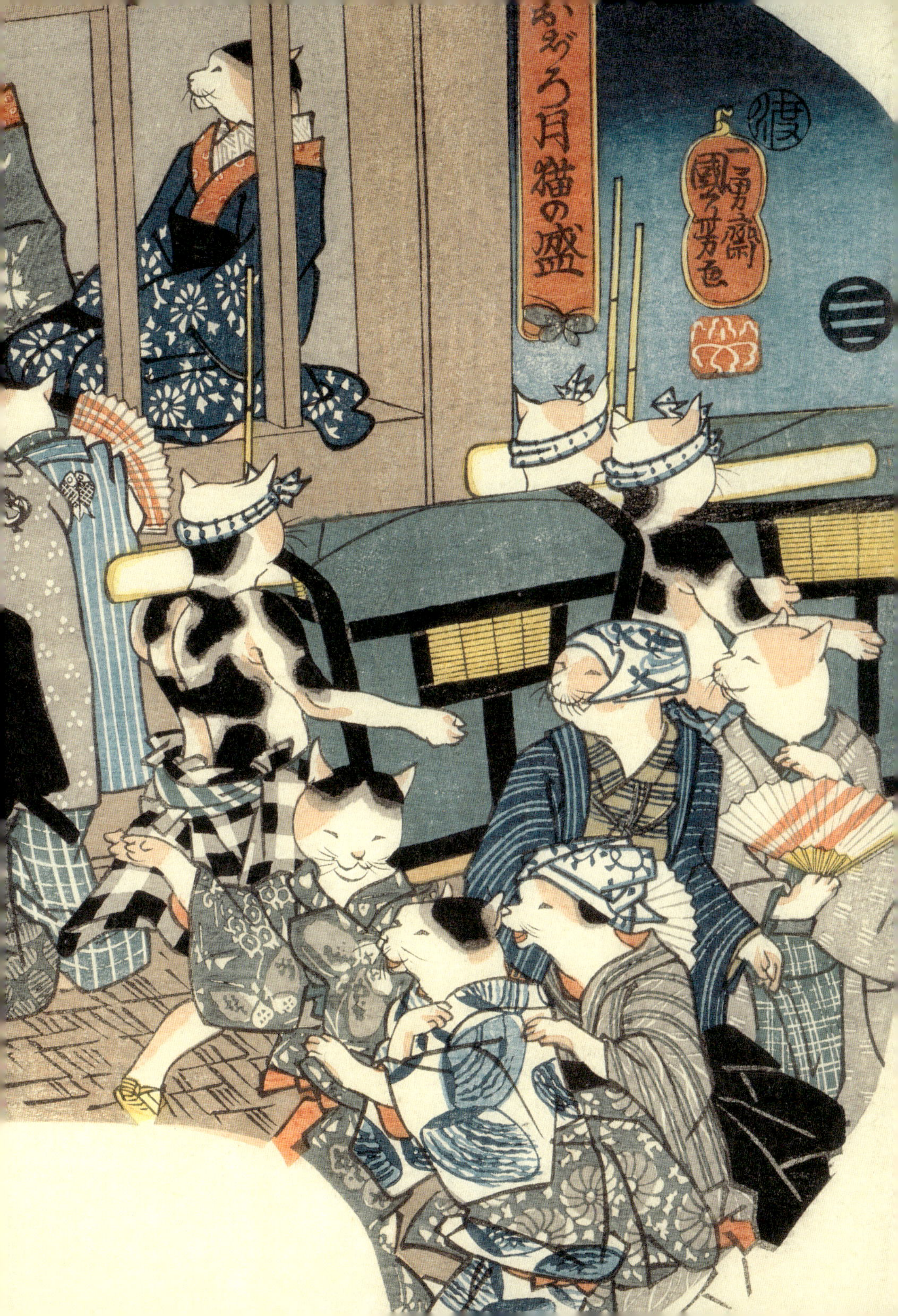
かぢろう月猫の盛
一勇齋國芳畫

おわりに

　写真家の八二一さんの愛猫「はっちゃん」が、写真集やブログで大人気。私の家にも、はっちゃんの「肉球本」、つまり直筆サイン本がある。自慢話はさておき、国芳のことをあれこれ考えていて思い出したのが、はっちゃんは絵になる猫だという、八二さんの言葉である。たくさんの猫や動物にカメラを向けてきた方の言葉だけに、たいへん興味深い。はっちゃんはきっと、歌舞伎役者が最高のポーズを見せてくれるのと同じように、猫好きの心を鷲づかみにする仕草やポーズを次々と決める「千両役者」なのだろう。

　私も飼い猫にカメラを向けた経験があるが、つたない腕では、絵になるどころか、かわいく撮ることすらむずかしい。写真だけではなく、猫のかわいらしさを「絵」にするのは簡単ではない。江戸時代の浮世絵師たちも猫を描いているが、国芳の域に達している画家は見当たらない。そればかりか、「これが猫？」と悩んでしまうような絵さえある。なぜだろうか。

　そもそも、猫は描きにくい動物である。現代人は、すでにパターン化されている「猫の絵」や「猫の描き方」を知っているから、そう感じないかもしれない。しかし、私たちは無意識に、パターン化された「猫の絵」を通して猫の姿かたちを見ている面さえあるだろう。そこで、かつての人々になったつもりで、改めて猫の姿を観察してみよう。歩いているところ、寝ているところ、変てこりんな姿勢、骨があるのかないのか考え込んでしまうような動きもする。伸縮自在な体の大きさを測るには、一体どういう状態の時にどこを測ればよいのだろうか。

　不思議な動物だからこそ、描き方の定番が確立していなかった時代に猫を描けば、奇妙になったり、お世辞にもかわいいとは言えない残念な結果になったりするのは無理もないことである。

　そうした時代に、人々の望むとおりの、心を揺さぶる猫の絵を描いたのが国芳というわけだが、その仕事は、単なる猫の絵の名手というにとどまらない。日本の動物絵画史上、重大な業績なのである。少し歴史を振り返ってみよう。

　日本は、西洋と比べても豊かな動物絵画の歴史をもっている。なぜ古くから動物が描かれてきたかといえば、動物の神秘性に対する畏怖、あるいは、亀は長寿を意味するというような中国伝来の動物観などがあったから。つまり、信仰や、人生における利益と結びつけて、多くの絵が描かれてきた。

　もちろんその一方で、人々は動物に対して愛情やかわいらしさも感じてきた。猫に関しては、『源氏物語』の女三宮の話からしても、平安時代にはすでに「かわいい動物」として認められていたのは間違いない。しかし、信仰や現世利益のための絵は描かれても、「かわいい猫の絵」は、なかなか実現しなかった。その大きな理由が、やはり「猫を絵にするむずかしさ」だろう。

　国芳が登場したのは、19世紀前半のこと。対象を精密に、正確に描こうとする18世紀以来の絵画界の全般的な風潮が、一層高まり、浸透した時代だった。本書3章の国芳のスケッ

Afterword

"Hatch-chan," much-loved pet of photographer couple Hani Hajime has acquired star status through various media including photography books and even his own blog. I too am the proud owner of a volume autographed (or rather "pawtographed") personally(?) by Hatch-chan. Enough bragging for the moment: musing on Kuniyoshi and his work I was reminded of the couple's description of Hatch-chan as "extremely photogenic." Coming from professionals who've pointed cameras at countless cats, not to mention many other animals, this was intriguing. Hatch-chan must be a great actor capable of affecting pose after gesture to enrapture cat-lovers, in the same way that kabuki actors like to revisit their finest moments for the fans.

I too have photographed pet cats, but in my clumsy hands they come off looking far from photogenic; rarely even cute. Nor is it a challenge confined to photography: capturing a cat's appeal by drawing or painting is no easier. Edo period ukiyo-e artists did depict cats, but none comes anywhere close to Kuniyoshi in skill. Perhaps this is why in some of his paintings, we worry whether those cats are actually cats. Why should this be?

Cats are inherently tricky creatures to draw or paint. Today we can all think of cat pictures and ways of drawing cats that adhere to certain rules, so perhaps do not sense this difficulty. It could also be that we have come to view the feline form through the prism of such cat picture templates. So let us return to an earlier age, and make a fresh study of cats: walking, sleeping, adopting strange attitudes, the movements that make us wonder if cats actually have bones. If we were to measure a cat's body in all its freedom to stretch and contract, where would we measure, and in what state?

Cats being such amazing animals, it's hardly surprising then that depicting cats at a time when there were no standard ways of doing so led to some unfortunate results: cats that looked very odd, or could not, by any stretch of the imagination, be described as endearing.

It was Kuniyoshi who in such an era painted the kind of heartwarming cat pictures the public craved. Nor was he simply an expert painter of cats: his pictures represent a significant body of work in the annals of Japanese animal painting. Let us therefore take a brief trip back in time.

Japan has a rich history of animal painting easily rivaling that of the west. This depiction of animals from the earliest times is attributable to an awe of the mysterious nature of the animal kingdom, and a view of animals that came from China, for example the linking of turtles to longevity. Thus many pictures were connected to religious belief, or the quest for a better life.

Meanwhile, naturally people also felt a simple, doting affection for their animals. When it comes to cats, the story of Onna Sannomiya in *The Tale of Genji* suggests that by the Heian period they were already recognized as endearing in their own right. But although pictures were painted as an expression of religious belief, or to acquire spiritual benefit in this world, plain old cute pictures of cats failed to materialize. The biggest reason no doubt was the difficulty of pinning down cats on paper.

Kuniyoshi appeared in the first half of the 19th century, at a time when the general trend in the world of painting since the 18th century to render subjects accurately and in detail was becoming even more dominant, penetrating widely. Looking at Kuniyoshi's sketches in chapter three one can see how he grasped, incisively and concisely, the most subtle contours and movements of the feline form. The emergence of a painter combining a thoroughly modern rendering technique with an extraordinary love of cats, finally resulted, for the first time in Japanese painting, in pictures to truly tickle the fancy of cat-lovers.

In every work, Kuniyoshi's cats are truly realistic. One suspects this intense realism to have largely

チを見れば、猫の体のきわめて微妙な起伏や動きまで、鋭く、無駄なくつかみ取っているのがわかる。もはや完全に近代的といえる描写技術を身につけ、並々ならぬ猫への愛を抱いた一人の画家が現れた時、ようやく日本絵画史上初の「猫好きのかゆいところに手が届く絵」が誕生したのである。

　どんな作品でも、国芳の猫は本当にリアルである。そのリアリティーが何から生まれているのか、さらに考えてみると、人間観察によるところが大きいのでは、と思われてならない。
　猫好きは、猫の「いやっちさ」を喜ぶが、それは、猫に人と同じ心理や、まなざしを見い出しているからだろう。１章に登場した美人画の中の猫たちが、単なる美人画の点景を越えた、もう一人の主役たり得るゆえんは、猫好きたちの目に叶う「性格描写」の明確さにある。そして、《猫のすゞみ》(73)をはじめとする猫世界の風俗画の数々。酸いも甘いも噛み分け、人生を知り尽くした、滑稽ささえ滲ませた猫たちが織りなす光景は、まさに人間世界の縮図。それも、人を描くより濃厚に滲み出ているように感じられる。

　ところで、家に通ってくる猫と親しくなった人の体験談だが、ある日、猫が「こっちへ来い」という仕草をするので、ついていったという。すると、そこは猫たちの「集会」だったそうである。彼は猫仲間として認められ、参加を許されたということなのだろうか。
　人は猫を「飼っている」と思っているが、猫はそう思っていないのかもしれない。今でこそ室内飼いが多くなったが、そもそもは家の中から縁の下、人の布団の中から屋根の上まで、自分の空間を自分の都合で闊歩するのが猫である。そして彼らには彼らの社会がある。飼い猫でありながら、飼い主の知らない世界に生きる猫たち。家の中での猫の様子から、人に取って代わったかのような「猫世界」の風俗画まで描いた国芳にも、猫の集会に参加した経験の一度や二度はあったかもしれない。

　描写の技術、人間観察、そして猫世界への想像……現代人をも魅了してやまない国芳の猫の絵だが、展覧会などでは「戯画」に分類され、後ろの方で扱われることが多い。ただ、誤解のないように付け加えれば、その場合の「戯画」という言葉は、「余技」とか「本気ではない」という意味で使われているわけではない。「戯れ絵」、つまり人を笑わせるような滑稽な絵という意味である。あの絵巻物の名作《鳥獣戯画》を、ただ戯れに描いたものと思う人がいないのと同じように、国芳の猫の絵の数々を、単なる余興とは誰も考えてはいないだろう。それにもかかわらず、武者絵で名をあげた画家だからか、猫の絵は、少々軽く扱われているのではないだろうか。「武者絵か、猫の絵か」。国芳の真骨頂を、そんな風に論じ合ってもよいくらいだと思うのである。
　最後に、私事で恐縮だが、この本が世に出ることを、今は亡き愛猫の「うし」も喜んでいるのではないかと思う。長く人とともにあった動物、猫。一人でも多くの人が慈しみ、そして、世の猫たちが安泰であることを心から祈っている。

been born out of the artist's penchant for observing human nature.

Those who love cats rejoice in their irresistable ways, probably because they perceive in cats similar psychological processes and expressions to humans. The reason the cats appearing in the *bijinga* in chapter one have the potential to become more than incidental details – instead playing a major role themselves – lies in a clarity to these "character studies" that pleases cat-lovers. Then there are the myriad genre paintings of the cat world, such as *Cats Enjoying the Cool of Evening* (73). These tapestries woven by characters who have tasted both bitter and sweet, studied a great deal in the school of life, and are even suffused with a degree of humor, form a realm that is no less than the human world writ small. Moreover one senses in these pictures a richness greater than anything achieved using human figures.

Incidentally, talking to someone who became friendly with a cat that started turning up at their house, I learned that one day the cat gestured for him to follow, so he did. There he came upon a group of cats having a "meeting." Does this mean he was acknowledged as a fellow cat, and permitted to participate in proceedings?

People think they "keep" cats, but it's doubtful cats concur with this notion. Though these days many cats are kept exclusively indoors, originally they are creatures that strut from inside house to under veranda, from snuggled in someone's futon to up on the roof, moving through their own space at their own pace. Plus they have a whole society of their own. Pet they may be, yet they inhabit a world unknown to their owners. Kuniyoshi too, who depicted everything from the cats in his home to genre paintings of a feline world in which cats completely took the place of people, may well have attended the odd one of these cat meetings.

With their superb rendering skills, observation on humans and human nature, and feline flights of fancy, Kuniyoshi's cat paintings are every bit as alluring to modern-day viewers as they were to his contemporaries, but at exhibitions they tend to be classed as *giga* and relegated to the last part of the show. To avoid misunderstanding, may I add that the term *giga* here does not refer to a sideline, or something not undertaken seriously. It refers to comical pictures designed to make people laugh. Just as few think that the famous *Choju giga* (Scrolls of Frolicking Animals) were painted simply for fun, probably nobody views Kuniyoshi's many paintings of cats as mere entertainment. Despite this, perhaps because he made his name with pictures of samurai, Kuniyoshi's cat pictures are treated a little lightly, when in fact one could debate whether it was his warrior paintings or cat paintings that displayed the artist at his best.

Finally, on a personal note, let me say I'm sure my late and dearly loved cat Ushi will be glad to see the publication of this book. Cats have lived alongside us for a long time. Let us hope that more and more people grow to love them, and that all the cats of the world can live in peace and security.

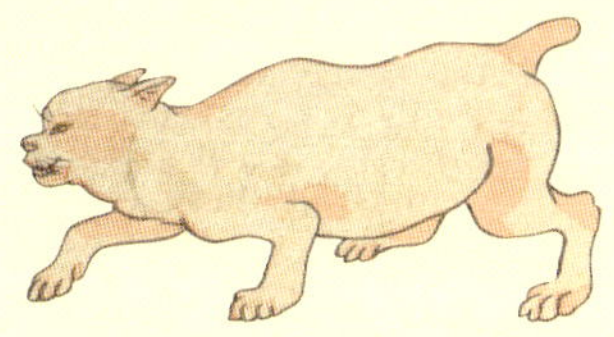

作品リスト　List of Works

作品番号　作品名　大きさ　版元　制作時期　所蔵（表記のないものは個人蔵）

No., Title, Size, Date, Collection (Those without mention belong to private collections.)

01　風流六花撰 百合　大判　和泉屋市兵衛　天保末〜弘化期
Fashionable Selection of Six Flowers (Furyu rokkasen): Lilies, Oban, late Tenpo to Koka period

02　時世粧菊揃 こどもがあるかときく　大判　小島屋重兵衛　弘化2年（1845）　国立国会図書館
Modern Chrysanthemum Varieties: News of potential little ones
(Kodomo ga aru ka to kiku), Oban, 1845, National Diet Library

03　当世商人日斗計 日九時　大判　津村屋三郎兵衛　文政期　ボストン美術館
Sundial of Modern Tradesmen: Noon,
Oban, Bunsei period, Museum of Fine Arts, Boston
(Photograph © 2012 Museum of Fine Arts, Boston. All rights reserved. William Sturgis. Bigelow
Collection, 1911 11_36368)

04　艶姿十六女仙 初平　大判　有田屋清右衛門　弘化末〜嘉永初期
Beautiful Figures of Women Linked to the Sixteen Taoist Immortals: Tai Sin,
Oban, late Koka to early Kaei period

05　艶姿十六女仙 豊干禅師　大判　有田屋清右衛門　弘化末〜嘉永初期
Beautiful Figures of Women Linked to the Sixteen Taoist Immortals: Bukan, a Zen Buddhist,
Oban, late Koka to early Kaei period

06　妙でんす十六利勘 降那損者　大判　遠州屋又兵衛　弘化3年（1846）
Sixteen Wonderful Considerations of Profit (Myodensu juroku rikan): Furuna Sonja,
Oban, 1846

07　女三宮　大判2枚続　丸屋甚八　天保13年（1842）頃
Onna Sannomiya, Oban diptych, c. 1842

08　新良万造　団扇絵判　伊場屋仙三郎　天保14年（1843）〜弘化3年（1846）
Shinra manzo, fan print, 1843-46

09　五行之内 針の金性　団扇絵判　駿河屋作次郎　天保末〜弘化3年（1846）
The Five Elements: Needle, Metal, fan print, late Tenpo to 1846

10　賢女烈婦伝 大納言行成女　大判　伊場屋仙三郎　弘化期　東京都立中央図書館東京誌料文庫
Biographies of Wise Women and Virtuous Wives: The Daughter of Dainagon Yukinari,
Oban, Koka period, The Tokyo Metropolitan Central Library

11　嘘真言心之裏表　大判　湊屋小兵衛　弘化4年（1847）〜嘉永元年（1848）
Falsehood and Truth: Both Sides of the Heart, Oban, 1847-48

12　子供遊八行のうち 仁　大判　伊賀屋勘右衛門　天保後期
The Eight Virtues in Children at Play: Benevolence, Oban, late Tenpo period

13　子供遊八行の内 礼　大判　天保後期
The Eight Virtues in Children at Play: Courtesy, Oban, late Tenpo period

14　於竹大日如来の由来　大判　海老屋林之助　嘉永2年（1849）頃
Origin of Otake Dainichi Nyorai, Oban, c. 1849

15　八代目市川団十郎死絵　大判2枚続　嘉永7年（1854）
Memorial Portrait of Actor Ichikawa Danjuro VIII, Oban diptych, 1854

16   風俗女水滸伝 百八番之内 炬燵　色紙判　文政末期　東京国立博物館
Elegant Women's Water Margin –One Hundred and Eight Sheets: In the Kotatsu,
Shikishi-ban, late Bunsei period, Tokyo National Museum (Image:TNM Image Archives)

17   譬諭草をしへ早引 輪　大判　有田屋清右衛門　天保 14 年 (1843) 頃
北海道立近代美術館 (髙橋博信コレクション)
Instructive Index of All Sorts of Proverbs: Wheel (Wa), Oban, c. 1843,
The Hokkaido Museum of Modern Art (Collection of TAKAHASHI Hironobu)

18   譬諭草をしへ早引 砥　大判　有田屋清右衛門　天保 14 年 (1843) 頃　ボストン美術館
Instructive Index of All Sorts of Proverbs: Whetstone (To), Oban, c. 1843,
Museum of Fine Arts, Boston (Photograph © 2012 Museum of Fine Arts, Boston.
All rights reserved. William Sturgis. Bigelow Collection, 1911 11_36368)

19   貞操千代の鑑 義　大判　古賀屋勝五郎　弘化期　平木浮世絵美術館
Mirror of Eternal Feminine Virtues: Righteousness (Gi), Oban, Koka period,
Hiraki Ukiyo-e Museum

20   源氏雲浮世画合 柏木　大判　伊勢屋市兵衛　弘化期　国立国会図書館
Genji Clouds Matched with Ukiyo-e Pictures: Kashiwagi,
Oban, Koka period, National Diet Library

21   源氏雲浮世画合 若菜 下　大判　伊勢屋市兵衛　弘化期
Genji Clouds Matched with Ukiyo-e Pictures: Wakana, Oban, Koka period

22   園中八せん花 菊　団扇絵判　伊場屋仙三郎　天保末～弘化期　平木浮世絵美術館
Selection of Eight Beautiful Flowers in the Garden: Chrysanthemum,
fan print, late Tenpo to Koka period, Hiraki Ukiyo-e Museum

23   猫と遊ぶ娘　団扇絵判　伊場屋仙三郎　弘化 2 年 (1845) 頃
Girl Playing with a Cat, fan print, c. 1845

24   艶曲揃　団扇絵判　三平　嘉永 6 年 (1853)
Women Reading Kabuki Lyrics, fan print, 1853

25   絵兄弟やさすかた　大判　海老屋林之助　弘化期
Graceful Sibling Pictures, Oban, Koka period

26   七婦久人 寿老人　大判　遠州屋彦兵衛　弘化 4 年 (1847) ～ 嘉永元年 (1848)
Women Compared with the Seven Gods of Good Fortune: Juro-jin, Oban, 1847-48

27   見立挑灯蔵 三段目　大判　山本平吉　弘化末～嘉永元年 (1848)
Parody of the Chushingura in Lanterns: Act Three, Oban, late Koka to 1848

28   山海愛度図会 ヲゝいたい 越中滑川大蛸　大判　蔦屋吉蔵　嘉永 5 年 (1852)
Auspicious Pictures of Land and Sea: Ouch! – Giant Octopus at Namerikawa, Etchu, Oban, 1852

29   うろたへた小猫盆画へ屎をたれ　小判　天保後期
Urotaeta koneko bonga e kuso o tare (A wandering kitten does its business in the sand picture),
Koban, late Tenpo period

30   雪月花 月　大判　江崎屋吉兵衛　文政後期
Snow, Moon and Flowers: Moon, Oban, Late Bunsei period

31   尾上菊五郎の玉屋新兵衛 関三十郎の鵜飼九十郎　大判　東屋大助　文政 7 年 (1824)
Onoe Kikugoro as Tamaya Shinbei and Seki Sanjuro as Ukai Kujuro, Oban, 1824

32   通俗水滸伝豪傑百八人之一個 活閻羅阮小七　大判　加賀屋 (加賀吉)　文政 10 年 (1827) 頃
One of the 108 Heroes of the Popular Water Margin: Living King Yama Ruan Xiaoqi, Oban, about 1827

33   坂田怪童丸　大判　加賀屋 (加賀吉)　天保中期
Sakata Kaidomaru, Oban, middle Tenpo period

34　東都橋場之図　大判　山口屋藤兵衛　天保前期
The Eastern Capital: Picture of Hashiba, Oban, early Tenpo period

35　魚の心　大判　川口屋宇兵衛　天保後期
Actors as Fish, Oban, late Tenpo period

36　道外獣の雨やどり　大判　山口屋藤兵衛　天保後期
Fool Beasts Taking Shelter From the Rain, Oban, late Tenpo period

37　かゑるづくし　大判　越村屋平助　天保後期
Frogs Playing Various Roles, Oban, late Tenpo period

38　百亀家久 かるわざ・四天王の見立　中判　ふうよ(瓢形印)　天保後期
One Hundred Turtles of Good Luck (Hyakki yakyu):
Acrobatics / Representation of the Four Great Retainers, Chuban, late Tenpo period

39　金魚づくし 玉や玉や　中判　村田　天保後期　東京国立博物館
Set of Goldfish: Blowing Soap Bubbles, Chuban, late Tenpo period,
Tokyo National Museum (Image:TNM Image Archives)

40　きん魚づくし ぼんぼん　中判　村田　天保後期
Set of Goldfish: Singing 'Bonbon' Song, Chuban, late Tenpo period

41　みかけハこハゐがとんだいゝ人だ　大判　藤岡屋彦太郎　嘉永元年 (1848) 頃
He Looks Fierce but He's a Really Great Man, Oban, c. 1848

42　讃岐院眷属をして為朝をすくふ図　大判 3 枚続　住吉屋政五郎　嘉永 4 年 (1851) 頃
Tametomo Rescued by Tengu Sent by Sanuki-in, Oban Triptych, c. 1851

43-51　ねこの写生および画稿類　国立ライデン民族学博物館
Study of cats, National Museum of Ethnology Leiden

52　たとゑ尽の内　大判 3 枚組　加賀屋安兵衛　嘉永 5 年 (1852)
Proverbs Illustrated by Cats, Oban Triptych, 1852

53　其まゝ地口猫飼好五十三疋　大判 3 枚続　伊場屋仙三郎　嘉永初期
Cats for the 53 Stations of the Tokaido, Oban Triptych, eary Kaei period

54　猫の百面相　団扇絵判　天保 12 年 (1841) 頃
One Hundred Faces of Cats, fan print, c. 1841

55　猫の源氏 賢木　団扇絵判　天保後期
Cat Version of the Tale of Genji: Sakaki, fan print, late Tenpo period

56　流行猫の戯 梅が枝無間の真似　大判　山本平吉　弘化 4 年 (1847) 頃
Fashionable Cat Games: Parody of Umegae Striking the Bell of Limitless [Hell], Oban, c. 1847

57　流行猫の戯 おしゆん伝兵衛 身の臭婬色時　大判　山本平吉　弘化 4 年 (1847) 頃
Fashionable Cat Games: Oshun and Denbei, Oban, c. 1847

58　流行猫のおも入　大判　川口屋宇兵衛　天保後期
Fashionable Cats Doing Mime Performances (Ryuko neko no omoire), Oban, late Tenpo period

59　五拾三次之内 岡崎の場　大判 3 枚続　和泉屋市兵衛　天保 6 年 (1835)
Scene from the 53 Stations of the Tokaido: Okazaki, Oban Triptych, 1835

60　古幸猫のよふくハい　大判　清水屋直次郎　弘化 4 年 (1847) 頃　早稲田大学演劇博物館 (100-8849)
Furu neko no youkai, Oban, c. 1847, The Tsubouchi Memorial Theatre Museum Waseda University

61　猫の当字 ふぐ　大判　伊場屋仙三郎　天保 13 年 (1842) 頃
Cat Letters: Pufferfish (Neko no ateji: Fugu), Oban, c. 1842

62　猫の当字 たこ　大判　伊場屋仙三郎　天保 13 年（1842）
Cat Letters: Octopus (Neko no ateji: Tako), Oban, 1842

63　猫の当字 かつを　大判　伊場屋仙三郎　天保 13 年（1842）
Cat Letters: Bonito (Neko no ateji: Katsuo), Oban, 1842
(©The Trustees of the British Museum c/o DNPartcom)

64　猫の当字 なまづ　大判　伊場屋仙三郎　天保 14 年（1843）
Cat Letters: Catfish (Neko no ateji: Namazu), Oban, 1843

65　流行猫の曲手まり　大判　川口屋宇兵衛　天保 12 年（1841）
Fashionable Cat Juggler with a Ball, Oban, 1841

66　猫の曲まり　団扇絵判　天保 12 年（1841）頃
Cats Juggling Balls, fan print, c. 1841

67　猫の歌舞伎 出語り図　団扇絵判　伊場屋仙三郎　天保後期　東京都江戸東京博物館
Cat Kabuki: Degatari, fan print, late Tenpo period, Edo-Tokyo Museum
(Image: 東京都歴史文化財団イメージアーカイブ)

68　荷宝蔵壁のむだ書　大判　伊場屋仙三郎　弘化 4 年（1847）〜嘉永元年（1848）頃
Scribbles on a Storehouse Wall, Oban, c. 1847-1848

69　絵鏡台合かゞ身（みみずく・獅子・般若面 ）　団扇絵判 2 枚組　伊場屋仙三郎　天保後期
Mirror Images: Owl, Lion, and Female Demon, a set of fan print, late Tenpo period

70　朧月猫の草紙　版本　山本平吉（栄久堂）　初編・2 編　天保 13 年（1842）
袋：礫川浮世絵美術館、本：国立国会図書館
The Cat's Tale, book, 1842, Koishikawa Ukiyo-e Museum (paper bag), National Diet Library (book)

71　猫のけん　団扇絵判　天保後期　渡辺木版画舗
Cats Playing a Hand Game, fan print, late Tenpo period, Watanabe Color Prints Co.

72　猫のけいこ　団扇絵判　天保後期　渡辺木版画舗
Cats Taking a Lesson, fan print, late Tenpo period, Watanabe Color Prints Co.

73　猫のすゞみ　団扇絵判　天保後期　東京国立博物館
Cats Enjoying the Cool of Evening, fan print, late Tenpo period, Tokyo National Museum
(Image:TNM Image Archives)

74　くつろぐ夏の猫美人たち　団扇絵判　天保後期
Cat Beauties Relaxing in Summer, fan print, late Tenpo period

75　当流猫の六毛撰　団扇絵判　伊場屋仙三郎　弘化期　東京国立博物館
Six Poetic Geniuses of the Heian Period, fan print, Koka period,
Tokyo National Museum (Image:TNM Image Archives)

76　おぼろ月猫の盛　団扇絵判　伊場屋仙三郎　弘化 3 年（1846）
Pale Moon, Cats in Season, fan print, 1846

サイズの目安 Standard print dimensions (roughly)

団扇絵判	Fan print:	22.5 × 29㎝
大判	Oban:	39 × 26.5㎝
中判	Chuban:	26 × 19㎝
小判	Koban:	23 × 16.5㎝
色紙判	Shikishiban:	21 × 18.5㎝

金子信久　KANEKO Nobuhisa

1962年、東京都生まれ。府中市美術館学芸員。著書は『旅する江戸絵画 琳派から銅版画まで』（PIE BOOKS、2010）、『かわいい江戸絵画』（共著、府中市美術館編、求龍堂、2013）、『おこまの大冒険〜朧月猫の草紙〜』（パイ インターナショナル、2013）、『たのしい日本美術 江戸かわいい動物』（講談社、2015）、『めでる国芳ブック ねこ』（大福書林、2015）、『たのしい日本美術 日本おとぼけ絵画史』（講談社、2016）『歌川国芳 21世紀の絵画力』（共著、府中市美術館編、講談社、2017)、『めでる国芳ブック どうぶつ』（大福書林、2017)、『あの名画に会える美術館ガイド 江戸絵画篇』（講談社、2017）ほか。

Born 1962 in Tokyo. Curator, Fuchu Art Museum. Author of Tabi suru Edo kaiga: Rinpa kara dohanga made (The journey in Edo painting: From Rinpa to copperplate prints) (PIE Books, 2010), Cute Edo Paintings (coauthored, Fuchu Art Museum and Kyuryudo, 2013), Okoma no daiboken: Oborozuki neko no soshi (Okoma's Great Adventure: The Cat's Tale) (PIE International, 2013), Tanoshii Nihon bijutsu: Edo kawaii dobutsu (Fun Japanese art: Charming animals from Edo) (Kodansha, 2015), Ukiyo-e Paper Book: Cats by Kuniyoshi (Daifuku Shorin, 2015), and Tanoshii Nihon bijutsu: Nihon otoboke kaigashi (Fun Japanese art: Another Side of the Japanese Art World — Innocent, Naive, Non-Polished...) (Kodansha, 2016) UTAGAWA Kuniyoshi His pictorial Eloquence in the 21st Century(Kodansha, 2017), Animals by Kuniyoshi(Daifukushorin, 2017), and Japan Museums Guide: A Complete Guide to Edo Paintings(Kodansha, 2017), among others.

ねこと国芳　Cats in Ukiyo-e: Japanese Woodblock Prints of UTAGAWA Kuniyoshi

2012 年 10 月 13 日　　初版　第 1 刷発行
2024 年 10 月 5 日　　第 2 版第 5 刷発行

著者：金子信久
翻訳：パメラ三木、カーステン・マッカイバー
アートディレクション：柿木原 政広（10 inc.）
デザイン：石黒 潤（FRASCO）
協力：ギャラリー紅屋
撮影：鈴木静華
編集：瀧 亮子（大福書林）

Written by KANEKO Nobuhisa
Translated by Pamela Miki and Kirsten McIvor
Art direction by KAKINOKIHARA Masahiro
Designed by ISHIGURO Jun
With cooperation from Gallery Beniya
Edited by TAKI Akiko

発行人　　三芳寛要
発行元　　株式会社 パイ インターナショナル
〒 170-0005　東京都豊島区南大塚 2-32-4
TEL　03-3944-3981
FAX　03-5395-4830
sales@pie.co.jp

PIE International
2-32-4, Minami-Otsuka, Toshima-ku, Tokyo, 170-0005 Japan
TEL　+81-3-5395-4811
FAX　+81-3-5395-4812
sales@pie.co.jp

印刷・製本　アベイズム株式会社